Mathematics of Manpower Planning

Mathematics
of
Manpower Planning

S. Vajda

Visiting Professor,
Universities of
Birmingham and Sussex

A Wiley–Interscience Publication

JOHN WILEY & SONS
Chichester · New York · Brisbane · Toronto

Library of Congress Cataloging in Publication Data:

Vajda, S.
Mathematics of manpower planning.

Bibliography: p.
Includes index.
1. Manpower planning – Mathematical models.
2. Linear programming. I. Title.
HF5549.5.M3V34 331.1'1'0151 77-26104

ISBN 0 471 99627 0

Typeset in IBM Press Roman by Preface Ltd, Salisbury, Wilts.
Printed in Great Britain by Unwin Brothers Ltd, The Gresham Press, Old Woking, Surrey.

Contents

Preface

The origins of this book go back to the middle 1940s, when the author was Statistician in the Admiralty, and to work done in the middle 1970s, when he was a Senior Research Fellow in the University of Sussex.

The earlier work is described, with the necessary background, and with extensive additions, in Part I, while the later work is contained – again with extensions – in Part II.

We give here a summary of the contents.

In Part I we deal with long-term development, with the algebraic or analytic description of structures, and with the application of discrete or continuous rates of transfer, dependent on age, grade or seniority, and with entries into one or more states.

In Part II we deal with short-term, step to step aspects, where the rates may change from step to step, and the question of optimality arises when a desired result can be obtained in a variety of ways.

We investigate also the case of transfer rates under the control of management.

In this part our main tools are techniques of linear programming.

Chapter 1 introduces the concept of a cohort, first with a single state, and then within a hierarchy of states. The rates of transfer may depend on the time in the organization, or in a grade. Career prospects are considered, as are the probabilities of reaching a state from another. Finally, a continuous model is introduced, while the state parameter remains discontinuous.

In Chapter 2 we deal with a population whose total is kept constant by new entrants. The main tool is Markov theory. Difference equations are introduced for the numbers of members in the various states, and for the number of new entrants. We prove the convergence, with increasing time, to a stationary structure, under given conditions.

In Sections 2.23 to 2.27 we describe a model (the 'Kent model') which has been used for planning purposes, and we prove that with its rules the population converges again to a stationary one. We have not seen any proof of this fact in the literature.

In Sections 2.28 ff. we turn once more to continuous time, and the final Section 2.34 mentions a few results concerning continuous state characteristics.

The topic of Chapter 3 is the stationary population, i.e. a hierarchic structure where all state totals are repeated at each step, with entries into one or into more states. Continuous parameters are introduced in the last sections of this chapter.

Chapter 4 deals with the concept of semi-stationarity, a concept which was introduced by the author in 1947, but has not been dealt with since then. It is here approached from various algebraic points of view.

Chapter 5 deals with changing totals of membership. First, we consider expansion or contraction and establish bounds on their rates. The stable population is defined, and use is made of results of matrix theory (the Perron–Frobenius theorem). We then proceed to cases of given input (push models) or given changes of size (pull models). Finally, instead of a constant total, a constant weighted total is considered.

In Part II, we deal with developments during a finite number of steps, and our methods – mainly those of linear programming – allow us to use recruitment rates which need not be independent of time. After a brief introduction and a fundamental lemma in Chapter 6, we deal in Chapter 7 with the question of which structures are attainable after 1,2, . . . steps, and from which structures a structure aimed at can be obtained. The relationship between the set of structures from which this can be done in one step, and those from which it is possible in two steps is examined.

In Chapter 8 we consider the question of re-attaining a structure and, in particular, the problem of re-attainability after $t + 1$ steps, when re-attainability after t steps is known. In Chapter 7 as well as in Chapter 8 we assume that either the total membership, or the weighted total membership, with weights dependent on the states, is being kept constant throughout.

Chapter 9 is concerned with re-attaining the total of a subset of two states out of three, after one or after two steps, or both and, briefly, with retaining a given total of two out of three states, using the transition matrix $\mathbf{P}_0$ (given in Appendix III), as in most of our examples.

In Chapter 10 we determine the set of those structures which can be expanded at a rate $1 + \alpha$ at each of t steps, with an example for $t = 2$.

The topic of Chapter 11 is optimization. If there are a number of ways of going from one structure to another, then we might ask for the most preferable one. This is investigated by applying the theory of linear programming, including in one case that of duality. An infinite horizon is also considered, and examples of goal programming are given.

In all these chapters it was assumed that the transition rates were given. In Chapter 12 we consider the choice of transition rates, to solve problems analogous to those in Chapters 7 and 8, for one step, and we show that with the control of transition rates any structure can be reached, arbitrarily closely, from any other, in a suitable number of steps, even if demotion is not allowed.

The mathematical pre-requisites are those of high-school level. An appendix deals with relevant parts of matrix theory, with remarks about difference and differential equations, and another with the simplex method of linear programming and with the transportation problem, the latter being relevant when the transition rates are subject to choice.

Appendix III gives, for easy reference, matrix $\mathbf{P}_0$ with some of its powers, and the product of these with the wastage vector. $(\mathbf{I} - \mathbf{P}_0)^{-1}$ is also quoted.

Notation

Matrices are denoted by bold face capital letters, scalars by lower case letters, and vectors by bold face lower case letters. Transposition is indicated by a prime.

A vector $\mathbf{v} = (v_1, \ldots, v_k)$ is a row vector, a vector $\mathbf{w} = [w_1, \ldots, w_k]$ is a column vector. Hence, for instance, the matrix $[\mathbf{u}_1', \ldots, \mathbf{u}_m']$, where $\mathbf{u}_i = [u_{i1}, \ldots, u_{ik}]$ and hence $\mathbf{u}_i' = (u_{i1}, \ldots, u_{ik})$, equals

$$\begin{pmatrix} u_{11} & \cdots & u_{1k} \\ \vdots & \ddots & \vdots \\ u_{m1} & \cdots & u_{mk} \end{pmatrix}$$

Introduction

Manpower planning is concerned with arranging for the right number of individuals to be allocated to various well-defined activities. The structure best adapted to the purposes of an organization – industrial, military, educational, or others – changes with time, and planning has to take account of changing circumstances, to arrive at a structure most appropriate in its own time, at least as nearly as possible.

In this sense, manpower planning is not identical with personnel management (which must take a much more intimate account of the individual), but it is an important part of it. It is indeed obvious that no member of an organization can be satisfied with his or her contribution to its work, if the structure of that organization is distorted, perhaps top-heavy in its manning, or if it is dangerously contracting, due to circumstances which had not been foreseen.

The tools of manpower planning include transfers, promotion, and recruiting. Such tools are mostly under the control of management. The results of managerial decisions depend also on influences not under the management's control, such as demographic facts, competition for manpower by other organizations, etc.

In this book we deal with the control of manpower by mathematical methods. Because the numbers of people to be transferred, recruited or promoted, and those of people retiring or resigning are not negative, we can say that we are dealing here with a case of the theory of non-negative control.

Those numbers are also integers. However, we shall, in our analysis use rates of transfer, promotion and so on, and these fractions might be interpreted as probabilities, leading to expected (mean) values, or they might be thought to apply to large units, when fractions in the results of computations may be ignored.

The earliest mathematical and statistical investigations relevant to forecasting the development of populations were due to actuaries; they go back at least as far as to Graunt (1662).

In its most elementary form, the actuarial approach was concerned with the development of a group of entrants, a cohort, without grading, though the more recent development of sickness insurance and of disability insurance considers a splitting up of a population in its development into subpopulations of different characteristics, e.g. those healthy and those sick. Transfers in either direction are possible between such subpopulations.

The consideration of hierarchies, of graded or stratified populations is of more recent origin. Early papers in this field are those of Seal (1945), Vajda (1947, 1948), Young and Almond (1961), Gani (1963). The book by Bartholomew (1973) deals with this topic in detail, in particular in Chapters 4, 5 and 8.

Actuaries have also been concerned with the estimation of the values of relevant parameters, such as mortality rates. We do not deal with this problem here. Nor do we deal with probabilistic considerations. Deviations from the underlying assumptions, their variances and covariances, are important in small organizations, but they remain outside the scope of this book: our treatment is deterministic. For the statistical aspects we refer, in particular, to Bartholomew (1974) and to Pollard (1973), Chapter 9, pp. 112–35).

Other aspects of manpower planning such as behavioural and organizational problems, and their influence on efficiency, problems of selection and of enrolment as well as of emoluments, are described in Proceedings of conferences, e.g. Wilson (1969), Smith (1970), Bartholomew and Smith (1971), Clough, Lewis, and Oliver (1974).

PART I

1

The Cohort

1.1

We consider a group of individuals, consisting at (nominal) time 0 of $n(0)$ members. We shall call this group a 'cohort' and we shall follow the development of its membership through time.

Assume that during the next time period, which we shall take to be one year, a proportion q_1 of members leaves. Generally, the proportion of leavers during the tth year will be q_t.

We call q_t the loss rate, and $1 - q_t = p_t$, say, the survival rate.

If all members of the cohort are initially of age 0, then t equals the age of the remaining members at time t, and p_t will then be their age-dependent survival rate. However, we shall not, in general, assume that all members are of the same age, or that they have any other characteristic in common, except that we started observing them all at the same time.

In some contexts the rates q_t and p_t will be interpreted as probabilities. In that case the numbers of surviving members will be expected values, and there will be no problem about the meaning of fractions. However, we shall for convenience use deterministic concepts, and in that case fractional values might be considered to be approximations. Alternatively, we might consider $n(0)$ to be large enough to make its product with any fractions which appear in an argument to be integers.

At the end of t years the number of members still in the cohort will be

$$n(t) = n(0)p_1p_2 \ldots p_t \tag{1.1}$$

and during the next year, the $(t + 1)$th year,

$$n(t) - n(t + 1) = n(t)q_{t+1} \tag{1.2}$$

members will leave the cohort.

We shall throughout this book illustrate the theoretical development by examples, and introduce now

Example 1.

Let the survival and less rates be as follows:

t	p_t	q_t
1	0.875	0.125
2	0.583	0.417
3	0.306	0.694
4	0.217	0.783
5	0.077	0.923
6	0.000	1.000

After six years, no member of the cohort will still be left in it.
If we start with $n(0) = 1000$, then at the end of year

	0	1	2	3	4	5	6
$n(t) =$	1000	875	510	156	34	3	0

1.2

Imagine now that a cohort enters a population which is partitioned into grades, or ranks, and that during each year a given proportion of members of a rank are promoted into the next higher rank (if there is one). We assume that the promotion rates depend on time as well as on rank, while the loss rate depends only on time.

The cohort enters, at time 0, into rank 1; the highest rank is rank R.

The number of members in rank r at the end of the tth year is denoted by $n_r(t)$. The rate of promotion from rank r to rank $r + 1$ during that year is $p_{r,r+1}(t)$, and the rate of those remaining in rank r is

$$p_{r,r}(t) = 1 - p_{r,r+1}(t) - q_t \tag{1.3}$$

when $r = 1, \ldots, R - 1$, and

$$p_{R,R}(t) = 1 - q_t \tag{1.4}$$

The promotion rates will again, in some contexts, be interpreted as probabilities.

To determine the numbers in the various ranks, at given times, we have to solve the system

$$n_1(t + 1) = p_{1,1}(t + 1)n_1(t) \tag{1.5}$$

$$n_r(t + 1) = p_{r,r}(t + 1)n_r(t) + p_{r-1,r}(t + 1)n_{r-1}(t) \tag{1.6}$$

for $r = 2, \ldots, R$.

This system holds for all non-negative integer values of t. However, we know that only a finite number of the $n_r(t)$ will be different from zero, if for some t we have $q_t = 1$, and consequently $p_{r,r}(t) = p_{r,r+1}(t) = 0$.

For $t = 0$ we have

$$n_2(0) = \ldots = n_R(0) = 0 \tag{1.7}$$

and $n_1(0)$ is the original membership of the cohort. Also, $n_i(t) = 0$ if $i > t + 1$.

The system (1.5), (1.6) can be solved step by step, as we now show by an example.

1.3

Example 2.

Let there be three ranks, with the same loss and survival rates, dependent on time only, as in Example 1. The promotion rates are as shown in Table 1.

Table 1

Time	From rank 1 to rank 2	Hence $p_{1,1}(t)$	From rank 2 to rank 3	Hence $p_{2,2}(t)$	$p_t = p_{3,3}(t)$
1	0.050	0.825	–	–	–
2	0.033	0.550	0.303	0.280	–
3	0.022	0.284	0.102	0.204	0.306
4	0.007	0.210	0.117	0.100	0.217
5	0.000	0.077	0.032	0.045	0.077

With these values, the matrix of coefficients of the system (1.5), (1.6) is as follows, after transferring all left-hand sides to the right-hand side, with changed sign:

$n_1(0)$	$n_1(1)$	$n_1(2)$	$n_1(3)$	$n_1(4)$	$n_1(5)$	$n_2(1)$	$n_2(2)$	$n_2(3)$	$n_2(4)$	$n_2(5)$	$n_3(2)$	$n_3(3)$	$n_3(4)$	$n_3(5)$
0.825	−1													
	0.550	−1												
		0.284	−1											
			0.210	−1										
				0.077	−1									
0.050						−1								
	0.033					0.280	−1							
		0.022					0.204	−1						
			0.007					0.100	−1					
				0.000					0.045	−1				
						0.303					−1			
							0.102				0.306	−1		
								0.117				0.217	−1	
									0.032				0.077	−1

(1.8)

Starting with $n_1(0)$, we determine the successive values of the $n_r(t)$. The complete development is illustrated by Figure 1, where we have taken 1000 to be the initial total membership:

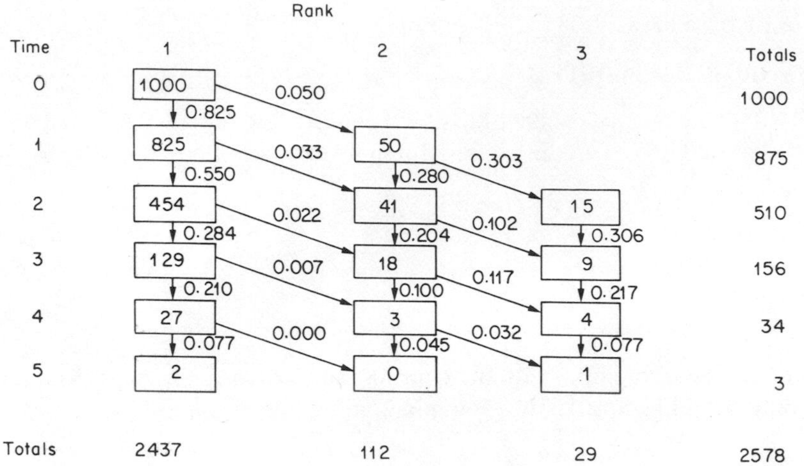

Figure 1

The arrows between ranks are marked with the promotion rates, and the vertical arrows with $p_{r,r}(t)$.

The last column 'Totals' reproduces the values of $n(t)$ from Section 1.1.

1.4

It would be more realistic to assume that the rates of promotion depend, in addition to rank and time, also on the seniority s, i.e. the time spent in the rank.

If we denote the promotion rate from rank r to rank $r+1$ dependent on s and on time t by $p_{r,r+1}(t,s)$, then the number $n_{r,s}(t)$ of members of the cohort at time t with seniority s in their rank r can be computed from the following system (note that after promotion the seniority in the new rank is, of course, zero)

$$n_{r+1,0}(t+1) = \sum_{s=1} p_{r,r+1}(t+1,s)n_{r,s}(t) \tag{1.9}$$

$$n_{r,s+1}(t+1) = p_{r,r}(t+1,s+1)n_{r,s}(t) \quad (s = 0,1,2,\ldots) \tag{1.10}$$

$t = 0,1,\ldots.$

Starting with $n_{1,0}(0)$, we can again determine the successive values step by step.

1.5

We do not claim that the rates chosen in Examples 1 and 2 are realistic. The loss rates, in particular, do not necessarily reflect mortality or incapacity, as they do in many actuarial calculations. A cohort may consist of members of various ages, different sex and background, and other considerations may in fact be overriding in their effect on the propensity of members to leave.

The dependence of the loss rates on the completed length of service in an organization has been frequently investigated. The rates have been approximated successfully by a log-normal distribution with density

$$\exp[-(\ln t - m)^2/2\sigma^2]/\sigma x\sqrt{2\pi}$$

(see, for example, Lane and Andrew, 1955; Young 1971).

Bartholomew (1973, pp. 184ff.), discusses also exponential and mixed exponential densities of the form $\Sigma_i p_i \alpha_i \exp(-\alpha_i t)$.

The more general question of how a time-independent transition matrix fits observed data is considered by Forbes (1971).

1.6

In Examples 1 and 2 all members of the cohort had left after a finite number of years. We shall now consider a cohort where members have no finite limited life-span.

Example 3.

Let the transition rates between three ranks be as follows:

		To rank 1	2	3
From rank	1	0.590	0.036	0
	2	0	0.214	0.187
	3	0	0	0.276

A cohort of 1000 entrants into rank 1 will then develop as in Figure 2.

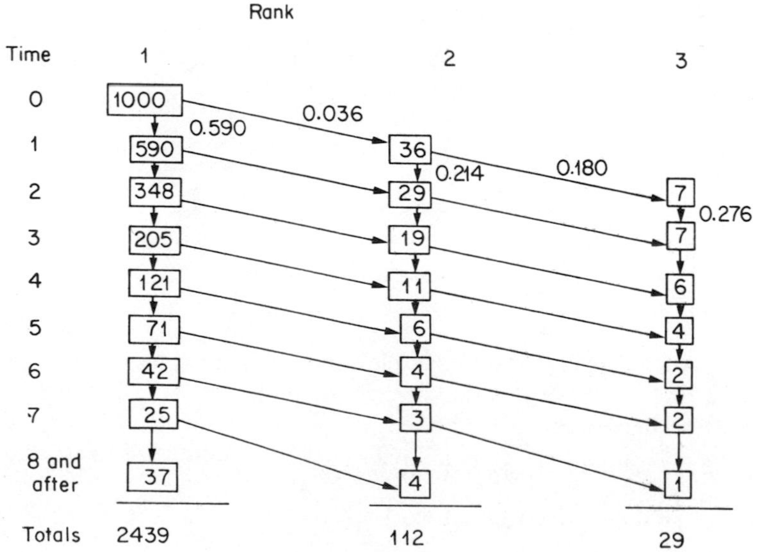

Figure 2

1.7

In Examples 2 and 3 we have assumed that promotions were possible only into the next higher rank, and that no rank could be jumped over. We shall now consider the more general case, where transitions are possible between any two states.

We shall, accordingly, not refer to ranks any more, but we shall speak of states, which are characterized, perhaps, by age, trade, rank, seniority, or a number of other features.

We shall consider transition rates (or probabilities) p_{ij} of transitions from state i to state j, and now we shall assume that they are independent of time, as in Example 3.

If we wished to make transition rates dependent on time as well, then we could add time as a characteristic, as we have done in Example 2. Of course, in such a case a transition from a state with characteristic time t, would only be possible into a state with time characteristic $t + 1$. Also, in our present framework we should want to take discrete values only, though later we shall consider continuous characteristics as well.

In Part II of this book, when we shall be interested in short-time developments, i.e. in the structures arrived at after a finite, and usually after a small number of steps, we shall use methods of linear programming (Appendix II) which are particularly convenient for that type of analysis.

1.8

Let a cohort of $n_1(0)$ enter state 1 at time 0. The development in time is then given by the system

$$n_i(t+1) = p_{1i}n_1(t) + p_{2i}n_2(t) + \ldots + p_{ki}n_k(t) \text{ for } i = 1, \ldots, k \tag{1.11}$$

and $n_2(0) = \ldots = n_k(0) = 0$.

Appendix I gives details about a method of solving such a set of linear difference equations, and we illustrate it here by an example.

Example 4.

We take now as our transition matrix.

$$\mathbf{P}_0 = \begin{pmatrix} 0.3 & 0.4 & 0.1 \\ 0.1 & 0.5 & 0.3 \\ 0.2 & 0.1 & 0.4 \end{pmatrix}$$

(This matrix will be used for many examples, and we list a number of its features in Appendix III.)

We have now the system

$$\begin{aligned} n_1(t+1) &= 0.3n_1(t) + 0.1n_2(t) + 0.2n_3(t) \\ n_2(t+1) &= 0.4n_1(t) + 0.5n_2(t) + 0.1n_3(t) \\ n_3(t+1) &= 0.1n_1(t) + 0.3n_2(t) + 0.4n_3(t) \end{aligned} \tag{1.12}$$

(Note that the matrix of coefficients of the right-hand side is the transpose of the transition matrix $\mathbf{P}_0$.)

To solve the system, we determine the latent roots of the matrix of coefficients, i.e. the roots of

$$\begin{vmatrix} 0.3-\lambda & 0.1 & 0.2 \\ 0.4 & 0.5-\lambda & 0.1 \\ 0.1 & 0.3 & 0.4-\lambda \end{vmatrix} = -\lambda^3 + 1.2\lambda^2 - 0.38\lambda + 0.05 = 0 \quad (1.13)$$

The latent roots are

$$\lambda_1 = 0.805 \quad \lambda_2 = 0.1975 + 0.1517\mathrm{i} \quad \lambda_3 = 0.1975 - 0.1517\mathrm{i}$$

and the corresponding latent vectors are proportional to

$$\begin{pmatrix} 0.0935 \\ 0.1720 \\ 0.1505 \end{pmatrix} \quad \begin{pmatrix} 0.0082 - 0.0766\mathrm{i} \\ -0.0710 + 0.0607\mathrm{i} \\ 0.0898 + 0.0152\mathrm{i} \end{pmatrix} \quad \begin{pmatrix} 0.0082 + 0.0766\mathrm{i} \\ -0.0710 - 0.0607\mathrm{i} \\ 0.0898 - 0.0152\mathrm{i} \end{pmatrix}$$

so that

$$n_1(t) = 0.0935(0.805)^t A + (0.0082 - 0.0766\mathrm{i})(0.1975 + 0.1517\mathrm{i})^t B + (0.0082 + 0.0766\mathrm{i})(0.1975 - 0.1517\mathrm{i})^t C \quad (1.14)$$

$$n_2(t) = 0.1720(0.805)^t A + (-0.0710 + 0.0607\mathrm{i})(0.1975 + 0.1517\mathrm{i})^t B + (-0.0710 - 0.0607\mathrm{i})(0.1975 - 0.1517\mathrm{i})^t C \quad (1.15)$$

$$n_3(t) = 0.1505(0.805)^t A + (0.0898 + 0.0152\mathrm{i})(0.1975 + 0.1517\mathrm{i})^t B + (0.0898 - 0.0152\mathrm{i})(0.1975 - 0.1517\mathrm{i})^t C \quad (1.16)$$

In order to have $n_1(0) = 1$, $n_2(0) = 0$, $n_3(0) = 0$, we must take

$$A = 2.569 \quad B = -1.274 + 5.119\mathrm{i} \quad C = -1.274 - 5.119\mathrm{i}$$

With these values we obtain

$$n_1(t) = 0.240(0.805)^t + (0.380 + 0.140\mathrm{i})(0.1975 + 0.1517\mathrm{i})^t + (0.380 - 0.140\mathrm{i})(0.1975 - 0.1517\mathrm{i})^t \quad (1.17)$$

$$n_2(t) = 0.442(0.805)^t + (-0.221 - 0.431\mathrm{i})(0.1975 + 0.1517\mathrm{i})^t + (-0.221 + 0.431\mathrm{i})(0.1975 - 0.1517\mathrm{i})^t \quad (1.18)$$

$$n_3(t) = 0.384(0.805)^t + (-0.192 + 0.440\mathrm{i})(0.1975 + 0.1517\mathrm{i})^t + (-0.192 - 0.440\mathrm{i})(0.1975 - 0.1517\mathrm{i})^t \quad (1.19)$$

We can write this in a different form, using trigonometric functions, because

$$0.380 + 0.140\mathrm{i} = 0.405 \exp(0.353\mathrm{i})$$

$$-0.221 - 0.431\mathrm{i} = -0.484 \exp(1.097\mathrm{i})$$

$$-0.192 + 0.440\mathrm{i} = -0.480 \exp(-1.159\mathrm{i}) \quad \text{and}$$

$$0.1975 + 0.1517\mathrm{i} = 0.249 \exp(0.64\mathrm{i})$$

and appropriate changes for their conjugate complex values. It follows that

$$n_1(t) = 0.240(0.805)^t + 0.810(0.249)^t \cos(0.353 + 0.64t) \quad (1.20)$$

$$n_2(t) = 0.442(0.805)^t - 0.968(0.249)^t \cos(1.097 + 0.64t) \quad (1.21)$$

$$n_3(t) = 0.384(0.805)^t - 0.960(0.249)^t \cos(-1.159 + 0.64t) \quad (1.22)$$

1.9

Table 2 shows the development of a cohort of 1000 starting in state 1.

Table 2

Time	State 1	2	3	Total
0	1000			1000
1	300	400	100	800
2	150	330	190	670
3	116	244	190	550
4	97	187	161	445
5	80	148	130	358
6	65	119	104	288
7	52	96	84	232
8	42	77	68	187
9	34	62	54	150
10	27	50	44	121
11	22	40	35	97
12	18	32	28	78
13	14	28	23	65
14	12	22	19	53
15	10	18	15	43
16+	38	70	63	171
Totals	2077	1923	1308	5308

1.10

If we interpret the transition rates as probabilities, then we can deduce the time a new entrant is expected to spend in the various states.

The time spent, on the average, in state i, will be $\Sigma_t n_i(t)$, where the summation is to be extended from $t = 0$ to infinity.

In general, given the system (1.11), we shall be looking for the solution of the system

$$\sum_{t=0} n_1(t+1) = p_{1i} \sum_{t=0} n_1(t) + \ldots + p_{ki} \sum_{t=0} n_k(t) \quad (1.23)$$

If all members of the cohort are initially in state 1, then

$$\sum_{t=0} n_1(t) = 1 + \sum_{t=1} n_1(t) \quad (1.24)$$

$$\sum_{t=0} n_i(t) = \sum_{t=1} n_i(t) \quad (i = 2, \ldots, k) \tag{1.25}$$

and, of course,

$$\sum_{t=0} n_i(t+1) = \sum_{t=1} n_i(t) \quad \text{for all } i \tag{1.26}$$

It follows that we have to solve the system

$$\sum_{t=1} n_i(t) = p_{1i}\left(1 + \sum_{t=1} n_1(t)\right) + p_{2i} \sum_{t=1} n_2(t)$$
$$+ \ldots + p_{ki} \sum_{t=1} n_k(t) \quad \text{for } i = 1, 2, \ldots, k \tag{1.27}$$

or

$$p_{1i} = \sum_{t=1} n_i(t) - p_{1i} \sum_{t=1} n_1(t) - \ldots - p_{ki} \sum_{t=1} n_k(t) \tag{1.28}$$

If we write $\mathbf{p}_1$ for the first column of the transition matrix $\mathbf{P}'$, then equation (1.28) can be written

$$\mathbf{p}_1 = (\mathbf{I} - \mathbf{P}') \sum_{t=1} \mathbf{n}(t) \tag{1.29}$$

where $\mathbf{n}(t)$ is the vector $[n_1(t), \ldots, n_k(t)]$

From equation (1.29) we obtain

$$\sum_{t=1} \mathbf{n}(t) = (\mathbf{I} - \mathbf{P}')^{-1} \mathbf{p}_1 \tag{1.30}$$

i.e. the first column of $(\mathbf{I} - \mathbf{P}')^{-1}\mathbf{P}'$, provided the inverse $(\mathbf{I} - \mathbf{P}')^{-1}$ exists. This will be the case (see Appendix I, Section 1.4) when all columns of $\mathbf{P}'$ add up to less than unity, as they do in Example 3.

To obtain $\sum_{t=0} \mathbf{n}(t)$, we add the first column of the identity matrix $\mathbf{I}$. Now

$$(\mathbf{I} - \mathbf{P}')^{-1} \mathbf{P}' + \mathbf{I} = (\mathbf{I} - \mathbf{P}')^{-1}$$

(to see this, multiply both sides by $(\mathbf{I} - \mathbf{P}')$). In other words, the $\Sigma_{t=0}\, n_i(t)$ are the elements of the first column of $(\mathbf{I} - \mathbf{P}')^{-1}$, or of the first row of $(\mathbf{I} - \mathbf{P})^{-1}$ (sometimes called the 'fundamental matrix').

1.11

Because in general the states do not form a hierarchy, we can permute the rows and columns of the transition matrix and make any state that into which the cohort enters. For entries into state i, the elements of the ith row of $(\mathbf{I} - \mathbf{P})^{-1}$ give the expected times which a member will spend in the various states.

For the transition matrix $\mathbf{P}_0$ of Example 3, $(\mathbf{I} - \mathbf{P}_0)^{-1}$ is given in Appendix III. By adding the respective rows, we find that an individual entering state 1 has an expected time of 5.308 years of remaining in the population, in whatever state. For entrants into state 2 (or 3), this time is 5.692 (or 4.385).

1.12

In Section 1.10 we have, essentially, solved the system (1.28) in the following form:

$$0.7N_1 - 0.1N_2 - 0.2N_3 = 0.3$$
$$-0.4N_1 + 0.5N_2 - 0.1N_3 = 0.4$$
$$-0.1N_1 - 0.3N_2 + 0.6N_3 = 0.1$$

where N_i stands for $\Sigma_{t=1} n_i(t)$.

The answer is

$$N_1 = 1.077 \left(\text{hence } \sum_{t=0} n_1(t) = 2.077\right) \qquad N_2 = 1.923 \qquad N_3 = 1.308$$

We have seen that if the cohort starts in state 1, then the result depends only on the first row of $(\mathbf{I} - \mathbf{P})^{-1}$. We want to stress this argument by taking now another transition matrix, with the same first row of $(\mathbf{I} - \mathbf{P})^{-1}$.

When

$$\mathbf{P} = \begin{pmatrix} 0.484 & 0.092 & 0.030 \\ 0.026 & 0.837 & 0.046 \\ 0.017 & 0.093 & 0.884 \end{pmatrix}$$

then

$$(\mathbf{I} - \mathbf{P})^{-1} = \begin{pmatrix} 2.077 & 1.923 & 1.308 \\ 0.542 & 8.473 & 3.530 \\ 0.740 & 7.063 & 11.626 \end{pmatrix}$$

Using these elements of $\mathbf{P}$ in equation (1.28), we solve

$$0.516N_1 - 0.026N_2 - 0.017N_3 = 0.484$$
$$-0.092N_1 + 0.163N_2 - 0.093N_3 = 0.092$$
$$-0.030N_1 - 0.046N_2 + 0.116N_3 = 0.030$$

and obtain again $N_1 = 1.077$, $N_2 = 1.923$, $N_3 = 1.308$.

1.13

When a state is equivalent to a rank, as in Examples 2 and 3, with loss rates and promotion rates independent of time, and when transitions are only possible into the next higher rank, then the transition matrix is triangular, with zero entries below the diagonal; $p_{ij} = 0$ when $j < i$ or $j > i + 1$.

In such a case the time spent in a rank is the time until either promotion, or leaving the population, because no return is possible to a state which has been left earlier. (In the general case, with other types of transition being allowed, the time spent without interruption in a state can be obtained in the same way, by giving to a state a different name when reached the second, the third, . . . , time.)

In the special case which we are considering now, the matrix $(\mathbf{I}-\mathbf{P})^{-1}$ has the form (q_{ij}), where

$$q_{ii} = 1/(1-p_{ii})$$

and for $i \neq j$

$$q_{ij} = (p_{i,i+1} \ldots p_{j-1,j})/(1-p_{ii})(1-p_{i+1,i+1}) \ldots (1-p_{jj})$$

Grinold and Marshall (1977) derive the diagonal element $1/(1-p_{ii})$ for this special case by a method which differs from ours.

In the case treated in Section 1.6 the inverse of the matrix $(\mathbf{I}-\mathbf{P})$ is

$$\begin{pmatrix} 2.439 & 0.112 & 0.029 \\ 0 & 1.272 & 0.238 \\ 0 & 0 & 1.381 \end{pmatrix}$$

and the entries in its first row are the totals mentioned in that Section (times 10^{-3}).

1.14

A related question is that of the probability of reaching a state $j > i$ from state i, at some time, with the assumptions of Section 1.13. In such a case there is only one single path from state i to state j, consisting of one or more steps.

This probability is easily seen to be

$$q_{ij}(1-p_{jj}) = (p_{i,i+1} \ldots p_{j-1,j})/(1-p_{ii}) \ldots (1-p_{j-1,j-1}) \qquad (1.31)$$

These expressions are, also, the off-diagonal entries in the matrix product

$$[(\mathbf{I}-\mathbf{P})^{-1} - \mathbf{I}] \begin{pmatrix} 1-p_{11} & 0 & \ldots & 0 & 0 \\ 0 & 1-p_{22} & \cdots & 0 & 0 \\ \vdots & \vdots & & \vdots & \vdots \\ 0 & 0 & \ldots & 0 & 1-p_{kk} \end{pmatrix} \qquad (1.32)$$

We can also describe the off-diagonal elements of the matrix $(\mathbf{I}-\mathbf{P})^{-1}$ as being the probabilities of ever being in state j, if the member is now in state i and this holds also for more general transition matrices (see, e.g., Kemeny and Snell 1960, pp. 61ff.).

The diagonal elements of the matrix product (1.32) are p_{ii}.

1.15

In the previous sections we have considered transitions between the various states to happen at the end of finite time intervals, which we took to be years. In many cases this will describe the development of a population well enough. We have to understand that, for instance, the rate of promotion is the rate of those promoted during the year who have not left during the same year.

However, we might wish to follow the development within the finite time intervals more closely. This we can do by shortening the interval from a year to six months, or to three months, and so on, and by considering in the limit a continuous flow of entries and of losses as well as of transitions.

Of course, this approach implies again an approximation, but it produces results which are sufficiently close to reality to be of help to planners, apart from very exceptional circumstances. Moreover, the continuous model is convenient mathematically, because the analytical tools for handling it are readily available and they are familiar in many fields of control.

The next few sections will therefore reconsider the problem dealt with in earlier sections, using a model in which the time variable is continuous. The states, on the other hand, are finite, and so the corresponding parameter is still discontinuous.

1.16

A cohort enters at time $t = 0$ (t is a continuous variable). Let the proportional loss during the interval $(t, t + \Delta t)$ be $\mu_t \Delta t$. Then the number of members at time $t + \Delta t$ is

$$n(t + \Delta t) = n(t)(1 - \mu_t \Delta t) \tag{1.33}$$

and

$$\frac{n(t + \Delta t) - n(t)}{n(t)\Delta t} = -\mu_t \tag{1.34}$$

When $\Delta t \to 0$, we obtain

$$\mathrm{d}n(t)/n(t)\mathrm{d}t = \mathrm{d}\ln n(t)/\mathrm{d}t = -\mu_t \tag{1.35}$$

and hence

$$n(t) = n(0) \exp\left(-\int_0^t \mu_t \mathrm{d}t\right) \tag{1.36}$$

(Actuaries call μ_t the force of mortality when t is the age, and death is the cause of leaving the population.)

When $\mu_t = \mu$ (a constant), then $n(t) = n(0)\exp(-\mu t)$ and the time a member of the cohort remains in the population is

$$\int_0^T n(t)\mathrm{d}t = n(0)[1 - \exp(-\mu T)]/\mu \tag{1.37}$$

if T is the highest possible age of survival.

The connection between p_t (the discrete survival rate) and μ_t is given by

$$p_t = n(t)/n(t-1) = \exp\left(-\int_{t-1}^t \mu_t \mathrm{d}t\right) \tag{1.38}$$

A constant μ_t during $(t-1,t)$ satisfies therefore $p_t = \exp(-\mu)$, and if for some t we have $p_t = 0$, then the equivalent μ equals infinity.

1.17

Consider now a cohort of 1000 entrants into state 1, at time 0. Denote the rate of flow from state i into state j during an interval of length Δt by $p_{ij}\Delta t$, and $1 - \Sigma_{j=1}^{k} p_{ij}$ by w_i. We take p_{ij} to be independent of t, as in the analogous case of Section 1.7. Then

$$n_j(t+\Delta t) = n_j(t)\left(1 - \sum_{\substack{i=1\\ i\neq j}}^{k} p_{ij}\Delta t - w_j\Delta t\right) + \sum_{\substack{i=1\\ i\neq j}}^{k} n_i(t)p_{ij}\Delta t \tag{1.39}$$

Add $-n_j(t)p_{jj}\Delta t + n_j(t)p_{jj}\Delta t$ to the right-hand side, and replace $(-\Sigma_i p_{ij} - w_j)\Delta t$ by $-\Delta t$. Then transfer $n_j(t)$ to the left-hand side and divide both sides by Δt. When $\Delta t \to 0$, then we obtain the system

$$\begin{aligned}
\mathrm{d}n_1(t)/\mathrm{d}t &= n_1(t)(p_{11}-1) + n_2(t)p_{21} + \ldots + n_k(t)p_{k1}\\
\mathrm{d}n_2(t)/\mathrm{d}t &= n_1(t)p_{12} + n_2(t)(p_{22}-1) + \ldots + n_k(t)p_{k2}\\
&\vdots\\
\mathrm{d}n_k(t)/\mathrm{d}t &= n_1(t)p_{1k} + n_2(t)p_{2k} + \ldots + n_k(t)(p_{kk}-1)
\end{aligned} \tag{1.40}$$

Appendix I shows how such a system can be solved. We take an example for illustration.

1.18

Example 5.

We use again the matrix $\mathbf{P}_0$, now as the matrix of flow rates, and have

$$\begin{aligned}
\mathrm{d}n_1(t)/\mathrm{d}t &= -0.7n_1(t) + 0.1n_2(t) + 0.2n_3(t)\\
\mathrm{d}n_2(t)/\mathrm{d}t &= 0.4n_1(t) - 0.5n_2(t) + 0.1n_3(t)\\
\mathrm{d}n_3(t)/\mathrm{d}t &= 0.1n_1(t) + 0.3n_2(t) - 0.6n_3(t)
\end{aligned} \tag{1.41}$$

The latent roots of the matrix of coefficients of the right-hand sides are clearly those of equation (1.13) in Section 1.8, Example 4, reduced by unity, i.e.

$\lambda_1 = -0.195 \quad \lambda_2 = -0.8025 + 0.1517\mathrm{i} \quad \lambda_3 = -0.8025 - 0.1517\mathrm{i}$

with the same latent vectors, viz. (proportional to)

0.0935	0.0082 – 0.0766i	0.0082 + 0.0766i
0.1720	–0.0710 + 0.0607i	–0.0710 – 0.0607i
0.1505	0.0898 + 0.0152i	0.0898 – 0.0152i

Therefore the system (1.41) is solved by

$$n_1(t) = 0.0935 \exp(-0.195t)A + (0.0082 - 0.0766\text{i})\exp[(-0.08025 + 0.1517\text{i})t]B + (0.0082 + 0.0766\text{i})\exp[(-0.8025 - 0.1517\text{i})t]C \tag{1.42}$$

$$n_2(t) = 0.1720 \exp(-0.195t)A + (-0.0710 + 0.067\text{i})\exp[(-0.8025 + 0.1517\text{i})t]B + (-0.0710 - 0.0607\text{i})\exp[(-0.8025 - 0.1517\text{i})t]C \tag{1.43}$$

$$n_3(t) = 0.1505 \exp(-0.195t)A + (0.0898 + 0.0152\text{i})\exp[(-0.8025 + 0.1517\text{i})t]B + (0.0898 - 0.0152\text{i})\exp[(-0.8025 - 0.1517\text{i})t]C \tag{1.44}$$

These three equations are the analogues of equations (1.14) to (1.16). In order to have $n_1(0) = 1$, $n_2(0) = n_3(0) = 0$, we must make

$$A = 2.569 \quad B = -1.274 + 5.119\text{i} \quad C = -1.274 - 5.119\text{i}$$

as in Section 1.8. With these values we obtain

$$n_1(t) = 0.240 \exp(-0.195t) + (0.380 + 0.140\text{i})\exp(-0.8025t)[\cos(0.1517t) + \text{i}\sin(0.1517t)] + (0.380 - 0.140\text{i})\exp(-0.8025t)[\cos(0.1517t) - \text{i}\sin(0.1517t)] \tag{1.45}$$

$$n_2(t) = 0.442 \exp(-0.195t) + (-0.221 - 0.431\text{i})\exp(-0.8025t)[\cos(0.1517t) + \text{i}\sin(0.1517t)] + (-0.221 + 431\text{i})\exp(-0.8025t)[\cos(0.1517t) - \text{i}\sin(0.15176)] \tag{1.46}$$

$$n_3(t) = 0.384 \exp(-0.195t) + (-0.192 + 0.440\text{i})\exp(-0.8025t)[\cos(0.1517t) + \text{i}\sin(0.1517t)] + (-0.192 - 0.440\text{i})\exp(-0.8025t)[\cos(0.1517t) - \text{i}\sin(0.1517t)] \tag{1.47}$$

Multiplying the complex expressions and thus losing the imaginary parts, we obtain finally

$$n_1(t) = 0.240 \exp(-0.195t) + \exp(-0.8025t)[0.760 \cos(0.1517t) - 0.280 \sin(0.1517t)] \tag{1.48}$$

$$n_2(t) = 0.442 \exp(-0.195t) + \exp(-0.8025t)[-0.442 \cos(0.1517t) + 0.862 \sin(0.1517t)] \tag{1.49}$$

$$n_3(t) = 0.384 \exp(-0.195t) + \exp(-0.8025t)[-0.384 \cos(0.1517t) - 0.880 \sin(0.1517t)]. \tag{1.50}$$

The numbers in the various grades add up to

$$\int_0^\infty n_1(t)\mathrm{d}t = 2.077 = 27/13 \qquad \int_0^\infty n_2(t)\mathrm{d}t = 1.923 = 25/13$$

$$\int_0^\infty n_3(t)\mathrm{d}t = 1.308 = 17/13$$

(recollecting that $\int_0^\infty \exp(-at)\mathrm{d}t = 1/a$, $\int_0^\infty \exp(-at)\cos(bt)\mathrm{d}t = a/(a^2 + b^2)$, and $\int_0^\infty \exp(-at)\sin(bt)\mathrm{d}t = b/a^2 + b^2)$) and we observe that these are the values in the first row of $(\mathbf{I} - \mathbf{P})^{-1}$.

1.19

Table 3 lists $n_i(t)$ for $i = 1,2,3$ and for values of t which were chosen so as to facilitate the computation using tables of trigonometric functions.

Table 3

t	$1000n_1(t)$	$1000n_2(t)$	$1000_3(t)$	Totals
0	1000	0	0	1000
2.30	251	263	140	654
4.60	108	185	136	429
6.90	63	117	96	276
9.20	40	74	63	177
11.50	25	47	41	113
13.80	16	30	26	72
16.10	10	19	17	46
18.40	7	12	11	30
20.71	4	8	7	19
23.01	3	5	4	12
25.31	2	3	3	8
27.61	1	2	2	5
29.91	1	1	1	3
32.21	0	1	1	2
34.51	0	0	0	0
		and so on		

(Compare with Table 2 in Section 1.9.)

1.20

To establish the expected time spent in the various states in the continuous case, we integrate both sides of each equation in (1.40), for t from 0 to ∞. Assuming that $n_i(\infty) = 0$ for all i, this gives

$$(p_{11} - 1)\int_0^\infty n_1(t)\mathrm{d}t + p_{21}\int_0^\infty n_2(t)\mathrm{d}t + \ldots + p_{k1}\int_0^\infty n_k(t)\mathrm{d}t = -n_1(0) \tag{1.51}$$

$$p_{12}\int_0^\infty n_1(t)\mathrm{d}t + (p_{22}-1)\int_0^\infty n_2(t)\mathrm{d}t + \ldots + p_{k2}\int_0^\infty n_k(t)\mathrm{d}t = -n_2(0) \tag{1.52}$$

$$\vdots$$

$$p_{1k}\int_0^\infty n_1(t)\mathrm{d}t + p_{2k}\int_0^\infty n_2(t)\mathrm{d}t + \ldots + (p_{kk}-1)\int_0^\infty n_k(t)\mathrm{d}t = -n_k(0) \tag{1.53}$$

i.e. the product of the matrix $(\mathbf{P}' - \mathbf{I})$ and the vector

$$\left[\int_0^\infty n_1(t)\mathrm{d}t, \ldots, \int_0^\infty n_k(t)\mathrm{d}t\right] = \mathbf{v} \text{ say} \tag{1.54}$$

equals the vector

$$[-n_1(0), \ldots, -n_k(0)]$$

If the cohort enters state j, then $n_i(0) = 0$ for $i \neq j$, and therefore

$$\mathbf{v} = (\mathbf{I} - \mathbf{P}')^{-1}\,[n_1(0), \ldots, n_k(0)] \tag{1.55}$$

will equal the jth column of $(\mathbf{I} - \mathbf{P}')^{-1}$, multiplied by $n_j(0)$, or the jth row of $(\mathbf{I} - \mathbf{P})$, multiplied by $n_j(0)$.

1.21

We introduce yet another example, more realistic in a hierarchic environment, in that it considers only promotions, and only into the next higher rank.

Example 6.

Let the transition matrix be that of Section 1.6, viz.

$$\begin{pmatrix} 0.590 & 0.036 & 0 \\ 0 & 0.214 & 0.187 \\ 0 & 0 & 0.276 \end{pmatrix}$$

so that the vector of losses is $[0.374, 0.599, 0.724]$.

The system (1.40) to be solved is now

$$\mathrm{d}n_1(t)/\mathrm{d}t = -0.410n_1(t)$$

$$\mathrm{d}n_2(t)/\mathrm{d}t = 0.036n_1(t) - 0.78n_2(t)$$

$$\mathrm{d}n_3(t)/\mathrm{d}t = 0.187n_2(t) - 0.724n_3(t)$$

The latent roots are

$$-0.410 \quad -0.786 \quad -0.724$$

with latent vectors

$$\begin{pmatrix}1.0000\\0.0957\\0.0570\end{pmatrix}\quad\begin{pmatrix}0\\-0.0957\\0.2882\end{pmatrix}\quad\begin{pmatrix}0\\0\\1.0000\end{pmatrix}$$

We have chosen these vectors so as to facilitate the computation of the multipliers which we have to use to obtain

$$n_1(0) = 1000 \qquad n_2(0) = n_3(0) = 0$$

The multipliers are $A = 1000$, $B = 1000$, $C = -345.2$. Then

$$n_1(t) = 1000 \exp(-0.410t)$$

$$n_2(t) = 95.7 \exp(-0.410t) - 95.7 \exp(-0.786t)$$

$$n_3(t) = 57.0 \exp(-0.410t) + 288.2 \exp(-0.786t) - 345.2 \exp(-0.724t)$$

We give a list for selected values of t in Table 4.

Table 4

t	$n_1(t)$	$n_2(t)$	$n_3(t)$
0	1000	0	0
2	440	22	4
4	194	14	4
6	85	7	3
8	37	3	2
10	16	2	1
12	7	1	0
14	3	0	0
16	1	0	0
18	1	0	0

The numbers in the various ranks add up to

$$\int_0^\infty n_1(t)\mathrm{d}t = 2439 \qquad \int_0^\infty n_2(t)\mathrm{d}t = 112. \qquad \int_0^\infty n_3(t)\mathrm{d}t = 29$$

This can be checked by inspecting the first row of the inverse of $(\mathbf{I} - \mathbf{P})$, where $\mathbf{P}$ is the transition matrix which we have used, thus:

$$\begin{pmatrix}2.439 & 0.112 & 0.029\\0 & 1.272 & 0.328\\0 & 0 & 1.381\end{pmatrix}$$

(See also the totals in Example 3, Section 1.6.)

1.22

It is sometimes of interest to envisage a somewhat simplified situation where a proportion of members of a cohort are simultaneously promoted, and no further promotion takes place from that rank.

Suppose the proportion to be promoted from rank i is r_i, and that simultaneous promotions happen, once and for all, at time t_i. With the loss rates of Example 6, in Section 1.21, the effect on an initial cohort of 1000 would be

$$n_1(t) = \begin{cases} 1000\exp(-0.374t) & \text{for } 0 \leqslant t \leqslant t_1 \\ 1000(1-r_1)\exp(-0.374t) & \text{for } t > t_1 \end{cases} \tag{1.56}$$

$$n_2(t) = \begin{cases} 0 & \text{for } t \leqslant t_1 \\ 1000r_1\exp(-0.374t_1)\exp[-0.599(t-t_1)] & \\ \quad = 1000r_1\exp(-0.599t + 0.225t_1) & \text{for } t_1 < t \leqslant t_2 \\ 1000r_1(1-r_2)\exp(-0.599t + 0.225t_1) & \text{for } t > t_2 \end{cases} \tag{1.57}$$

$$n_3(t) = \begin{cases} 0 & \text{for } t \leqslant t_2 \\ 1000r_1r_2\exp(-0.724t + 0.225t_1 + 0.125t_2) & \text{for } t > t_2 \end{cases}$$

We can choose $t_1, t_2, \ldots$ as an average time of promotion, and $r_1, r_2, \ldots$ as average promotion rates. These assumptions would fix the proportions of sojourn in the various ranks. The latter proportions depend on t_i and r_i, because the loss rates are different from the different ranks.

Alternatively, we could fix the proportions in the ranks, choose the average promotion rates (or the average promotion times) and this would result in the appropriate promotion times (or the appropriate promotion rates).

To solve the last mentioned problems, we would have to solve transcendental equations. We shall here illustrate the situation where the average promotion times, and the average promotion rates have been chosen, and from these we compute the times which the cohort's members are expected to spend in the various ranks.

1.23

For the average rates and times we choose, in the following illustration, averages which are implicit in the assumptions of Example 6.

Example 7.

We make once more the assumptions of Section 1.13. The probability of being some time promoted from rank i is

$$\begin{aligned} \int_0^\infty \exp\left(-\int_0^t (p_{i,i+1} + w_i)\mathrm{d}t\right) p_{i,i+1}\mathrm{d}t &= p_{i,i+1}/(p_{i,i+1} + w_i) \\ &= p_{i,i+1}/(1 - p_{i,i}) \end{aligned} \tag{1.58}$$

and in Example 6 this is

$0.036/0.410 = 0.088$ from rank 1. We choose this as r_1

$0.187/0.786 = 0.238$ from rank 2. We choose this as r_2

The expected time to promotion is $1/(1 - p_{ii})$, i.e.

for rank 1 $\quad 2.437 = t_1$

for rank 2 $\quad 1.272 = t_2 - t_1, \quad$ hence $t_2 = 3.709$

The total times spent in the various ranks are then

in rank 1 $\quad \int_0^{2.437} \exp(-0.374t)\,dt + 0.912 \int_{2.437}^{\infty} \exp(-0.374t)\,dt$

$$= 2.674[1 - \exp(-0.912)] + 2.439[\exp(-0.912)]$$

$$= 2.580$$

in rank 2 $\quad 0.088 \exp(0.225 \times 2.437) \int_{2.437}^{3.709} \exp(-0.599t)\,dt$

$$+ 0.088 \times 0.762 \exp(0.225 \times 2.437) \int_{3.709}^{\infty} \exp(-0.599t)\,dt$$

$$= 0.147 \exp(-0.912) + 0.035 \exp(-1.674)$$

$$= 0.065$$

in rank 3 $\quad 0.088 \times 0.238 \exp(0.225 \times 2.437) + 0.125$

$$\times 3.709) \int_{3.709}^{\infty} \exp(-0.724t)\,dt$$

$$= 0.029 \exp(-0.1674) = 0.006$$

The proportions in the various ranks turn out to be 2.580 to 0.065 to 0.006. They differ, of course, from 2.439 to 0.112 to 0.029, but as we have pointed out, we could not expect a precise match.

1.24

In Examples 1 and 2 the survival and loss rates depended on the time completed within the organization, while in Examples 3 to 7 they depended on the state only. This is the reason why the totals remaining in the population after given times depend on the times when transitions between states take place.

We go now one step further in simplifying our assumptions: let the loss rate be independent of time as well as of state.

In such a case the total in the population depends only on time, and not on the transitions which have taken place.

Example 8.

Let the transition matrix be

$$\mathbf{P} = \begin{pmatrix} 0.590 & 0.036 & 0 \\ 0 & 0.500 & 0.126 \\ 0 & 0 & 0.626 \end{pmatrix}$$

with losses

$$\begin{pmatrix} 0.374 \\ 0.374 \\ 0.374 \end{pmatrix}$$

In this case $(\mathbf{I} - \mathbf{P})^{-1}$ equals

$$\begin{pmatrix} 2.437 & 0.177 & 0.060 \\ 0 & 2.000 & 0.674 \\ 0 & 0 & 2.674 \end{pmatrix}$$

We choose average promotion rates and promotion times, and then assume that promotions take place simultaneously. Thus:

$$r_1 = 0.036/0.410 = 0.088 \qquad r_2 = 0.126/0.500 = 0.252$$

and

$$t_1 = 1/0.410 = 2.437 \qquad t_2 = t_1 + 1/0.500 = 4.437$$

The total times spent in the various ranks are, with these assumptions,

in rank 1

$$\int_0^{2.437} \exp(-0.374t)\,\mathrm{d}t + 0.912 \int_{2.437}^{\infty} \exp(-0.374t)\,\mathrm{d}t$$

in rank 2

$$0.088 \int_{2.437}^{4.437} \exp(-0.374t)\,\mathrm{d}t + 0.088 \times 0.748 \int_{4.437}^{\infty} \exp(-0.374t)\,\mathrm{d}t$$

in rank 3

$$0.088 \times 0.252 \int_{4.437}^{\infty} \exp(-0.374t)\,\mathrm{d}t$$

These values are:

in rank 1 2.580 (as in Example 7)

in rank 2 0.083

in rank 3 0.011

The total of these values is 2.674. This is also the total of the stationary population from the original transition matrix, i.e. the totals in the first row of $(\mathbf{I} - \mathbf{P})^{-1}$.

2

The Constant Population

2.1

In Chapter 1 we considered a cohort and its development in time. Due to positive loss rates the numbers were reduced as time increased, and this was demonstrated in tables 2, 3 and 4 in Sections 1.9, 1.19 and 1.21, respectively.

We suppose now that it is required to keep the total number in the population constant. This can be achieved by letting a new cohort enter each year, with a total membership which equals the losses during the year which has just passed.

Denote the number of members at time t who had been in the population for i years by $n_i(t)$. This notation does not contradict that introduced in Section 1.2, where $n_i(t)$ was the number of members in state (rank) i at time t. We simply define now a state by the completed length of service (CLS) in the organization.

If q_i and p_i are the loss and survival rates in state i, then the number of new entrants at time $t + 1$ will be

$$n_0(t+1) = n_0(t)q_1 + n_1(t)q_2 + \ldots + n_{k-1}(t)q_k + n_k(t) \tag{2.1}$$

where k is the highest CLS, and therefore $q_{k+1} = 1, p_{k+1} = 0$.

The numbers of those who have entered before time $t + 1$ and who are still in the population are given by

$$\begin{aligned} n_1(t+1) &= n_0(t)p_1 \\ n_2(t+1) &= n_1(t)p_2 \\ &\vdots \\ n_k(t+1) &= n_{k-1}(t)p_k \end{aligned} \tag{2.2}$$

To solve this system of difference equations (see Appendix I), we determine the latent roots of the characteristic equation

$$\begin{vmatrix} q_1 - \lambda & q_2 & q_3 & \cdots & q_k & 1 \\ p_1 & -\lambda & 0 & \cdots & 0 & 0 \\ 0 & p_2 & -\lambda & \cdots & 0 & 0 \\ 0 & 0 & p_3 & \cdots & 0 & 0 \\ \vdots & \vdots & \vdots & \ddots & \vdots & \vdots \\ 0 & 0 & 0 & \cdots & p_k & -\lambda \end{vmatrix} = 0 \tag{2.3}$$

The entries in each column add up to $1 - \lambda$ and hence $\lambda = 1$ is one of the latent roots.

The characteristic equation is

$$(-1)^{k+1}(\lambda^{k+1} - q_1\lambda^k - p_1q_2\lambda^{k-1} - \ldots - p_1p_2 \ldots p_{k-1}q_k\lambda - p_1p_2 \ldots p_k)$$
$$= (-1)^k(1-\lambda)[\lambda^k + p_1\lambda^{k-1} + p_1p_2\lambda^{k-2} + \ldots + p_1p_2 \ldots p_k] = 0 \tag{2.4}$$

All coefficients within the square brackets of the right-hand side of equation (2.4) are positive, and therefore any real root different from 1 must be negative. This follows also from the sign rule of Descartes, because in the first line of (2.4) only one change of sign occurs in the polynomial. Moreover, by formula (I.11) in Appendix I no latent root can have an absolute value exceeding 1. This follows also from the Eneström–Kakeya theorem (Kakeya 1912/3), because the coefficients within the square brackets of the right-hand side of (2.4), viz. $1, p_1, \ldots, p_1p_2 \ldots p_k$ are not increasing, and the last is positive.

2.2

Leslie (1945) deals with a matrix of the same type as that with which we are concerned here, but instead of loss rates he considers 'fertility rates'; these non-negative rates are responsible for new entries in his case, while in our case new entries are due to replacement of losses. Work similar to that of Leslie's was published slightly earlier by Bernardelli (1941) and by Lewis (1942), but these papers were unknown in Britain until later, due to circumstances prevailing at that time.

2.3

We assume here, as generally in this book, that all latent roots $\lambda_0 = 1, \lambda_1, \ldots, \lambda_k$ are different. The general solution of the set of difference equations (2.2) is then

$$n_i(t) = a_0c_{i0} + a_1c_{i1}\lambda_1^t + \ldots + a_kc_{ik}\lambda_k^t \tag{2.5}$$

where the vectors

$$\mathbf{c}_j = [c_{0j}, \ldots, c_{kj}]$$

are the latent vectors corresponding to the λ_j respectively. The constants $a_0, \ldots, a_k$ depend on the initial structure

$$\mathbf{n}(0) = \begin{pmatrix} a_0c_{00} + a_1c_{01} + \ldots + a_kc_{0k} \\ \vdots \\ a_0c_{k0} + a_1c_{k1} + \ldots + a_kc_{kk} \end{pmatrix} \tag{2.6}$$

2.4

Because the latent vectors, corresponding to different latent roots, are linearly independent (Appendix I, Section 1.7), we can always find multiples of the latent vectors which add up to a given $(k + 1)$-vector. (However, it might not be possible to stipulate an arbitrary population to be reached after t steps, since this might imply an initial population with negative components. We return to this point in Section 2.10.)

It is clear that for $j \neq 0$ we must have $\sum_{i=0}^{k} c_{ij} = 0$. Otherwise it would be impossible to have $\sum_{i=0}^{k} n_i(t)$ independent of t. This follows also formally from the fact that the components of the left-hand latent vectors of a stochastic matrix, corresponding to a latent root other than 1, add up to zero (Appendix I, Section 1.14). The matrix we are dealing with here is the transpose of a stochastic matrix, and hence the statement refers here to the right-hand latent vectors.

If we choose the a_i in equation (2.6) to obtain a required structure, then the vector $[c_{00}, \ldots, c_{k0}]$ will have a positive multiplier a_0, because $\sum_{i=0}^{k} n_i(0)$ is not zero.

The coefficient a_0 can be chosen to make $\sum_{i=0}^{k} n_i(t) = a_0 \sum_{i=0}^{k} c_{i_0}$ equal to any desired total.

2.5

If the absolute values of λ_i $(i = 1, \ldots, k)$ are smaller than unity, then the structure $n(t)$ will converge, with increasing t, to

$$[a_0 c_{00}, a_0 c_{10}, \ldots, a_0 c_{k0}] \tag{2.7}$$

If this were the initial structure, then it would remain unchanged in time. We call the structure (2.7) 'stationary'. We shall deal with such structures in greater detail, in Chapter 3.

The structure (2.7) is a latent vector of (2.3), corresponding to $\lambda_0 = 1$ (latent vectors are only defined with an arbitrary factor of proportionality). It is therefore a solution of the set of equations

$$\begin{aligned}
(q_1 - 1)y_0 + q_2 y_1 + q_3 y_2 + \ldots + q_k y_{k-1} + y_k &= 0 \\
p_1 y_0 - y_1 \qquad\qquad\qquad\qquad &= 0 \\
p_2 y_1 - y_2 \qquad\qquad &= 0 \\
&\ \vdots \\
p_k y_{k-1} + y_k &= 0
\end{aligned} \tag{2.8}$$

The first equation is linearly dependent on the others, because each column of coefficients adds up to zero. Therefore, if $y_0 = a_0 c_{00} = n_0(0)$, then

$$[y_0, y_1, \ldots, y_k] = [n_0(0), n_0(0)p_1, \ldots, n_0(0)p_1 \ldots p_k] \tag{2.9}$$

A comparison with (1.1) shows that the components of the stationary structure are also the numbers of survivors of a cohort in successive years. This is to be expected. If we observe a succession of cohorts, with the same number of members when they enter, and if the survival and loss rates depend on the time a member has been in the population, then after the first cohort has run its course, a stationary population will have been established.

2.6

If the characteristic equation has, apart from its latent root 1, another latent root with absolute value unity, then no stationary structure will be approached.

To give a rather obvious example, let $p_1 = p_2 = \ldots = p_k = 1$, i.e. there is no loss until the highest age is reached. The characteristic equation (2.4) reduces then to $(\lambda^{k+1} - 1) = 0$, and the latent roots are the roots of unity.

Unless the initial structure is stationary (corresponding to $\lambda = 1$), the initial structure will re-appear periodically.

2.7

For $t = 0$, equation (2.1) reads

$$n_0(1) = n_0(0)q_1 + n_1(0)q_2 + \ldots + n_{k-1}(0)q_k + n_k(0)$$

From this we obtain, substituting successively from equations (2.2),

$$\begin{aligned}
n_0(2) &= n_0(1)q_1 + n_0(0)p_1q_2 + n_1(0)p_2q_3 + \ldots + n_{k-1}(0)p_k \\
n_0(3) &= n_0(2)q_1 + n_0(1)p_1q_2 + n_0(0)p_1p_2q_3 + n_1(0)p_2p_3q_4 \\
&\quad + \ldots + n_{k-2}(0)p_{k-1}p_k \\
&\vdots \\
n_0(k) &= n_0(k-1)q_1 + n_0(k-2)p_1q_2 + n_0(k-3)p_1p_2q_3 + \ldots \\
&\quad + n_1(0)p_2p_3 \cdots p_k \\
n_0(k+1) &= n_0(k)q_1 + n_0(k-1)p_1q_2 + n_0(k-2)p_1p_2q_3 + \ldots \\
&\quad + n_0(1)p_1p_2 \ldots p_{k-1}q_k + n_0(0)p_1p_2 \ldots p_k
\end{aligned}$$

This follows also from first principles. The new entrants replace present loss from those who are still left of the initial population, and the present loss of those who have entered since time 0, to replace earlier losses.

Generally, for $t > k$, i.e. when all initial members have left,

$$\begin{aligned}
n_0(t+1) &= n_0(t)q_1 + n_0(t-1)p_1q_2 + n_0(t-2)p_1p_2q_3 + \ldots \\
&\quad + n_0(t-k+1)p_1 \ldots p_{k-1}q_k + n_0(t-k)p_1 \ldots p_k
\end{aligned} \tag{2.11}$$

This difference equation for n_0 has the characteristic equation (see Appendix I, Section I.17)

$$\lambda^{k+1} - \lambda^k q_1 - \lambda^{k-1}p_1q_2 - \ldots - \lambda p_1p_2 \ldots p_{k-1}q_k - p_1p_2 \ldots p_k = 0$$

which is again equation (2.4).

We shall see in Section 2.16 that it is generally true that the characteristic equation of the difference equation of new entrants is the same as that defining the structures at times t. The values of $n_0(t)$ are therefore

$$n_0(t) = b_0\lambda_0^t + b_1\lambda_1^t + \ldots + b_k\lambda_k^t \tag{2.12}$$

where the λ_j are the latent roots of equation (2.4), and in particular $\lambda_0 = 1$. The constants $b_0, \ldots, b_k$ can be found from $n_0(0), \ldots, n_0(k)$.

If $[n_0(0), \ldots, n_k(0)]$ is given, then the $n_0(0), \ldots, n_0(k)$ are thereby implied. A comparison of equations (2.5) and (2.12) shows that $b_j = a_j c_{0j}$. Thus, if the numbers of new entrants are known for $k + 1$ successive years, then we have an alternative method of determining the a_j multipliers. This is particularly easy if we take $c_{0j} = 1$ for all j, which we can do, because latent vectors are defined up to a factor of proportionality only.

2.8

Example 9.

Let $k = 5$, and let the survival and loss rates be those of Example 1 in Section 1.1. Let the initial population consist of 1000 members who have just joined. The development of this population will then be as shown in Table 5.

Table 5

i \ End of year	0	1	2	3	4	5	6	7	8	9	10	
0	1000	125	381	447	361	390	392	386	388	388	388	
1		875	109	333	391	316	341	343	340	340	340	
2			510	64	194	228	184	199	197	198	198	etc.
3				156	20	59	70	56	61	60	60	
4					34	4	13	15	13	13	13	
5						3	0	1	1	1	1	
Totals	1000	1000	1000	1000	1000	1000	1000	1000	1000	1000	1000	

The structures approach a stationary one. We notice also that the bottom values of the first six columns are those of $n(t)$ in Example 1.

If we wanted a structure whose new entrants converge to 1000, then we would start with 2578 members. This would make the components of the stationary structure equal to the $n(t)$ of Example 1.

Now consider the following example.

Example 10.

It differs from Example 9 in that the structure with which we start consists of members who have been in the population for differing numbers of years, thus:

t	$n_t(0)$
0	859
1	1269
2	229
3	50
4	115
5	56
	2578

With survival and loss rates equal to those in Examples 1 and 9 this population will develop as in Table 6.

Once more, the structure approaches a stationary one.

Table 6

i \ After years	1	2	3	4	5	6	7	8	9	
0	996	1025	989	1002	1001	999	1000	1000	1000	
1	752	872	897	865	876	876	874	875	875	
2	740	438	508	523	505	511	511	510	510	etc.
3	70	227	134	156	160	155	156	156	156	
4	11	15	49	29	34	34	34	34	34	
5	9	1	1	4	2	3	3	3	3	
Totals	2578	2578	2578	2578	2578	2578	2578	2578	2578	

2.9

In Examples 9 and 10 the characteristic equation (2.4)

$$(1-\lambda)(\lambda^5+0.875\lambda^4+0.510\lambda^3+0.156\lambda^2+0.034\lambda+0.003)=0 \qquad (2.13)$$

has the latent roots

j	0	1	2	3	4	5
λ_j	1	-0.125	$-0.25+iv$	$-0.25-iv$	$-0.125+iw$	$-0.125-iw$

where $v=(5/48)^{1/2}$ and $w=(7/64)^{1/2}$, i.e. $v\simeq 0.3225$, $w\simeq 0.3307$.

The latent vectors are proportional to the entries in Table 7.

To obtain the initial structure of Example 10 we have to solve equation (2.6)

Table 7

i \ j	0	1	2	3	4	5
0	1000	1000	1000	1000	1000	1000
1	875	−7000	−1313 − 1693i	−1313 + 1693i	−875 − 2315i	−875 + 2315i
2	510	32664	−763 + 2962i	−763 − 2962i	−3062 + 2701i	−3062 − 2701i
3	156	−79992	2108 − 907i	2108 + 907i	3125 + 1654i	3125 − 1654i
4	34	138656	−1066 − 589i	−1066 + 589i	271 − 2150i	271 + 2150i
5	3	−85328	34 + 227i	34 − 227i	−459 + 110i	−459 − 110i
	2578	0	0	0	0	0

and obtain

$$a_0 = 1 \quad a_1 = -0.001 \quad a_2 = -0.07 + 0.06\mathrm{i} \quad a_3 = -0.07 - 0.06\mathrm{i}$$
$$a_4 = 0 \quad a_5 = 0$$

and

$$\begin{aligned} n_0(t) &= 1000\,[1 - 0.001(-0.125)^t + (-0.07 + 0.06\mathrm{i})(-0.25 + 0.3225\mathrm{i})^t \\ &\quad + (-0.07 - 0.06\mathrm{i})(-0.25 - 0.3225\mathrm{i})^t] \\ &= 1000\,[1 - 0.001(-0.125)^t \\ &\quad + (-0.1844)(-0.408)^t \cos(0.6911 + 0.9110t)] \end{aligned} \tag{2.14}$$

If we take

$$a_0 = 1 \quad a_1 = -0.000125 \quad a_2 = -0.002 - 0.038\mathrm{i}$$
$$a_3 = -0.002 + 0.058\mathrm{i} \quad a_4 = 0 \quad a_5 = 0$$

then we obtain the structure of Example 10 after 1 year. With $a_0 = 1, a_i = 0$ for $i \neq 0$ we obtain the stationary structure, with $n(t)$ independent of time.

2.10

If we fixed a structure required after t years, then the appropriate values of a_i could be derived; however, this could imply an initial population with some negative components. Hence not any arbitrary structure can be stipulated to hold after a given number of years.

For instance, if it were required that the population after three years should be

[1000, 876, 506, 166, 17, 13]

(total membership 2578), then this would imply an initial population

[1064, 427, 2600, –4963, 8908, –5458]

(The effect of the last three components will have disappeared after three years.)

The question of which populations can be reached after a given number of years will be dealt with in Chapter 7, by applying techniques of linear programming.

2.11

In Chapter 1 we considered a cohort and its development in time. We then observed a splitting up of the cohort into ranks, with promotion rates between them.

In the present chapter we assume that the population is being replenished, replacing losses so that the total membership remains constant. But we have not yet considered any hierarchy.

We do this now. Since we take notice of new members as well, the treatment will not be identical with that in Chapter 1, but the contents of the two chapters will be based on the same aspects of matrix theory: latent roots and latent vectors.

The connection between the two chapters is most easily established by imagining that there is a transition from each rank back to rank 1. The rate of 'transition' equals the loss rates, since these are the new entry rates, caused by the losses in the several ranks.

Now the transition rates from each rank add up to unity, while in Chapter 1 they added up to unity less the loss rate.

2.12

We denote the number of members with completed time i at time t, now in rank r, by $n_{ri}(t)$. Let k be the longest possible time to remain in the population, and R the highest rank. Let the promotion rates from rank r to rank $r + 1$, after completed time $i + 1$, be $p_{r,\,r+1}(i + 1)$, and the rates of remaining in rank r, after completion of time $i + 1$, be $p_{rr}(i + 1)$. Also, the loss rate after time i is q_i, which we assume to be independent of time, and of rank.

Then

$$n_{10}(t + 1) = \sum_{i=0}^{k-1} (n_{1i}(t) + n_{2i}(t) + \ldots + n_{Ri}(t))q_{i+1} \tag{2.15}$$

where, however, $n_{uv}(t) = 0$ when v is less than $u - 1$,

$$n_{1,i+1}(t + 1) = p_{11}(i + 1)n_{1i}(t) \quad (i = 0, \ldots, k - 1) \tag{2.16}$$

and for $r = 2, \ldots, R, i = r - 1, \ldots, k - 1$

$$n_{r,i+1}(t + 1) = p_{rr}(i + 1)n_{ri}(t) + p_{r-1,r}(i + 1)n_{r-1,i}(t) \tag{2.17}$$

Example 11.

We assume the same loss, survival, and promotion rates, dependent on time in the organization, as in Example 2 in Section 1.3. Also $R = 3$ and $k = 5$, as in that example.

Then the matrix of coefficients on the right-hand side of equations (2.15), (2.16), and (2.17) is as follows:

n_{10}	n_{11}	n_{12}	n_{13}	n_{14}	n_{15}	n_{21}	n_{22}	n_{23}	n_{24}	n_{25}	n_{32}	n_{33}	n_{34}	n_{35}
0.125	0.417	0.694	0.783	0.923	1.00	0.417	0.694	0.783	0.923	1.00	0.694	0.783	0.923	1.00
0.825														
	0.550													
		0.284												
			0.210											
				0.077										
0.050														
	0.033					0.280								
		0.022					0.204							
			0.007					0.100						
				0.000					0.045					
						0.303								
							0.102				0.306			
								0.117				0.217		
									0.032				0.077	

Comparing this matrix with matrix (1.8) in Chapter 1, we find that we have now an additional row (the first), and we have omitted the entries 1 in the diagonal. This will be significant at a later stage.

All columns add up to unity, hence 1 is a latent root. The characteristic equation is

$$(1-\lambda)\lambda^9(\lambda^5 + 0.875\lambda^4 + 0.510\lambda^3 + 0.156\lambda^2 + 0.034\lambda + 0.003) = 0 \quad (2.18)$$

Apart from the irrelevant latent root 0 (which leads to a latent null-vector), the latent roots are the same as those of equation (2.13) for Example 9 and 10.

This was to be expected. We have seen in Section 2.7 that the characteristic equation of the transition matrix is the same as that of the difference equation which is satisfied by the numbers of new entrants. These numbers are functions of the loss rates. Now the loss rates in Example 11 depend only on the length of time in the organization, as in Examples 9 and 10, and the fact that we consider now a hierarchy has no effect on the numbers of new entrants, since the losses are the same as in the previous examples.

However, we have now more states, so that the latent vectors have more components than they had earlier. They are proportional to the entries in Table 8.

If we add the entries referring to the same second subscript, viz. to the same completed time, then we obtain the columns of the latent vectors of Example 10 (multiplied by some power of 10, and with a different number of significant figures).

Table 8

	$\lambda_0 = 1$	$\lambda_1 = -0.125$	$\lambda_{2,3} = -0.25 \pm 0.3225i$	$\lambda_{4,5} = -0.125 \pm 0.3307i$
n_{10}	1000	1	100	100
n_{11}	825	−7	$-123 \mp 160i$	$-82 \mp 219i$
n_{12}	454	29	$-68 \pm 264i$	$-272 \pm 240i$
n_{13}	129	−66	$174 \mp 75i$	$258 \pm 137i$
n_{14}	27	111	$-85 \mp 47i$	$22 \mp 172i$
n_{15}	2	−68	$2 \pm 18i$	$-37 \pm 9i$
Subtotals	2437	0	0	$-11 \mp 5i$
n_{21}	50	0	$-8 \mp 10i$	$-5 \mp 13i$
n_{22}	41	3	$-6 \pm 24i$	$-25 \pm 22i$
n_{23}	18	−9	$23 \mp 10i$	$37 \pm 20i$
n_{24}	3	10	$-9 \mp 5i$	$2 \mp 18i$
n_{25}	0	−4	$\pm i$	$-2 \pm i$
Subtotals	112	0	0	$7 \pm 12i$
n_{32}	15	1	$-2 \pm 9i$	$-9 \pm 8i$
n_{33}	9	−5	$12 \mp 5i$	$17 \pm 9i$
n_{34}	4	17	$-12 \mp 7i$	$3 \mp 26i$
n_{35}	1	−13	$2 \pm 3i$	$-7 \pm 2i$
Subtotals	29	0	0	$4 \mp 7i$
Grand totals	2578	0	0	0

The significance of the subtotals will emerge when we deal, in Chapter 4, with 'semi-stationary' structures.

2.14

Because the latent vectors are linearly independent, it is possible to find suitable multipliers to construct any initial population. This is the same argument as that used in Section 2.4. As in Section 2.5, we can conclude that if the absolute values of all latent vectors apart from the first (of value 1) are smaller than unity, then any structure will converge, with increasing time, to a stationary one. We illustrate these points by the following example.

Example 12.

Multiply the column for $\lambda_0 = 1$ in Table 8 by 1, and those for λ_4 and for λ_5 by −0.2. We obtain Table 9.

This structure will develop as shown in Table 10, while the grand total is being kept constant at 2578.

The structure converges to a stationary one, viz. to the latent vector corresponding to $\lambda_0 = 1$. The grand total remains constant throughout, though not the numbers in the several states.

Table 9

Time in service	Rank 1	2	3	Totals
0	960			960
1	858	52		910
2	563	51	18	632
3	26	3	2	31
4	18	2	3	23
5	17	1	4	22
Totals	2442	169	27	2578

Table 10

After one year				After two years			
Rank				Rank			
1	2	3	Totals	1	2	3	Totals
1006			1006	1003			1003
792	48		840	830	50		880
472	45	16	531	436	40	15	491
160	23	11	194	134	19	9	162
5	0	1	6	34	3	5	42
1	0	0	1	0	0	0	0
2436	114	28	2578	2437	112	29	2578
After three years				**After four years**			
Rank				Rank			
1	2	3	Totals	1	2	3	Totals
999			999	1000			1000
827	50		877	824	50		874
456	41	15	512	455	41	15	511
124	18	9	151	130	18	9	157
28	3	4	35	26	3	4	33
3	0	1	4	2	0	1	3
2437	112	29	2578	2437	112	29	2578

2.15

Example 13.

In another example, we multiply the columns of the latent vectors in Section 2.13 by 1 for λ_0, 1 for λ_1, $-0.7 + 0.6i$ for λ_2, $-0.7 - 0.6i$ for λ_3 and by 0 for λ_4 and for λ_5. We have then the succession of structures shown in Table 11.

Again the structure converges to the stationary one, and the total membership remains constant at 2578. However, this example exhibits yet another feature: the totals in the ranks – though not in the states composing them – also remain constant throughout time. This characteristic will occupy us in Chapter 4. It defines the concept of a 'semi-stationary' structure.

Table 11

859			859	996			996
1196	73		1269	709	43		752
204	18	7	229	658	60	22	740
41	6	3	50	58	8	4	70
92	11	12	115	9	0	2	11
45	4	7	56	7	1	1	9
2437	112	29	2578	2437	112	29	2578
1025			1025	989			989
822	50		872	845	52		897
390	35	13	438	452	41	15	508
187	26	14	227	111	14	9	134
12	1	2	15	39	5	5	49
1	0	0	1	1	0	0	1
2437	112	29	2578	2437	112	29	2578
1001			1001	1001			1001
816	49		865	826	50		876
465	43	15	523	449	40	16	505
129	18	9	156	132	19	9	160
23	2	4	29	27	3	4	34
3	0	1	4	2	0	0	2
2437	112	29	2578	2437	112	29	2578
999			999	1000			1000
826	50		876	824	50		874
455	41	15	511	455	41	15	511
128	18	9	155	129	18	9	156
27	3	4	34	27	3	4	34
2	0	1	3	2	0	1	3
2437	112	29	2578	2437	112	29	2578

and so on

2.16

Examples 11, 12 and 13 were still rather special. We assumed that all new entrants joined rank 1, and that transitions took place only between certain pairs of states. Also, there were states from which there were no further transfers, because their loss rates were unity.

We shall now drop those simplifying assumptions. We shall not speak of rank any more, but generally of states. However we shall still deal with only a finite number of states, for the time being.

Let the transition rate from state i ($i = 1, \ldots, k$) to state j ($j = 1, \ldots, k$) be p_{ij} ($\geqslant 0$) and let the loss rate of state i be denoted by $w_i = 1 - p_{i1} - \ldots - p_{ik}$.

If n_i is the number of members of state i, then the total number of those leaving the population, and hence of the yearly new entrants to keep the total constant, will be $\Sigma_{i=1}^{k} n_i w_i$. If we denote the transition matrix (p_{ij}) by $\mathbf{P}$, and the vector $[w_1, \ldots, w_k]$ by $\mathbf{w}$, then

$$\mathbf{w} = (\mathbf{I} - \mathbf{P})\mathbf{e} \tag{2.19}$$

where $\mathbf{I}$ is the identity matrix, and $\mathbf{e}$ is the vector $[1, \ldots, 1]$.

2.17

Assume that a proportion ρ_j of new entrants joins state j. We assume these proportions to be independent of t, of the n_i and of the w_i (as does, for instance, Gani (1963)). We have then

$$n_j(t+1) = p_{1j}n_1(t) + \ldots + p_{kj}n_k(t) + \rho_j \sum_{i=1}^{k} n_i(t)w_i \quad \text{for } j = 1, \ldots, k \tag{2.20}$$

More generally, we might make ρ_j also dependent on t, and this is the situation which we shall envisage in Part II.

Introducing the notation

$$r_{ij} = p_{ij} + \rho_j w_i \tag{2.21}$$

we write equation (2.20) as follows:

$$n_j(t+1) = r_{1j}n_1(t) + r_{2j}n_2(t) + \ldots + r_{kj}n_k(t) \qquad \text{for } j = 1, \ldots, k \tag{2.22}$$

To solve this system (see Appendix I) we find the latent roots of the matrix

$$\mathbf{R}(\rho) = \begin{pmatrix} r_{11} & r_{21} \cdots r_{k1} \\ r_{12} & r_{22} \cdots r_{k2} \\ \vdots & \\ r_{1k} & r_{2k} \cdots r_{kk} \end{pmatrix} = \mathbf{P}' + \begin{pmatrix} \rho_1 \\ \rho_2 \\ \vdots \\ \rho_k \end{pmatrix} (w_1, w_2, \ldots, w_k) \tag{2.23}$$

(Note that in this matrix the first subscripts refer to the columns, and the second to the rows.)

The columns add up to

$$\sum_{j=1}^{k} r_{ij} = \sum_{j=1}^{k} p_{ij} + w_i \sum_{j=1}^{k} \rho_j = \sum_{j=1}^{k} p_{ij} + w_i = 1 \tag{2.24}$$

Hence one latent root will be unity. The matrix is non-negative, and hence its transpose, $\mathbf{R}(\rho)'$, will be stochastic. If no other latent root except that of real value 1 has absolute value 1, then any initial structure converges to a stationary one, and if that structure is $[n_1, \ldots, n_k]$, then $\mathbf{R}(\rho)^t$ converges to the matrix (see Appendix I, Section I.15)

$$\begin{pmatrix} n_1 & n_1 & \ldots & n_1 \\ \vdots & \vdots & & \vdots \\ n_k & n_k & & n_k \end{pmatrix}$$

We can write for equations (2.22)

$$\mathbf{n}(t+1) = \mathbf{R}(\rho)\mathbf{n}(t) \tag{2.25}$$

so that

$$\mathbf{n}(t) = [\mathbf{R}(\rho)]^t \mathbf{n}(0) \tag{2.26}$$

$\mathbf{R}(\rho)$ satisfies its own characteristic equation, as every matrix does (Appendix I, Section I.3) and hence this is also the characteristic equation which $\mathbf{n}(t)$ satisfies.

The new entrants number

$$\mathbf{n}(t)'(\mathbf{I} - \mathbf{P})\mathbf{e} = \{[\mathbf{R}(\rho)]^t \mathbf{n}(0)\}'(\mathbf{I} - \mathbf{P})\mathbf{e} \tag{2.27}$$

so that the numbers of new entrants satisfy, also, the same difference equation.

A special case of this, concerning structures where the first state consists of entrants only, was mentioned in Section 2.7

2.18

Example 14.

To illustrate these general ideas, we use again the matrix $\mathbf{P}_0$, introduced in Section 1.8.

If all new entrants join state 1 (that state to which the first row and the first column refer), then we have to solve the system

$$\begin{aligned} n_1(t+1) &= 0.5n_1(t) + 0.2n_2(t) + 0.5n_3(t) \\ n_2(t+1) &= 0.4n_1(t) + 0.5n_2(t) + 0.1n_3(t) \\ n_3(t+1) &= 0.1n_1(t) + 0.3n_2(t) + 0.4n_3(t) \end{aligned} \tag{2.28}$$

The characteristic equation of this system is

$$\lambda^3 - 1.4\lambda^2 + 0.49\lambda - 0.09 = 0 \tag{2.29}$$

and this equation has the roots

$$\lambda_0 = 1 \quad \lambda_1 = 0.2 + i(0.05)^{1/2} \quad \lambda_2 = 0.2 - i(0.05)^{1/2}$$

with corresponding latent roots proportional to

$$\begin{matrix} 0.27 & -0.02 - 0.1118i & -0.02 + 0.1118i \\ 0.25 & -0.07 + 0.0894i & -0.07 - 0.0894i \\ 0.17 & 0.09 + 0.0224i & 0.09 - 0.0224i \end{matrix} \tag{2.30}$$

If we want the original structure to be [1000, 0, 0], then we multiply the first latent vector by 1000/0.69 = 1444, and the second and third by −722 + 2602i and −722 − 2602i respectively.

We obtain

$$n_1(t) = 392 + (304 + 29i)[0.2 + i(0.05)^{1/2}]^t \tag{2.31}$$

$$n_2(t) = 362 + (-181 - 247i)[0.2 + i(0.05)^{1/2}]^t + (304 - 29i)[0.2 - i(0.05)^{1/2}]^t \tag{2.32}$$

$$n_3(t) = 246 + (-123 + 218i)[0.2 + i(0.05)^{1/2}]^t + (-123 - 2181i)[0.2 - i(0.05)^{1/2}]^t \tag{2.33}$$

As in Section 1.8, we can again write this in a different form. Because

$$304 + 29i = 305 \exp(0.095i)$$

$$-181 - 247i = -306 \exp(0.930i)$$

$$-123 + 218i = -250 \exp(-1.05i)$$

and

$$0.2 + \sqrt{0.05i} = 0.3 \exp(0.84i)$$

we have

$$n_1(t) = 392 + 610(0.3)^t \cos(0.095 + 0.84t) \tag{2.34}$$

$$n_2(t) = 362 - 612(0.3)^t \cos(0.930 + 0.84t) \tag{2.35}$$

$$n_3(t) = 246 - 500(0.3)^t \cos(-1.05 + 0.84t) \tag{2.36}$$

We quote the first eight structures, which converge to the stationary one:

$$\begin{pmatrix} 1000 \\ 0 \\ 0 \end{pmatrix} \to \begin{pmatrix} 300 + 200 \\ 400 \\ 100 \end{pmatrix} \to \begin{pmatrix} 210 + 170 \\ 410 \\ 210 \end{pmatrix} \to \begin{pmatrix} 197 + 180 \\ 378 \\ 245 \end{pmatrix} \to$$

$$\begin{pmatrix} 200 + 187 \\ 364 \\ 249 \end{pmatrix} \to \begin{pmatrix} 202 + 188 \\ 362 \\ 248 \end{pmatrix} \to \begin{pmatrix} 203 + 189 \\ 362 \\ 246 \end{pmatrix} \to \begin{pmatrix} 203 + 189 \\ 362 \\ 246 \end{pmatrix} \text{ and so on}$$

The successive structures satisfy the difference equation whose characteristic

$$377 - 1.4 \times 380 + 0.49 \times 500 - 0.09 \times 1000 = 0$$
$$378 - 1.4 \times 410 + 0.49 \times 400 = 0$$
$$245 - 1.4 \times 210 + 0.49 \times 100 = 0$$

Starting from a stationary structure, we would have

$$\begin{pmatrix} 392 \\ 362 \\ 246 \end{pmatrix} \rightarrow \begin{pmatrix} 203 + 189 \\ 362 \\ 246 \end{pmatrix} = \begin{pmatrix} 392 \\ 362 \\ 246 \end{pmatrix}$$

2.19

Every initial structure will converge to the same limit. To obtain possible structures we must take such weights that the weighted sum of the latent vectors does not contain any negative values.

In the case of Example 14 we must find weights proportional to 1, $u + iv$, $u - iv$ such that

$$27 - 4u + 22.36v \geqslant 0$$
$$25 - 14u - 17.88v \geqslant 0$$
$$17 + 18u - 4.48v \geqslant 0$$

The extreme values of u and v, i.e. the coordinates of the vertices of the admissible region in the (u, v)-plane can be found by solving any two of the inequalities as equations.

We obtain

from the second and third equation $u = -0.5, v = 1.802$

from the first and third equation $u = -1.303, v = -1.441$

from the first and second equation $u = 2.709, v = -0.723$

These values lead to initial structures with the second and third, with the first and third, with the first and second states without members.

For instance, we have used above the weights 1, –0.5 + 1.802i, –0.5 – 1.802i multiplied by 1444, to obtain [1000, 0, 0]. To obtain the initial structure [0, 1000, 0] we would use the weights 1444, 1444(–1.303 – 1.441i) = –1882 – 2081i, 1444(–1.303 + 1.441i) = –1882 + 2081i, and to obtain [0, 0, 1000] the weights would be 1444, 1444(2.705 – 0.723i) = 3912 – 1044i, 1444(2.705 + 0.723i) = 3912 + 1044i.

2.20

If not all the new entrants join state 1, then we have to find the latent roots of

$$\begin{pmatrix} 0.3 + 0.2\rho_1 & 0.1 + 0.1\rho_1 & 0.2 + 0.3\rho_1 \\ 0.4 + 0.2\rho_2 & 0.5 + 0.1\rho_2 & 0.1 + 0.3\rho_2 \\ 0.1 + 0.2\rho_3 & 0.3 + 0.1\rho_3 & 0.4 + 0.3\rho_3 \end{pmatrix}$$

If we eliminate ρ_1 through $\rho_1 + \rho_2 + \rho_3 = 1$, then the latent roots can be written

$$\lambda_0 = 1$$

$$\lambda_{1,2} = (0.2 - 0.05\rho_2 + 0.05\rho_3) \pm (-0.05 + 0.03\rho_2 + 0.04\rho_3 - 0.0025\rho_2\rho_3 + 0.0025\rho_2^2 + 0.0025\rho_3^2)^{1/2} \quad (2.37)$$

These latent roots are, in particular,

when $\rho_1 = 1$:	1	$0.2 + i(0.05)^{1/2}$	$0.2 - i(0.05)^{1/2}$	(as above)
when $\rho_2 = 1$:	1	$0.15 + i(0.0175)^{1/2}$	$0.15 - i(0.0175)^{1/2}$	
when $\rho_3 = 1$:	1	$0.25 + i(0.0075)^{1/2}$	$0.25 - i(0.0075)^{1/2}$	

The latent vectors are

$$\begin{pmatrix} \lambda^2 - 0.9\lambda - 0.1\rho_2\lambda - 0.3\rho_3\lambda - 0.05\rho_2 + 0.14\rho_3 + 0.17 \\ 0.4\lambda + 0.2\rho_2\lambda \qquad - 0.05\rho_2 - 0.10\rho_3 - 0.15 \\ 0.1\lambda \qquad + 0.2\rho_3\lambda + 0.05\rho_2 - 0.06\rho_3 + 0.07 \end{pmatrix} \quad (2.38)$$

and, in particular the vector corresponding to $\lambda_0 = 1$ is, for general ρ_j, proportional to

$$[0.27 - 0.15\rho_2 - 0.16\rho_3, 0.25 + 0.15\rho_2 - 0.10\rho_3, 0.17 + 0.05\rho_2 + 0.14\rho_3]$$

Thus, when all new entrants join the same state, the stationary structure will be proportional to

$$\begin{pmatrix} 27 \\ 25 \\ 17 \end{pmatrix} \text{ or to } \begin{pmatrix} 392 \\ 362 \\ 246 \end{pmatrix} \qquad \begin{pmatrix} 12 \\ 40 \\ 22 \end{pmatrix} \text{ or to } \begin{pmatrix} 162 \\ 541 \\ 297 \end{pmatrix} \qquad \begin{pmatrix} 11 \\ 15 \\ 31 \end{pmatrix} \text{ or to } \begin{pmatrix} 193 \\ 263 \\ 544 \end{pmatrix}$$

when $\rho_1 = 1$ when $\rho_2 = 1$ when $\rho_3 = 1$

(Compare with the matrix $(\mathbf{I} - \mathbf{P}_0)^{-1}$ in Appendix III. The relationship will become clear in Section 3.1.)

The components of the vector (2.38) add up to

$$\lambda^2 - 0.4\lambda + 0.1\rho_2\lambda - 0.1\rho_3\lambda - 0.05\rho_2 - 0.02\rho_3 + 0.09$$

Those latent roots different from 1 make this expression equal to 0 (see equation (2.37)).

For entries into state 1, we have seen the convergence in Section 2.18. With entries into other states, starting with [1000,0,0], we have:

state 2 entries

$$\begin{pmatrix} 1000 \\ 0 \\ 0 \end{pmatrix} \begin{pmatrix} 300 \\ 600 \\ 100 \end{pmatrix} \begin{pmatrix} 170 \\ 580 \\ 250 \end{pmatrix} \begin{pmatrix} 159 \\ 550 \\ 291 \end{pmatrix} \begin{pmatrix} 161 \\ 542 \\ 297 \end{pmatrix} \begin{pmatrix} 162 \\ 541 \\ 297 \end{pmatrix} \begin{pmatrix} 162 \\ 541 \\ 297 \end{pmatrix} \begin{pmatrix} 162 \\ 541 \\ 297 \end{pmatrix} \text{ and so on}$$

state 3 entries

$$\begin{pmatrix}1000\\0\\0\end{pmatrix}\begin{pmatrix}300\\400\\300\end{pmatrix}\begin{pmatrix}190\\350\\460\end{pmatrix}\begin{pmatrix}184\\297\\519\end{pmatrix}\begin{pmatrix}189\\274\\537\end{pmatrix}\begin{pmatrix}192\\266\\542\end{pmatrix}\begin{pmatrix}193\\264\\543\end{pmatrix}\begin{pmatrix}193\\263\\544\end{pmatrix}$$

and so on.

If entries take place in proportions 0.3/0.5/0.2, say, then we obtain, starting again from [1000, 0, 0], the correspondingly weighted means of the values in the three series above (the first in Section 2.18, and the two just quoted). Thus the development will be, after three steps,

$$\begin{pmatrix}1000\\0\\0\end{pmatrix}\to\begin{array}{c}300+\ 60\\400+100\\100+\ 40\end{array}=\begin{pmatrix}360\\500\\140\end{pmatrix}\to\begin{array}{c}186+51\\408+75\\242+38\end{array}=\begin{pmatrix}237\\483\\280\end{pmatrix}\to\begin{array}{c}175+54\\364+84\\281+42\end{array}=$$

$$\begin{pmatrix}229\\448\\323\end{pmatrix}$$

which equals

$$(0.3)\begin{pmatrix}377\\378\\245\end{pmatrix}+(0.5)\begin{pmatrix}159\\550\\291\end{pmatrix}+(0.2)\begin{pmatrix}184\\297\\519\end{pmatrix}$$

2.21

In another example, we follow the development of [0.32, 0.43, 0.25]. With entries into the various states, we find

$$\begin{array}{l}0.189+0.182\\\to 0.368\\0.261\end{array}=\begin{pmatrix}0.371\\0.368\\0.261\end{pmatrix}\to\begin{array}{l}0.200+0.190\\0.358\\0.252\end{array}=\begin{pmatrix}0.390\\0.358\\0.252\end{pmatrix}$$

$$\begin{array}{l}0.189\\\to 0.368+0.182\\0.261\end{array}=\begin{pmatrix}0.189\\0.550\\0.261\end{pmatrix}\to\begin{array}{l}0.164\\0.377+0.171\\0.288\end{array}=\begin{pmatrix}0.164\\0.548\\0.288\end{pmatrix}$$

$$\begin{array}{l}0.189\\\to 0.368+\\0.261+0.182\end{array}=\begin{pmatrix}0.189\\0.368\\0.443\end{pmatrix}\to\begin{array}{l}0.182\\0.304\\0.306+0.208\end{array}=\begin{pmatrix}0.182\\0.304\\0.514\end{pmatrix}$$

Any non-negatively weighted average of these values can be obtained after one, and after two years respectively.

On the other hand, we cannot obtain, from [0.32, 0.43, 0.25], after two years, [0.200, 0.548, 0.252], because

$$\begin{pmatrix}200\\548\\252\end{pmatrix} = w_1\begin{pmatrix}390\\358\\252\end{pmatrix} + w_2\begin{pmatrix}164\\548\\288\end{pmatrix} + w_3\begin{pmatrix}182\\304\\514\end{pmatrix}$$

with $w_1 = 0.1698$, $w_2 = 0.9624$, $w_3 = -0.1322$.

It is important to realize, though, that this negative result arose because we assumed that entries will, after each year, be those in the example, multiplied by w_i.

If we allow changes in this respect, then we can in fact reach [0.200, 0.548, 0.252] from [0.32, 0.43, 0.25], for instance thus:

$$\begin{pmatrix}0.32\\0.43\\0.25\end{pmatrix} \to \begin{matrix}0.189+0.182\\0.368\\0.261\end{matrix} = \begin{pmatrix}0.371\\0.368\\0.252\end{pmatrix} \to \begin{matrix}0.200\\0.358+0.190\\0.252\end{matrix} = \begin{pmatrix}0.200\\0.548\\0.252\end{pmatrix}$$

The question of which structures can be obtained, after a given number of years, from some other structure, with suitable entries into the various states, will be one of our main considerations in Part II of this book.

2.22

As we have seen, it is the matrix $\mathbf{R}(\rho)$ which transforms a structure into that of the next step. It takes account of the distribution of new entrants into the various states, by containing the terms $\rho_j w_i$.

A given matrix $\mathbf{R}$ can be interpreted in various ways, though. For example, instead of considering.

$$\begin{pmatrix}0.5 & 0.2 & 0.5\\0.4 & 0.5 & 0.1\\0.1 & 0.3 & 0.4\end{pmatrix}$$

to be the sum of the matrices

$$\begin{pmatrix}0.3 & 0.1 & 0.2\\0.4 & 0.5 & 0.1\\0.1 & 0.3 & 0.4\end{pmatrix} \text{ and } \begin{pmatrix}0.2 & 0.1 & 0.3\\0 & 0 & 0\\0 & 0 & 0\end{pmatrix}$$

(this is what we have done above, guiding all entrants into state 1), we can also take it to be the sum of the matrices

$$\begin{pmatrix} 0.4 & 0 & 0.4 \\ 0.3 & 0.3 & 0 \\ 0 & 0.1 & 0.3 \end{pmatrix} \text{ and } \begin{pmatrix} 0.1 & 0.2 & 0.1 \\ 0.1 & 0.2 & 0.1 \\ 0.1 & 0.2 & 0.1 \end{pmatrix}$$

This would be interpreted by assuming the transition matrix to be

$$\begin{pmatrix} 0.4 & 0.3 & 0 \\ 0 & 0.3 & 0.1 \\ 0.4 & 0 & 0.3 \end{pmatrix} \text{ with } \mathbf{w} = \begin{pmatrix} 0.3 \\ 0.6 \\ 0.3 \end{pmatrix}$$

and each state to be refilled by one third of the losses, i.e. by 0.1 of n_1, 0.2 of n_2, 0.1 of n_3.

The succession of structures is the same as in Section 2.18, thus:

$$\begin{pmatrix} 1000 \\ 0 \\ 0 \end{pmatrix} \to \begin{matrix} 400 + 100 \\ 300 + 100 \\ 0 + 100 \end{matrix} = \begin{pmatrix} 500 \\ 400 \\ 100 \end{pmatrix} \to \begin{matrix} 240 + 140 \\ 290 + 140 \\ 70 + 140 \end{matrix} = \begin{pmatrix} 380 \\ 410 \\ 210 \end{pmatrix} \quad \text{and so on}$$

The stationary structure depends only on $\mathbf{R}(\rho)$. With the latter interpretation we have

$$\begin{pmatrix} 392 \\ 362 \\ 246 \end{pmatrix} \to \begin{matrix} 256 + 136 \\ 226 + 136 \\ 110 + 136 \end{matrix} = \begin{pmatrix} 392 \\ 362 \\ 246 \end{pmatrix}$$

2.23

We consider now a hierarchy of ranks, with no demotion or redundancy, and mention another method of keeping the population total constant. In fact, we shall keep the membership of each rank constant as far as its total is concerned, though in general with changing age distributions.

The scheme is not as elegant, theoretically, as that which we have so far been dealing with, but it is quite straightforward and, in fact, practical: the highest rank loses members through retirement, resignation, death and other reasons. A given proportion of the number of lost members is replaced by recruitment, spread over a range of ages in given proportions, and the remainder is replaced by promotion from one or more lower ranks, again in given proportions spread over those ranks and over a range of ages. The age distribution of promotions is referred to as the 'promotion profile'.

The numbers lost to the lower ranks, through resignation etc., and also through promotion into higher ranks, are again replaced by recruitment or by promotion from lower ranks, if any, with given promotion profiles.

In general the proportion of members of given age and rank being promoted is not constant in time. It might happen that the number of promotees of a given age, required by the promotion profile, is not available in the lower rank. In such a case special rules apply.

A detailed description of such a scheme, programmed for computers, the 'Kent model', is given, for instance, in Smith (1976).

2.24

We show that with the scheme of Section 2.23 the structure will again converge to a stationary one. We prove it by assuming that promotions are only made from the next lower rank, but it will be seen that this is a simplification which does not affect the general argument.

The following notation will be used:

w_{ij} wastage rate of rank i, age j,
v_{ij} survival rate of rank i, age j, i.e. $1 - w_{ij}$,
ρ_i proportion of loss being recruited into rank i,
$\tau_{i1}, \tau_{i2}, \ldots$ promotion profile of rank i
$\sigma_{i1}, \sigma_{i2}, \ldots$ distribution of the proportion $\bar{\rho}_i = 1 - \rho_i$ of new entrants over ages 1,2, . . .

The ages of promotees are those at the beginning of that year, at the end of which they are promoted. Hence, if the highest age in the population is m, and hence $w_{im} = 1$ for all i, the subscript j of σ_{ij} ranges from 1 to $m - 1$.

2.25

Example 15.

Before we prove that any initial structure converges to a stationary one, we give an example for illustration. In this example $m = 6$, $\rho_1 = 1$, $\tau_{11} = 1$ (all recruits into the lowest rank are of age 1), $\rho_2 = \frac{1}{2}$, $\tau_2 = 1$ (one half of those joining rank 2 are by recruitment, all of age 2), $\sigma_{12} = \sigma_{13} = \frac{1}{2}$ (those promoted are, at the beginning of the year, of age 2 or 3, in equal numbers, $\rho_3 = 0$ (no recruitment into rank 3, only promotions), $\sigma_{23} = \sigma_{24} = \frac{1}{2}$ (those promoted from rank 2 into rank 3 were, at the beginning of the year, of age 3 or 4, in equal numbers).

We start from the initial population given in Table 12, with wastage rates, dependent on age only, given in the last column.

The highest rank loses through wastage. Adding promotees from ages 3 and 4, now aged 4 and 5, we have in rank 3

$$\begin{array}{lrcr} & \cdot\ + 183 & = & 183 \\ (300(0.5) =) & 150 + 183 & = & 333 \\ (210(0.4) =) & 84 & = & \underline{84} \\ & & & 600 \end{array}$$

Rank 2 loses through wastage, and those promoted to rank 3. It gains from recruitment, and from promotions

Table 12

column.

	Rank				
Age	1	2	3	Totals	Wastage rate
1	2000			2000	0.3
2	1500	1000		2500	0.1
3	1000	700		1700	0.3
4	800	500	300	1600	0.5
5	500	400	210	1110	0.6
6	200	400	90	690	1.0
Totals	6000	3000	600	9600	

	·	·		= ·
	·	+783		= 783
(1000(0.9) =)	900		+391	= 1291
(700(0.7) =)	490 – 183		+392	= 699
(500(0.5) =)	250 – 183			= 67
(400(0.4) =)	160			= 160
				3000

Rank 1 loses through wastage, and those promoted to rank 2. It gains from recruitment.

	·	2733	= 2733
(2000(0.7) =)	1400		1400
(1500(0.9) =)	1350 – 391		= 959
(1000(0.7) =)	700 – 392		= 308
(800(0.5) =)	400		= 400
(500(0.4) =)	200		= 200
			6000

Continuing in this manner, we obtain

rank 3			rank 2				rank 1			
·		·	·			·	·		2537	2537
·		·	·		695	695	1913			1913
·		·	705		347	1052	1260	– 347		913
·	+ 188	188	904	– 188	348	1064	671	– 348		323
91	+ 188	279	350	– 188		162	154			154
133		133	27			27	160			160
		600				3000				6000

At the fourth following stage we have

·	·	·		·	·	2431	2431
·	·	·	730	730	1690		1690
·	·	668	365	1033	1466 – 365		1101
· + 194	194	722 – 194	364	892	780 – 364		416
97 + 193	290	443 – 193		250	244		244
116	116	95		95	118		118
	600			3000			6000

From now on rank 3 is stationary. After another six steps we reach

·	·	·		·	·	2414	2414
·	·	·	732	732	1692		1692
·	·	658	367	1025	1517 – 367		1150
· + 194	194	718 – 194	366	890	800 – 366		434
97 + 193	290	445 – 193		252	220		220
116	116	101		101	90		90
	600			3000			6000

Now rank 2 has also reached its stationary structure. Seven more steps bring us to

·	·	·	·		·	·	2412	2412
·	·	·	·	732	732	1688		1688
·	·	·	658	367	1025	1519 – 367		1152
· + 194		194	718 – 194	366	890	806 – 366		440
97 + 193		290	445 – 193		252	220		220
116		116	101		101	88		88
		600			3000			6000

and this remains stationary within the accuracy of computation, retaining integers only.

The promotion rates are, of course, not unchanged during the succession of steps. They change from initially

	rank 2 to rank 3		rank 1 to rank 2
age 3	0.203	age 2	0.261
age 4	0.366	age 3	0.392

to finally

age 3	0.189	age 2	0.217
age 4	0.217	age 3	0.318

2.26

We turn now to the proof that in this system the structures converge to a stationary one. The proof consists in showing that unity is a latent root of the relevant matrix.

We exhibit the algebra for three ranks and three ages, but it will be readily understood that the result is true for any number of ranks and ages.

It will emerge that all columns of the matrix of the appropriate difference equation add up to unity, and that, therefore, any structure converges to the corresponding latent vector.

Consider the difference equation

$$\mathbf{n}(t+1) = \mathbf{Q}n(t) \tag{2.39}$$

and, to begin with, the columns of coefficients of $n_{31}(t)$, $n_{32}(t)$, $n_{33}(t)$, viz.

	$n_{31}(t)$	$n_{32}(t)$	$n_{33}(t)$
$n_{31}(t+1)$	$\rho_3\tau_{31}w_{31}$	$\rho_3\tau_{31}w_{32}$	$\rho_3\tau_{31}w_{33}$
$n_{32}(t+1)$	$(\rho_3\tau_{32}+\bar{\rho}_3\sigma_{21})w_{31}+v_{31}$	$(\rho_3\tau_{32}+\bar{\rho}_3\sigma_{21})w_{32}$	$(\rho_3\tau_{32}+\bar{\rho}_3\sigma_{21})w_{33}$
$n_{32}(t+1)$	$(\rho_3\tau_{33}+\bar{\rho}_3\sigma_{22})w_{31}$	$(\rho_3\tau_{33}+\bar{\rho}_3\sigma_{22})w_{32}+v_{32}$	$(\rho_3\tau_{33}+\bar{\rho}_3\sigma_{22})w_{33}$

(2.40)

The entries of these three rows add up to

$$(\rho_3+\bar{\rho}_3)w_{31}+v_{31}=1 \qquad (\rho_3+\bar{\rho}_3)w_{32}+v_{32}=1 \qquad (\rho_3+\bar{\rho}_3)w_{33}=1$$

(since $w_{33}=1$).

The next three rows of the set (2.39) are as follows, denoting the vector $[w_{i1}, w_{i2}, w_{i3}]$ by $\mathbf{w}_i$:

$$\begin{aligned} n_{21}(t+1) &= \rho_2\tau_{21}(n_2'(t)\mathbf{w}_2+\bar{\rho}_3n_3'(t)\mathbf{w}_3)\\ n_{22}(t+1) &= (\rho_2\tau_{22}+\bar{\rho}_2\sigma_{11})(n_2'(t)\mathbf{w}_2+\bar{\rho}_3n_3'(t)\mathbf{w}_3)+v_{21}n_{21}(t)\\ n_{23}(t+1) &= (\rho_2\tau_{23}+\bar{\rho}_2\sigma_{12})(n_2'(t)\mathbf{w}_2+\bar{\rho}_3n_3'(t)\mathbf{w}_3)+v_{22}n_{22}(t)\end{aligned} \tag{2.41}$$

If we write this out in full, we have non-zero entries in the columns of $n_{2j}(t)$ and of $n_{3j}(t)$, $j = 1, 2, 3$. The columns add up as follows:

those of n_{2j}

$$\rho_2\tau_{21}w_{2j}+(\rho_2\tau_{22}+\bar{\rho}_2\sigma_{11})w_{2j}+(\rho_2\tau_{23}+\bar{\rho}\sigma_{12})w_{2j}+v_{2j}=1$$

those of n_{3j}

$$\rho_2\bar{\rho}_3w_{3j}+\bar{\rho}_2\bar{\rho}_3w_{3j}-\bar{\rho}_3w_{3j}=0$$

The last three rows are as follows (ρ_1 is obviously 1):

$$\begin{aligned} n_{11}(t+1) &= \tau_{11}[n_1'\mathbf{w}_1+\bar{\rho}_2(n_2'\mathbf{w}_2+\bar{\rho}_3n_3'\mathbf{w}_3)]\\ n_{12}(t+1) &= \tau_{12}[n_1'\mathbf{w}_1+\bar{\rho}_2(n_2'\mathbf{w}_2+\bar{\rho}_3n_3'\mathbf{w}_3)]\\ &\quad -\bar{\rho}_2\sigma_{11}(n_2'\mathbf{w}_2+\bar{\rho}_3n_3'\mathbf{w}_3)+v_{11}n_{11}\\ n_{13}(t+1) &= \tau_{13}[n_1'\mathbf{w}_1+\bar{\rho}_2(n_2'\mathbf{w}_2+\bar{\rho}_3n_3'\mathbf{w}_3)]\\ &\quad -\bar{\rho}_2\sigma_{12}(n_2'\mathbf{w}_2+\bar{\rho}_3n_3'\mathbf{w}_3)+v_{12}n_{12}\end{aligned} \tag{2.42}$$

Written out in full, we find that these entries add up as follows:

in $n_{1j}(t)$	in $n_{2j}(t)$ ($j = 1, 2, 3$)	in $n_{3j}(t)$
$\tau_{11}w_{1j}$	$\tau_{11}\bar{\rho}_2 w_{2j}$	$\tau_{11}\bar{\rho}_2\bar{\rho}_3 w_{3j}$
$+\tau_{12}w_{1j}$	$-\bar{\rho}_2\sigma_{11}w_{2j}$	$-\bar{\rho}_2\sigma_{11}\bar{\rho}_3 w_{3j}$
$+\tau_{13}w_{1j}$	$+\tau_{12}\bar{\rho}_2 w_{2j}$	$+\tau_{12}\bar{\rho}_2\bar{\rho}_3 w_{3j}$
$+v_{1j}$	$+\tau_{13}\bar{\rho}_2 w_{2j}$	$+\tau_{13}\bar{\rho}_2\bar{\rho}_3 w_{3j}$
	$-\bar{\rho}_2\sigma_{12}w_{2j}$	$-\bar{\rho}_2\sigma_{12}\bar{\rho}_3 w_{3j}$
= 1	= 0	= 0

Adding the subtotals which we have just worked out, we find

	$n_{1j}(t)$	$n_{2j}(t)$	$n_{3j}(t)$
$n_{1j}(t+1)$	1	0	0
$n_{2j}(t+1)$	–	1	0
$n_{3j}(t+1)$	–	–	1
Grand total	1	1	1

2.27

The complete matrix for our Example 15 is as follows:

0.3	0.1	0.3	0.5	0.6	1.0	0.050	0.150	0.250	0.30	0.50	.	.	.
0.7	.	.	.	.	.	.	.	.	.	.	.	.	.
.	0.9	.	.	.	.	−0.025	−0.075	−0.125	−0.15	−0.25	.	.	.
.	.	0.7	.	.	.	−0.025	.	.	.	.	.	.	.
.	.	.	0.5	.	.	.	.	.	.	.	.	.	.
.	.	.	.	0.4	.	.	.	.	.	.	.	.	.
.	.	.	.	.	.	0.050	0.150	0.250	0.30	0.50	0.250	0.30	0.50
.	.	.	.	.	.	0.925	0.075	0.125	0.15	0.25	0.125	0.15	0.25
.	.	.	.	.	.	0.025	0.775	0.125	0.15	0.25	−0.125	−0.15	−0.25
.	.	.	.	.	.	.	.	0.500	.	.	−0.250	−0.30	−0.50
.	.	.	.	.	.	.	.	.	0.40	.	.	.	.
.	.	.	.	.	.	.	.	.	.	.	0.250	0.30	0.50
.	.	.	.	.	.	.	.	.	.	.	0.750	0.30	0.50
.	.	.	.	.	.	.	.	.	.	.	.	0.40	.

Unity is one of the latent roots, and it is easy to verify that a corresponding latent vector is proportional to

[2412, 1688, 1152, 440, 220, 88; 732, 1025, 890, 252, 101; 194, 290, 116]

2.28

We turn now to continuous time t.

Using the same notation as in Section 1.17, we have

$$n_j(t+\Delta t) = n_j(t)\left(1 - \sum_{\substack{i=1\\ i\neq j}}^{k} p_{ji}\Delta_t - W_j\Delta_t\right) + \sum_{\substack{i=1\\ i\neq j}}^{k} n_i(t)p_{ij}\Delta_t + \sum_{i=1}^{k} n_i(t)\rho_j w_i\Delta_t \tag{2.43}$$

i.e.

$$n_j(t+\Delta t) = n_j(t)\,(1-\Delta t) + \sum_{i=1}^{k} n_i(t)\,(p_{ij} + \rho_j w_i)\Delta t \tag{2.44}$$

In the same way as we obtained the system (1.40) from equation (1.39), we obtain from equation (2.44) the system

$$\begin{aligned}
\mathrm{d}n_1(t)/\mathrm{d}t &= n_1(t)(r_{11}-1) + n_2(t)r_{21} + \ldots + n_k(t)r_{k1}\\
\mathrm{d}n_2(t)/\mathrm{d}t &= n_1(t)r_{12} + n_2(t)r_{22} - 1) + \ldots + n_k(t)r_{k2}\\
&\vdots\\
\mathrm{d}n_k(t)/\mathrm{d}t &= n_1(t)r_{1k} + n_2(t)r_{2k} + \ldots + n_k(t)(r_{kk}-1)
\end{aligned} \tag{2.45}$$

This is the same as the system (1.40), except that p_{ij} is now replaced by $r_{ij} = p_{ij} + \rho_j w_i$.

When we add the equations of the system (2.45), we find

$$\sum_{j=1}^{k} \mathrm{d}n_j(t)/\mathrm{d}t = \sum_{i=1}^{k} n_1(t)\left(\sum_{j=1}^{k} r_{ij} - 1\right) = 0 \tag{2.46}$$

because of $\Sigma_{j=1}^{k} = 1$ for all i.

This confirms the fact that the sum of all $n_i(i)$ remains constant, for all t. Also, the matrix of coefficients of the right-hand side of equations (2.45) is singular, so that one of its latent roots is zero. It corresponds to the stationary solution: if we put all $\mathrm{d}n_i(t)/\mathrm{d}t$ equal to zero, the solution of the system will be the corresponding latent vector, independent of t.

It follows from the theorem of Brauer (1946) (see Appendix I, Section 1.5) that all latent roots are either 0, or have negative real parts.

2.29

Example 16

As a first example, let us again use the transition flow matrix $\mathbf{P}_0$. Then the matrix of coefficients of the set (2.45), with $\rho_1 = 1$, and hence $\rho_2 = \rho_3 = 0$ is

$$\begin{pmatrix} -0.5 & 0.2 & 0.5 \\ 0.4 & -0.5 & 0.1 \\ 0.1 & 0.3 & -0.6 \end{pmatrix}$$

Its latent roots are clearly those of the analogous system (2.28) of the discrete case, reduced by unity, i.e.

$$\lambda_0 = 0 \quad \lambda_1 = -0.8 + i(0.05)^{1/2} \quad \lambda_2 = -0.8 - i(0.05)^{1/2}$$

and the latent roots are the same as in that case, i.e. proportional to

$$\begin{matrix} 27 & -0.02 - 0.1118i & -0.02 + 0.1118i \\ 25 & -0.07 + 0.0894i & -0.07 - 0.0894i \\ 17 & 0.09 + 0.0224i & 0.09 - 0.0224i \end{matrix}$$

If we want the initial structure to be [1000, 0, 0], then we multiply the latent vectors, as in Section 2.18, by

$$1444 \quad -722 + 2602i \quad -722 - 2602i$$

and obtain

$$n_1(t) = 392 + (304 + 29i)\exp(-0.8t)(\cos 0.2236t + i\sin 0.2236t)$$
$$+ (304 - 29i)\exp(-0.8t)(\cos 0.2236t - \sin 0.2236t) \quad (2.47)$$

$$n_2(t) = 362 + (-181 - 247i)\exp(-0.8t)(\cos 0.2236t + i\sin 0.2236t)$$
$$+ (-181 + 247i)\exp(-0.8t)(\cos 0.2236t) - \sin 0.2236t) \quad (2.48)$$

$$n_3(t) = 246 + (-123 + 218i)\exp(-0.8t)(\cos 0.2236t - i\sin 0.2236t)$$
$$+ (-123 - 218i)\exp(-0.8t)(\cos 0.2236t - i\sin 0.2236t) \quad (2.49)$$

Multiplying the complex expressions and thus losing the imaginary parts, we obtain finally

$$n_1(t) = 392 + \exp(-0.8t)(608 \cos 0.2236t - 58 \sin 0.2236t) \quad (2.50)$$

$$n_2(t) = 362 + \exp(-0.8t)(-362 \cos 0.2236t + 492 \sin 0.2236t) \quad (2.51)$$

$$n_3(t) = 246 + \exp(-0.8t)(-246 \cos 0.2236t - 434 \sin 0.2236t) \quad (2.52)$$

These are the formulae if the initial structure is [1000, 0, 0]. To start from [0, 1000, 0] or from [0, 0, 1000] (but still with new entries into state 1 only), we have to use the weights mentioned in Section 2.19, and we obtain:

initial structure [0, 1000, 0]

$$n_1(t) = 392 + \exp(-0.8t)(-392 \cos 0.2236t - 506 \sin 0.2236t) \quad (2.53)$$

$$n_2(t) = 362 + \exp(-0.8t)(638 \cos 0.2236t + 45 \sin 0.2236t) \quad (2.54)$$

$$n_3(t) = 246 + \exp(-0.8t)(-246 \cos 0.2236t + 461 \sin 0.2236t) \quad (2.55)$$

initial structure [0, 0, 1000]

$$n_1(t) = 392 + \exp(-0.8t)(-392 \cos 0.2236t + 836 \sin 0.2236t) \quad (2.56)$$
$$n_2(t) = 362 + \exp(-0.8t)(-362 \cos 0.2236t - 849 \sin 0.2236t) \quad (2.57)$$
$$n_3(t) = 246 + \exp(-0.8t)(754 \cos 0.2236t + 13 \sin 0.2236t) \quad (2.58)$$

2.30

The following extract from extensive calculations shown in Table 13 gives an idea of the paths of $[n_1(t), n_2(t), n_3(t)]$.

If we wish to reach asymptotically another stationary structure, then we allocate new entrants to the various states as in the discrete case (see Section 2.20).

2.31

We add yet another illustration, in the form of the following example.

Example 17

The transition matrix is

$$\mathbf{P} = \begin{pmatrix} 0.2 & 0.2 & 0.3 \\ 0.1 & 0.6 & 0.1 \\ 0.1 & 0.2 & 0.6 \end{pmatrix} \qquad \mathbf{w} = \begin{pmatrix} 0.3 \\ 0.2 \\ 0.1 \end{pmatrix}$$

and we assume that all new entrants join state 1.

Now the system (2.41) has matrix of coefficients

$$\begin{pmatrix} -0.5 & 0.3 & 0.2 \\ 0.2 & -0.4 & 0.2 \\ 0.3 & 0.1 & -0.4 \end{pmatrix}$$

with characteristic equation $\lambda(\lambda + 0.6)(\lambda + 0.7) = 0$. Now all latent roots are real, thus:

$$\lambda_0 = 0 \quad \lambda_1 = -0.7 \quad \lambda_2 = -0.6$$

with corresponding latent vectors

$$\begin{pmatrix} 1 \\ 1 \\ 1 \end{pmatrix} \begin{pmatrix} 1 \\ 0 \\ -1 \end{pmatrix} \begin{pmatrix} 1 \\ 1 \\ -2 \end{pmatrix}$$

Starting from $[1, 0, 0]$, we have

$$n_1(t) = \tfrac{1}{3} + \exp(-0.7t) - \exp(-0.6t)/3 \quad (2.59)$$
$$n_2(t) = \tfrac{1}{3} - \exp(-0.6t)/3 \quad (2.60)$$
$$n_3(t) = \tfrac{1}{3} - \exp(-0.7t) + 2\exp(-0.6t)/3 \quad (2.61)$$

Table 13

	Entries into state 1								
	Start at								
	[1000, 0, 0]			[0, 1000, 0]			[0, 0, 1000		
0.2236t = $\pi/36$ times	n_1	n_2	n_3	n_1	n_2	n_3	n_1	n_2	n_3
0	1000	0	0	0	1000	0	0	0	1000
1	831	130	39	74	830	96	160	44	796
2	707	217	76	138	702	160	263	92	645
3	616	275	109	192	608	200	324	139	537
4	550	313	137	237	539	224	368	181	451
5	502	337	161	273	487	240	392	218	390
6	469	352	179	301	451	248	404	249	347
7	444	360	196	324	423	253	410	274	316
8	427	365	208	341	404	255	411	295	294
9	415	368	217	354	391	255	411	311	278
10	407	368	225	364	382	254	409	323	268
11	402	368	230	372	375	253	407	333	260
12	398	368	234	377	371	252	405	340	255
13	395	367	238	381	367	252	402	346	252
14	394	366	240	384	366	250	400	350	250
15	393	365	242	387	364	249	398	354	248
16	392	365	243	388	363	249	397	356	247
17	392	364	244	389	363	248	396	358	246
18	392	364	244	390	363	248	395	359	246
19	392	363	245	391	363	247	394	360	246
20	392	363	245	392	362	246	393	361	246
21	392	362	246	392	362	246	393	361	246
22	392	362	246	392	362	246	392	362	246

	Entries into state 2								
	Start at								
	[1000, 0, 0]			[0, 1000, 0]			[0, 0, 1000]		
	n_1	n_2	n_3	n_1	n_2	n_3	n_1	n_2	n_3
0	1000	0	0	0	1000	0	0	0	1000
1	643	286	71	56	798	146	93	211	696
2	436	427	137	94	684	222	137	342	521
3	317	495	188	119	620	261	156	422	422
4	249	525	226	136	584	280	163	471	366
5	211	538	251	146	564	290	165	500	335
6	189	543	268	152	554	294	165	517	318
7	177	544	279	156	548	296	165	527	308
8	170	544	286	159	544	297	164	533	303
9	166	543	291	160	543	297	163	537	300
10	164	543	293	161	542	297	163	538	299
11	163	542	295	162	541	297	163	540	297
12	162	542	296	162	541	297	162	541	297
13	162	542	296	162	541	297	162	541	297
14	162	541	297	162	541	297	162	541	297

Table 13 continued.

	Entries into state 3								
	Start at								
	[1000, 0, 0]			[0, 1000, 0]			[0, 0, 1000]		
	n_1	n_2	n_3	n_1	n_2	n_3	n_1	n_2	n_3
0	1000	0	0	0	1000	0	0	0	1000
1	526	235	239	82	633	285	129	94	777
2	327	295	378	131	447	422	175	163	662
3	245	299	456	160	353	487	191	206	603
4	212	290	498	175	307	518	195	232	573
5	199	280	521	184	284	532	195	247	558
6	195	273	532	188	273	539	195	254	551
7	193	269	538	191	268	541	194	259	547
8	193	265	542	192	265	543	194	261	545
9	193	264	543	192	264	544	193	262	545
0	193	264	543	192	264	544	193	262	545
1	193	263	544	193	263	544	193	263	544
2	193	263	544	193	263	544	193	263	544

Starting from [0, 1, 0]

$$n_1(t) = \tfrac{1}{3} - \exp(-0.7t) + 2\exp(-0.6t)/3 \tag{2.62}$$

$$n_2(t) = \tfrac{1}{3} + 2\exp(-0.6t)/3 \tag{2.63}$$

$$n_3(t) = \tfrac{1}{3} + \exp(-0.7t) - 4\exp(0.6t)/3 \tag{2.64}$$

Starting from [0, 0, 1]

$$n_1(t) = \tfrac{1}{3} - \exp(-0.6t)/3 \tag{2.65}$$

$$n_2(t) = \tfrac{1}{3} - \exp(-0.6t)/3 \tag{2.66}$$

$$n_3(t) = \tfrac{2}{3} + 2\exp(-0.6t)/3 \tag{2.67}$$

Table 14 gives an idea of the paths.

Table 14

	Start at								
	[1, 0, 0]			[0, 1, 0]			[0, 0, 1]		
t	n_1	n_2	n_3	n_1	n_2	n_3	n_1	n_2	n_3
0	1.000	0.000	0.000	0.000	1.000	0.000	0.000	0.000	1.000
1	0.647	0.150	0.203	0.203	0.700	0.097	0.150	0.150	0.700
3	0.400	0.278	0.322	0.322	0.444	0.234	0.278	0.278	0.444
5	0.347	0.317	0.336	0.336	0.366	0.298	0.317	0.317	0.366
7	0.335	0.328	0.337	0.337	0.344	0.319	0.328	0.328	0.344
9	0.334	0.332	0.334	0.334	0.336	0.330	0.332	0.332	0.336
∞	0.333	0.333	0.333	0.333	0.333	0.333	0.333	0.333	0.333

2.32

We have mentioned (see equation (2.46)) that $\Sigma_{i=1}^{k}\, \mathrm{d}n_i(t)/\mathrm{d}t = 0$. Therefore one of the differential equations is redundant. If, moreover, we replace $n_3(t)$ by $1 - n_1(t) - n_2(t)$, then the system (2.45) reduces for Example 16, entries into state 1, to

$$\mathrm{d}n_1(t)/\mathrm{d}t = -1.0n_1(t) - 0.3n_2(t) + 0.5 \quad (2.68)$$

$$\mathrm{d}n_2(t)/\mathrm{d}t = 0.3n_1(t) - 0.6n_2(t) + 0.1 \quad (2.69)$$

and for Example 17 to

$$\mathrm{d}n_1(t)/\mathrm{d}t = -0.7n_1(t) + 0.1n_2(t) + 0.2 \quad (2.70)$$

$$\mathrm{d}n_2(t)/\mathrm{d}t = \qquad\qquad -0.6n_2(t) + 0.2 \quad (2.71)$$

It will be noticed that if we substitute for $n_1(t)$ and $n_2(t)$ the stationary values, we obtain $\mathrm{d}n_1(t)/\mathrm{d}t = 0$ and $\mathrm{d}n_2(t)/\mathrm{d}t = 0$, as of course we must.

The sets (2.68), (2.69), and (2.70), (2.71) describe systems of streamlines in a plane. Their features depend on the latent roots, and in particular on $(\lambda_1 - \lambda_2)^2$. In Example 16 this expression is negative, and the streamlines are spirals. In Example 17 the expression is positive, and no spiralling takes place. (Note, for instance, from equations (2.65) and (2.66) that starting from [0, 0, 1], $n_1(t) = n_2(t)$ for all t, so that in this case the path is a straight line.)

A comprehensive description with illustrations will be found in many books, for instance in Brand (1966).

2.33

Starting in Section 1.16, we have introduced the consideration of continuous development in time t. However, we have not made t a characteristic of a state, as we have done in discrete time, in the first sections of the present chapter. Until now, the states were always distinguished by discrete parameters.

We shall now, briefly, consider a case where not only time is continuous, but also age x, which we take as the characteristic of the state. No other state characteristic will be considered: we take the transition flow to depend on age only.

For a cohort with all members starting at age 0, time is, of course, equivalent to age. However, when we consider populations whose totals are to be kept constant, then t and x have different meanings.

2.34

Assume now that all new entries happen at age 0, and denote the density of members at time t of age x by $n_x(t)$, and the loss density by μ_x.

In the initial population there is a density of $n_{x-t}(0)$ members of age $x - t$, say, Of these

$$n_{x-t}(0) \exp\left(-\int_{x-t}^{x} \mu_x \mathrm{d}_x\right) \quad (2.72)$$

have survived during time t, and their age is now x.

Also, at time $(t - \tau)$, there was a density of $n_0(t - \tau)$ new entrants, of whom

$$n_0(t-\tau)\exp\left(-\int_0^{\tau}\mu_x \mathrm{d}x\right) \tag{2.73}$$

have survived.

We want to keep the total membership constant, i.e. we want $\int_0^\infty n_x(t)\mathrm{d}x$ to equal $\int_0^\infty n_x(0)\mathrm{d}x$ for all t. This provides the integral equation of the first type

$$\int_0^\infty n_x(t)\mathrm{d}x = \int_t^\infty n_{x-t}(0)\exp\left(-\int_{x-t}^{x}\mu_x \mathrm{d}x\right)\mathrm{d}x$$

$$+\int_0^t n_0(t-\tau)\exp\left(-\int_0^t \mu_x \mathrm{d}x\right)\mathrm{d}\tau \tag{2.74}$$

The replacement of loss at time t, $n_0(t)$, satisfies the integral equation of second type

$$n_0(t) = \int_t^\infty n_x(0)\exp\left(-\int_x^{x+t}\mu_x \mathrm{d}x\right)\mu_{x+t}\mathrm{d}x$$

$$+\int_0^t n_0(t-\tau)\exp\left(-\int_0^{\tau}\mu_x \mathrm{d}x\right)\mathrm{d}\tau \tag{2.75}$$

This can be derived by an argument analogous to that used to explain the system (2.10). It can also be derived from equation (2.74), after some lengthy computation.

In certain cases the solution of equation (2.75) can be written

$$n_0(t) = \sum_{i=0}^{\infty} a_i \exp(-r_i t) \tag{2.76}$$

where the r_i are the roots of

$$\int_0^\infty f(t)\exp(-rt)\mathrm{d}t = 1 \tag{2.77}$$

and the a_i depend on the initial population. However, though the number of the a_i is infinite, it may still be impossible to reproduce an arbitrary initial structure.

We shall not deal here further with these problems, but we mention that Feller (1941) has proved that a solution of equation (2.75) exists, and he has also shown that for $n_0(t)$ to converge with increasing t to a constant (and for the structure to converge to a stationary one), it is necessary, but not sufficient, that the first integral in equation (2.75) converge to zero.

3

The Stationary Population

3.1

To find the stationary structure $[n_1; \ldots, n_k]$ when the transition matrix is $\mathbf{P} = (p_{ij})$, $w_i = 1 - \Sigma_{j=1}^{k} p_{ij}$, and ρ_j is the proportion of new entrants to join state j, we solve the system

$$n_j = p_{1j}n_1 + \ldots + p_{kj}n_k + u_j \tag{3.1}$$

where u_j is the number of new entrants into state j,

$$u_j = \rho_j \sum_{i=1}^{k} n_i w_i \tag{3.2}$$

so that the system to be solved is

$$\begin{aligned} n_1 &= r_{11}n_1 + r_{21}n_2 + \ldots + r_{k1}n_k \\ n_2 &= r_{12}n_1 + r_{22}n_2 + \ldots + r_{k2}n_k \\ &\vdots \\ n_k &= r_{1k}n_1 + r_{2k}n_2 + \ldots + r_{kk}n_k \end{aligned} \tag{3.3}$$

where $r_{ij} = p_{ij} + \rho_j w_i$.

The solution vector is clearly the latent vector of $\mathbf{R}(\rho)$ as defined in (2.23), corresponding to the latent root 1, and we have seen that if there is no other latent root with absolute value 1, then any structure will converge to the stationary one.

The system (3.3) has a non-trivial solution, because one equation is redundant (if we add them, we obtain $\Sigma_{i=1}^{k} n_i = \Sigma_{i=1}^{k} n_i$). The n_i which solve it are proportional to the signed minors of the elements of any row of the matrix $\mathbf{R}(\rho) - \mathbf{I}$. For instance, if $\rho_1 = 1$, and hence $\rho_i = 0$ for $i \neq 1$, then $(-1)^i n_i$ will be proportional to the subdeterminants of the matrix

$$\begin{pmatrix} p_{12} & p_{22} - 1 & p_{32} & \ldots & p_{k2} \\ p_{13} & p_{23} & p_{33} - 1 & \ldots & p_{k3} \\ \vdots & \vdots & \vdots & & \vdots \\ p_{1k} & p_{2k} & p_{3k} & \ldots & p_{kk} - 1 \end{pmatrix} \tag{3.4}$$

omitting the first, the second, . . . , the kth column respectively, because ρ_1 appears only in the first row of $\mathbf{R}(\rho)$.

These subdeterminants are, with alternating signs, proportional to the entries in the first column of $(\mathbf{P}' - \mathbf{I})^{-1}$, or also to those of the first row of $(\mathbf{I} - \mathbf{P})^{-1}$, where $\mathbf{I}$ is the identity matrix of order k.

Since the p_{ij} are common fractions, and the columns of $\mathbf{P}'$ (the rows of $\mathbf{P}$) add up to less than unity, i.e. $(\mathbf{I} - \mathbf{P}')\mathbf{e} > 0$, 1 is not latent root of $\mathbf{P}$, and the inverse of $(\mathbf{I} - \mathbf{P})$ exists (Appendix I, Section I.4). Moreover, because of

$$(\mathbf{I} - \mathbf{P})^{-1} = \mathbf{I} + \mathbf{P} + \mathbf{P}^2 + \ldots \tag{3.5}$$

all n_i will be non-negative.

Another way of obtaining the same result, and relating it to the number of new entrants, is as follows:

If $\mathbf{n}$ is stationary, then $\mathbf{n}' = \mathbf{n}'\mathbf{P} + \mathbf{u}'$, hence $\mathbf{n}'(\mathbf{I} - \mathbf{P}) = \mathbf{u}'$, and

$$\mathbf{n}' = \mathbf{u}'(\mathbf{I} - \mathbf{P})^{-1} \tag{3.6}$$

Let $(\mathbf{I} - \mathbf{P})^{-1} = (q_{ij})$, then if all entrants join state 1, we have

$$n_j = q_{1j} \sum_{i=1}^{k} n_i w_i \tag{3.7}$$

We see that if $\rho_j = 1$, then the stationary structure is given by the proportions of the elements in the jth row of $(\mathbf{I} - \mathbf{P})^{-1}$.

3.2

If the transition matrix has the special form which it had in Sections 2.1 ff., viz.

$$\bar{\mathbf{P}} = \begin{pmatrix} 0 & p_1 & 0 & \ldots & 0 & 0 \\ 0 & 0 & p_2 & \ldots & 0 & 0 \\ \vdots & \vdots & \vdots & & \vdots & \vdots \\ 0 & 0 & 0 & \ldots & 0 & p_k \\ 0 & 0 & 0 & \ldots & 0 & 0 \end{pmatrix}$$

then

$$(\mathbf{I} - \bar{\mathbf{P}})^{-1} = \begin{pmatrix} 1 & p_1 & (p_1 p_2) & \ldots & (p_1 \ldots p_{k-1}) & (p_1 \ldots p_k) \\ 0 & 1 & p_2 & \ldots & (p_2 \ldots p_{k-1}) & (p_2 \ldots p_k) \\ 0 & 0 & 1 & \ldots & (p_3 \ldots p_{k-1}) & (p_3 \ldots p_k) \\ \vdots & \vdots & \vdots & & \vdots & \vdots \\ 0 & 0 & 0 & \ldots & 1 & p_k \\ 0 & 0 & 0 & \ldots & 0 & 1 \end{pmatrix}$$

and the first row is proportional to the vector (2.9) in Section 2.5.

3.3

In Section 2.5 we have mentioned a relationship between the development of a cohort, and a stationary population. We shall do this now for the general case.

In Section 1.10 we have seen that the elements of the first row of $(\mathbf{I}-\mathbf{P})^{-1}$ are also the times which members of a cohort, subject to transitions given by the matrix $\mathbf{P}$, spend in the various states, if initially they are in state 1.

Those times were computed as $\Sigma_{t=0}^{\infty}\, n_i(t)$. The connection is readily seen: if we consider a succession of identical cohorts, starting in successive years, then they will eventually – i.e. when the last member of the first cohort has left (as e.g. in Example 2), or asymptotically (as e.g. in Example 3) – add up to a stationary population.

Conversely, the yearly entry into a stationary population $[n_i]$ must be $\Sigma_{i=1}^{k}\, n_i w_i$, and if all recruits join state 1, then this is also the initial membership of the cohort which produces that stationary population.

As regards Example 2, we interpret a state now as being characterized by rank (r) and time (t). Then after six steps the last member of the first cohort will have left, and the remaining members, from more recent cohorts, will add in number to n_{rt}, equal to the entries in the first column of the list in Section 2.13 (Example 11). They form a stationary population.

3.4

To illustrate the fact that the stationary structure depends only on the ratios in the first row of $(\mathbf{I}-\mathbf{P})^{-1}$ (if all entries are into state 1), consider again the transition matrix of Section 1.10, viz.

$$\mathbf{P}=\begin{pmatrix}0.484 & 0.092 & 0.036\\ 0.026 & 0.837 & 0.046\\ 0.017 & 0.093 & 0.884\end{pmatrix}\qquad \mathbf{w}=\begin{pmatrix}0.394\\ 0.091\\ 0.006\end{pmatrix}$$

so that

$$(\mathbf{I}-\mathbf{P})^{-1}=\begin{pmatrix}2.077 & 1.923 & 1.308\\ 0.542 & 8.473 & 3.530\\ 0.740 & 7.063 & 11.626\end{pmatrix}$$

The first row of $(\mathbf{I}-\mathbf{P})^{-1}$ is the same as that of $(\mathbf{I}-\mathbf{P}_0)^{-1}$, and the same stationary structure emerges:

$$\begin{pmatrix}392\\ 362\\ 246\end{pmatrix}\rightarrow\begin{matrix}203+189\\ 362\\ 246\end{matrix}=\begin{pmatrix}392\\ 362\\ 246\end{pmatrix}$$

where

$$(0.394)392+(0.091)362+(0.006)246=189$$

replaces the loss.

3.5

If we allow entries into more than one state, in proportions ρ_j, then the sub-determinants contain ρ_j linearly. Hence all stationary structures with given total and with given proportions of entrants into the various states will be in the convex hull of those structures corresponding to entries into just one single state, provided the total in each of the latter structures is that given.

If we denote the stationary structure with all entrants joining state j by $\mathbf{s}_j = [n_1^{(j)}, \ldots, n_k^{(j)}]$, then any structure in the convex hull of $\mathbf{s}_1, \ldots, \mathbf{s}_k$ is also stationary, with appropriate numbers of entrants into the states. Such a structure can be denoted by $\Sigma_{j=1}^k v_j \mathbf{s}_j$, where $\Sigma_{j=1}^k v_j = 1$, and all $v_j \geqslant 0$.

The number of entrants into state j is then $v_j \Sigma_{i=1}^k n_i^{(j)} w_i$. This can be seen as follows: $\mathbf{s}_j$ is defined to be the solution of

$$\begin{aligned}
n_1^{(j)} &= p_{11} n_1^{(j)} + \ldots + p_{k1} n_k^{(j)} \\
n_2^{(j)} &= p_{12} n_1^{(j)} + \ldots + p_{k2} n_k^{(j)} \\
&\vdots \\
n_j^{(j)} &= p_{1j} n_1^{(j)} + \ldots + p_{kj} n_k^{(j)} + \sum_{i=1}^{k} n_i^{(j)} w_i \\
&\vdots \\
n_k^{(j)} &= p_{1k} n_1^{(j)} + \ldots + p_{kk} n_k^{(j)}
\end{aligned} \tag{3.8}$$

and consequently

$$\begin{aligned}
\sum_{j=1}^{k} v_j n_1^{(j)} &= p_{11} \sum_{j=1}^{k} v_j n_1^{(j)} + \ldots + p_{k1} \sum_{j=1}^{k} v_j n_k^{(j)} + v_1 \sum_{i=1}^{k} n_i^{(1)} w_i \\
&\vdots \\
\sum_{j=1}^{k} v_j n_k^{(j)} &= p_{1k} \sum_{j=1}^{k} v_j n_1^{(j)} + \ldots + p_{kk} \sum_{j=1}^{k} v_j n_k^{(j)} + v_k \sum_{i=1}^{k} n_i^{(k)} w_i
\end{aligned} \tag{3.9}$$

This system exhibits the required numbers of entries in the last term of each equation.

We can also see that no structure outside the convex hull can be stationary, because if any v_j were negative, then this would require a negative number of new entrants into state j.

For illustrations, we use again the transition matrix $\mathbf{P}_0$. With entries into single states we obtain, starting with the structures defined by the rows of $130(\mathbf{I} - \mathbf{P}_0)^{-1}$,

Entries into state		
1	2	3
$\begin{pmatrix}70\\50\\70\end{pmatrix} \rightarrow \begin{matrix}140+130\\250\\170\end{matrix} = \begin{pmatrix}270\\250\\170\end{pmatrix}$	$\begin{pmatrix}120\\400\\220\end{pmatrix} \rightarrow \begin{matrix}120\\270+130\\220\end{matrix} = \begin{pmatrix}120\\400\\220\end{pmatrix}$	$\begin{pmatrix}110\\150\\310\end{pmatrix} \rightarrow \begin{matrix}110\\150\\180+130\end{matrix} = \begin{pmatrix}110\\150\\310\end{pmatrix}$

The fact that in all these three cases we had to add the same number of new entrants to establish the original structures is a consequence of our choice of the latter. After transformation, i.e. after multiplying $130(\mathbf{I}-\mathbf{P}_0)^{-1}$ by $\mathbf{P}_0$, thus obtaining

$$130(\mathbf{I}-\mathbf{P}_0)^{-1}\mathbf{P}_0$$

we have to add $130\mathbf{I}$ to obtain the original matrix $(\mathbf{I}-\mathbf{P}_0)^{-1}$. Indeed,

$$(\mathbf{I}-\mathbf{P}_0)^{-1}\mathbf{P}_0+\mathbf{I}=(\mathbf{I}-\mathbf{P}_0)^{-1} \tag{3.10}$$

since after pre-multiplying both sides of equation (3.10) by $(\mathbf{I}-\mathbf{P}_0)$, we have $\mathbf{P}_0+\mathbf{I}-\mathbf{P}_0=\mathbf{I}$.

3.6

We multiply the structures in Section 3.4 respectively by 1000/690, 1000/740, 1000/570 in order to obtain structures with totals 1000, thus:

s_1	s_2	s_3
392	162	193
362	541	263
246	297	544
1000	1000	1000

(This normalization is not necessary, but it is convenient for our argument.)

After one transition, the required new entries will be

	188.4	175.7	228.1
i.e.			
	13000/69	13000/74	13000/57

Now consider the structure $\mathbf{s}_1/2+\mathbf{s}_2/3+\mathbf{s}_3/6$, i.e.

$$\begin{pmatrix}282.2\\405.2\\312.6\end{pmatrix} \text{ which transforms into } \begin{pmatrix}187.7\\346.7\\274.8\end{pmatrix}$$

$$1000.0 \qquad\qquad 809.2$$

The missing 190.8 must be made up by

94.2 = 1/2 of 188.4 (but not of 190.8)

58.6 = 1/3 of 175.7 (but not of 190.8)

38.0 = 1/6 of 228.1 (but not of 190.8)

to re-establish the original structure.

We can also check equation (3.6):

$$\begin{pmatrix}282.2\\405.2\\312.7\end{pmatrix}=\begin{pmatrix}2.077 & 0.923 & 0.846\\1.923 & 3.077 & 1.154\\1.308 & 1.692 & 2.385\end{pmatrix}\begin{pmatrix}94.2\\58.6\\38.0\end{pmatrix}$$

3.7

The question reverse to that just dealt with, viz. the question of which proportions should enter into the various states so as to make a given structure stationary (if possible), is answered by ascertaining which non-negative weights (if any) attached to the vertices of the convex hull mentioned, produce that given structure as centre of gravity.

As we have pointed out in Section 3.6, the proportions of new entrants into the various states are not the same as the weights attached to the stationary structures with entries into a single state. If we wished, using $\mathbf{P}_0$, that the proportions of new entrants be as 1/2 to 1/3 to 1/6, then we have to find the latent vector corresponding to the latent root 1 of the matrix

$$\begin{pmatrix} 0.3 + 0.2(1/2) & 0.1 + 0.1(1/2) & 0.2 + 0.3(1/2) \\ 0.4 + 0.2(1/3) & 0.5 + 0.1(1/3) & 0.1 + 0.3(1/3) \\ 0.1 + 0.2(1/6) & 0.3 + 0.1(1/6) & 0.4 + 0.3(1/6) \end{pmatrix}$$

A latent vector is

$$\begin{pmatrix} 281 \\ 412 \\ 307 \end{pmatrix} \text{ which transforms into } \begin{matrix} 187 + 94 \\ 349 + 63 = \\ 275 + 32 \end{matrix} \begin{pmatrix} 281 \\ 412 \\ 307 \end{pmatrix}$$

$$\overline{1000} \qquad\qquad \overline{811 + 189} \quad \overline{1000}$$

3.8

In Section 2.34 we introduced a characteristic of a state which was continuous. We do this again here, using the earlier notation, but because we consider now a stationary population, $n_x(t)$ is independent of t, and we shall write simply n_x for the density of members of age x.

This allows some simplification. On the other hand, we allow new entries at ages different from 0, assuming a density of ρ_x of entrants at age x.

We have then

$$n_{x+\Delta x} = n_x + \left(\int_0^\infty n_y \mu_y \,\mathrm{d}y \right) \rho_x \Delta x - n_x \mu_x \Delta x \tag{3.11}$$

When $\Delta x \to 0$, we have

$$\mathrm{d}n_x/\mathrm{d}x = -n_x\mu_x + \int x \int_0^\infty n_y \mu_y \,\mathrm{d}y \tag{3.12}$$

The solution of this differential equation is

$$n_x = n_0 \exp\left(- \int_0^x \mu_x \,\mathrm{d}x \right) \int_0^x \rho_x \left(\int_0^\infty n_y \mu_y \,\mathrm{d}y \right) \exp\left(\int_0^x \mu_x \,\mathrm{d}x \right) \mathrm{d}x \tag{3.13}$$

If all entrants are of age 0, then equation (3.13) reduces to

$$n_x = n_0 \exp\left(-\int_0^x \mu_x \mathrm{d}x\right)$$

i.e. to equation (1.36).

3.9

We add one more example, where two parameters are continuous.

We consider discrete ranks, but assume now that the rate of promotion from rank r into rank $r+1$ (if any) depends on rank and on seniority in the rank, while the loss density depends only on time within the organization. We also assume that all new members enter rank 1, at age 0, so that the time in the organization is equivalent to age.

We can describe this model by saying that a state is defined by rank, seniority and age, the last two parameters being continuous.

The density of members in rank r, of seniority s, and of age x, is denoted by $n_r(s, x)$, the density of promotion from rank r to rank $r+1$ by $p_r(s)$, and the loss density by μ_x, dependent only on age x. Then

$$n_r(s, x) = n_r(0, s-x)\exp\left(-\int_0^s (\mu_{x-s+\tau} + p_r(\tau))\,\mathrm{d}\tau\right) \tag{3.14}$$

With regard to those just promoted, we have

$$n_{r+1}(0, x) = \int_0^x n_r(0, x-s)\exp\left(-\int_0^s (\mu_{x-s+\tau} + p_r(\tau))\mathrm{d}\tau\right)p_r(s)\mathrm{d}s$$

$$= \int_0^x n_r(0, x-s)\exp\left(-\int_0^s \mu_{x-s+\tau}\mathrm{d}\tau\right)h_r(s)\mathrm{d}s \tag{3.15}$$

where we have written $h_r(s)$ for $\exp(-\int_0^s p_r(\tau)\,\mathrm{d}\tau)p_r(s)$.

Now $n_1(0, x-s) = 0$ when $x \neq s$, and we write $n_1(0)$ for $n_1(0, 0)$. Hence

$$n_2(0, x) = n_1(0)\exp\left(-\int_0^x \mu_\tau \mathrm{d}\,\tau\right)h_1(x) \tag{3.16}$$

and generally, by induction

$$n_r(0, x) = n_1(0)\exp\Bigg(-\int_0^x \cdots \int_0^{x-y_1-\ldots-y_{r-3}} h_{r-1}(y_1)\ldots$$

$$h_2(y_{r-2})h_1(x-y_1-\ldots-y_{r-2})\,\mathrm{d}y_{r-2}\ldots\mathrm{d}y_1\Bigg) \tag{3.17}$$

We can obtain $n_r(s, x)$ from equation (3.17), through equation (3.14).

The detailed derivation, and examples, in particular concerning limited ranges for promotion and specific other requirements are given in Vajda (1948).

The special type of integral which appears in formula (3.17) is an integral of 'convolution', or '*faltung*'. We do not make any further remarks about this branch of analysis here. A systematic use of Laplace transforms to solve this type of problem is made in Seal (1945).

4

The Semi-stationary Population

4.1

We look again at Examples 12 and 13 in Sections 2.14 and 2.15. In both of these the times in service were 0 to 5, the ranks were 1, 2, and 3 and the total population amounted to 2578 members.

In Example 12 we started with rank totals 2442, 169, and 27 respectively, and these changed after one step into 2436, 114, and 28. Finally, they reached 2437, 112, and 29. These last were the rank totals of the intrinsic stationary structure.

In Example 13 we started with these rank totals, and they remained unaltered throughout, though the distribution within the population kept changing, converging to that of the stationary structure. In other words, not only the total membership was kept constant, but so were the totals of subsets, of the states within the same rank.

The existence of such structures is of interest. From the point of view of a member of the organization, his position is the same, regarding his career prospects, as if he had entered a stationary population, since his promotion prospects are unaffected by the ages of those ahead of him in the hierarchy, even if management wishes to keep the rank totals – these affect the efficiency of the organization – constant.

We call a structure where the total of the population, and also the totals of certain sets of states are kept constant, semi-stationary (see Vajda, 1947; where this concept was introduced and illustrated by our Example 13). We refer to the subset of states whose total remains constant as being 'preserved' (cf. Vajda, 1977).

A stationary structure is also semi-stationary: it preserves every single state.

In what follows we shall consider entries into state 1 only.

4.2

Let us now choose a set of states and see if it is possible to preserve it. By renumbering the states we can assume that the chosen states are the first r.

We have mentioned (equation (2.27)) that the number of new entrants after t years equals

$$\mathbf{n}(0)'(\mathbf{R}')^t\mathbf{w} \tag{4.1}$$

If this number is to preserve the set of the first r states by itself, then it must also equal

$$\mathbf{n}(0)'(\mathbf{R}')^t\mathbf{w}_{(r)} \tag{4.2}$$

where $\mathbf{w}_{(r)} = (\mathbf{I} - \mathbf{P})\mathbf{e}_{(r)}$ and $\mathbf{e}_{(r)}$ is the vector whose first r components are unity, and the remaining components are zero.

Consequently a semi-stationary structure $\mathbf{n}(0)$ which preserves the first r states must satisfy

$$\mathbf{n}(0)'(\mathbf{R}')^t(\mathbf{w} - \mathbf{w}_{(r)}) = 0 \tag{4.3}$$

for $t = 0, 1, \ldots, \infty$.

It would clearly be impractical to establish the existence of such a structure, if it were necessary to solve the infinite set of equations (4.3). However, this is not necessary, because every matrix satisfies its own characteristic equation (Appendix I, Section I.3), and therefore any power of $\mathbf{R}$, higher than the $(k - 1)$th, depends linearly on the 0th, 1st, . . . , $(k - 1)$th power if the matrix is of order k. Hence if $\mathbf{n}(0)$ satisfies equation (4.3) for $t = 0, \ldots, k - 1$, then it satisfies all subsequent equations as well.

4.3

The equations of the set (4.3) are homogeneous. We know that their rank is at most $k - 1$, because a non-trivial solution exists. It is the stationary solution, which is also semi-stationary, for any subset of states.

This is obvious from first principles, and it can be shown formally as follows:

If each single state is to be preserved, then we must have $\mathbf{n}(0)'(\mathbf{w} - \mathbf{w}_{(i)}) = 0$, for $i = 1, 2, \ldots, k$. (Note that $\mathbf{w}_{(k)} = \mathbf{w}$.) Now $\mathbf{w}_{(i)} = (\mathbf{I} - \mathbf{P})\mathbf{e}_{(i)}$, and comparing two successive equations we see that the scalar product of the sth column of $(\mathbf{I} - \mathbf{P})$ and $\mathbf{n}(0)$ must be zero for $s = 2, 3, \ldots, k$. Clearly the first row of $(\mathbf{I} - \mathbf{P})^{-1}$, i.e. the stationary structure, is such a vector $\mathbf{n}(0)$.

Thus one solution of the system (4.3) is the stationary structure. We want to find out if there are any other solutions. This depends on the rank of the system of the first k equations being less than $k - 1$.

4.4

Example 18

We use the transition matrix

$$\mathbf{P}_{18} = \begin{pmatrix} 0.2 & 0.1 & 0.6 & 0 \\ 0.2 & 0.2 & 0 & 0.4 \\ 0.3 & 0.1 & 0.2 & 0.1 \\ 0.3 & 0.3 & 0.2 & 0 \end{pmatrix}$$

where

$$\mathbf{w} = \begin{pmatrix} 0.1 \\ 0.2 \\ 0.3 \\ 0.2 \end{pmatrix} \qquad \mathbf{w}_{(2)} = \begin{pmatrix} 0.7 \\ 0.6 \\ -0.4 \\ -0.6 \end{pmatrix} \qquad \mathbf{w} - \mathbf{w}_{(2)} = \begin{pmatrix} -0.6 \\ -0.4 \\ 0.7 \\ 0.8 \end{pmatrix}$$

The first four equations of the set (4.3) are

$$6n_1 + 4n_2 - 7n_3 - 8n_4 = 0 \tag{4.4}$$

$$-20n_1 + 18n_3 + 28n_4 = 0 \tag{4.5}$$

$$48n_1 + 32n_2 - 56n_3 - 64n_4 = 0 \tag{4.6}$$

$$-160n_1 + 144n_3 + 224n_4 = 0 \tag{4.7}$$

Equation (4.6) is 8 times equation (4.4), and equation (4.7) is 8 times equation (4.5): the system has rank 2. Two independent solutions are proportional to

$$[10, 3, 8, 2] \qquad \text{and} \qquad [1, -1, -2, 2]$$

Any combination

$$[10a + b, 3a - b, 8a - 2b, 2a + 2b]$$

can serve as an initial structure, provided a and b are such that they produce non-negative values.

For instance, we may take $a = b = 43.5$, which makes the total equal to 1000. This choice produces the structure [478, 87, 261, 174] which develops as follows:

$$\begin{pmatrix} 478 \\ 87 \\ 261 \\ 174 \end{pmatrix} \to \begin{pmatrix} 243 + 179 \\ 143 \\ 374 \\ 61 \end{pmatrix} \to \begin{pmatrix} 243 + 196 \\ 126 \\ 340 \\ 95 \end{pmatrix} \to \begin{pmatrix} 243 + 191 \\ 131 \\ 350 \\ 85 \end{pmatrix} \to \begin{pmatrix} 243 + 192 \\ 130 \\ 348 \\ 87 \end{pmatrix}$$

$$\to \begin{pmatrix} 243 + 192 \\ 130 \\ 348 \\ 87 \end{pmatrix} \text{and so on.}$$

If we wanted to know whether the first state alone can be preserved, then we would compute $(\mathbf{I} - \mathbf{P})\mathbf{w}_{(1)}$ and consider

$$7n_1 - 4n_2 - 6n_3 - 5n_4 = 0 \tag{4.8}$$

$$-19n_1 + 21n_3 + 11n_4 = 0 \tag{4.9}$$

$$69n_1 - 32n_2 - 61n_3 - 53n_4 = 0 \tag{4.10}$$

$$-191n_1 + 207n_3 + 127n_4 = 0 \tag{4.11}$$

This system has rank 3, and only one solution, viz. the stationary structure.

4.5

We shall now show that if a semi-stationary structure, different from the stationary one, exists, then there must be a latent root with a subset of components adding up to zero.

Different latent vectors are linearly independent, so that any structure can be expressed as a linear combination of these vectors, and we concentrate our attention on a structure which is equal to a latent vector different from that corresponding to the latent root 1.

To obtain a latent vector, we have to solve the system

$$\begin{array}{llllll} (p_{11}-\lambda)n_1 + & p_{21}n_2 & + \ldots + & p_{k1}n_k & + n_1w_1 + \ldots + n_kw_k & = 0 \\ p_{12}n_1 & + (p_{22}-\lambda)n_2 & + \ldots + & p_{k2}n_k & & = 0 \\ \vdots & \vdots & & \vdots & & \vdots \\ p_{1k}n_1 & + \quad p_{2k}n_2 & + \ldots + & (p_{kk}-\lambda)n_k & & = 0 \end{array} \tag{4.12}$$

for λ, a latent root of $\mathbf{R}(\rho)$, when $\boldsymbol{\rho} = [1, 0, \ldots, 0]$

Adding the first r rows of these equations we obtain

$$\mathbf{n}'(\mathbf{I}-\mathbf{P})\mathbf{e} = n_1w_1 + \ldots + n_kw_k = \mathbf{n}'(\mathbf{I}\lambda - \mathbf{P})\mathbf{e}_{(r)} \tag{4.13}$$

The latent vector $\mathbf{n}$ satisfies the equation $\mathbf{R}^t\mathbf{n} = \lambda^t\mathbf{n}$. We want to find out whether it satisfies equation (4.3), which can be written

$$\lambda^t\mathbf{n}'(\mathbf{I}-\mathbf{P})\,(\mathbf{e}-\mathbf{e}_{(r)}) = 0$$

or, dividing by $\lambda^t \neq 0$,

$$\mathbf{n}'(\mathbf{I}-\mathbf{P})\mathbf{e} = \mathbf{n}'(\mathbf{I}-\mathbf{P})\mathbf{e}_{(r)} \tag{4.14}$$

If $\lambda = 1$, and hence $\mathbf{n}$ is the stationary structure, then we see from equation (4.13) that equation (4.14) is satisfied for any r. This we knew already. On the other hand, if $\lambda \neq 1$, then it follows from equations (4.13) and (4.14), that $\mathbf{n}$ must satisfy

$$\mathbf{n}'(\mathbf{I}-\mathbf{P})\mathbf{e}_{(r)} - \mathbf{n}'(\mathbf{I}\lambda - \mathbf{P})\mathbf{e}_{(r)} = 0 \tag{4.15}$$

But this means that $\mathbf{n}'(1-\lambda)\mathbf{e}_{(r)} = 0$, and if $1-\lambda \neq 0$, it means that $\mathbf{n}'\mathbf{e}_{(r)} = 0$. In words: the first r components of $\mathbf{n}$ add up to zero. This is the result required.

For the stationary structure the analogous result was mentioned in Section 2.4.

4.6

We have seen (Section 2.17) that to keep the total population constant, we multiply the structure at each step by the matrix $\mathbf{R}(\rho)$, which is defined there. If all new entrants join state 1, then the first row of $\mathbf{R}$ reads

$$\text{i.e.}\quad \frac{p_{11}+w_1}{1-p_{12}-\ldots-p_{1k}} \quad \frac{p_{21}+w_2}{1-p_{22}-\ldots-p_{2k}} \quad \ldots \quad \frac{p_{k1}+w_k}{1-p_{k2}-\ldots-p_{kk}} \tag{4.16}$$

Now let it be required to preserve the first r states, where r differs from k.

Before the new entrants arrive, these states total

$$(p_{11} + \ldots + p_{1r})n_1 + \ldots + (p_{k1} + \ldots + p_{kr})n_k,$$

and to make this again equal to $n_1 + \ldots + n_r$, we must add

$$(1 - p_{11} - \ldots - p_{1r})n_1 + \ldots + (1 - p_{r1} - \ldots - p_{rr})n_r$$
$$-(p_{r+1,1} + \ldots + p_{r+1,k})n_{r+1} \ldots - (p_{k1} + \ldots + p_{kr})n_k \tag{4.17}$$

It follows that the transition is given, at each step, by the matrix $\mathbf{R}^{(r)}$ with first row

$$1 \quad 0 \quad \ldots \quad 0$$

when $r = 1$, and when $r > 1$ by

$$1 - p_{12} - \ldots - p_{1r} \quad 1 - p_{22} - \ldots - p_{2r} \quad \ldots \quad 1 - p_{r2} - \ldots - p_{rr}$$
$$- (p_{r+1,2} + \ldots + p_{r+1,r}) \quad \ldots \quad - (p_{k2} + \ldots + p_{kr}) \tag{4.18}$$

while the other rows are those of $\mathbf{R}$.

$\mathbf{R}^{(r)}$ will not always keep the total population constant, but we shall find conditions which ensure that it does.

Consider the matrix $\mathbf{R}^{(r)} - \lambda\mathbf{I}$. If we add the 2nd, . . . , rth row to the first, then the latter will contain $1 - \lambda$ as the first r components, and 0 as the remaining $k - r$ components. Therefore $\lambda = 1$ will again be a latent root, as it is one of $\mathbf{R}$. There may be other common roots, and if they exist, then the corresponding latent vectors are also the same, because they depend on the 2nd, . . . , kth row only. In such a case it follows that $\mathbf{R}^{(r)}$ preserves the total of the population given by these latent vectors as well, just as $\mathbf{R}$ does.

4.7

To illustrate this by an example, more general than Example 13, we take again the transition matrix $\mathbf{P}_{18}$ of Section 4.4.

Example 19

The characteristic equation of the matrix

$$\mathbf{R} = \begin{pmatrix} 0.3 & 0.4 & 0.6 & 0.5 \\ 0.1 & 0.2 & 0.1 & 0.3 \\ 0.6 & 0 & 0.2 & 0.2 \\ 0 & 0.4 & 0.1 & 0 \end{pmatrix}$$

is

$$\lambda^4 - 0.7\lambda^3 - 0.38\lambda^2 + 0.056\lambda + 0.024$$
$$= (1 - \lambda)(\lambda + 0.3)(-\lambda^2 + 0.08) = 0 \tag{4.19}$$

The latent roots, and their corresponding latent vectors, are

$\lambda_0 = 1$	$\lambda_1 = -0.3$	$\lambda_2 = (0.08)^{1/2}$	$\lambda_3 = -(0.08)^{1/2}$
10	1	1	-1
3	-1	-2	2
8	-2	$10(0.08)^{1/2}$	$10(0.08)^{1/2}$
2	2	$1-10(0.08)^{1/2}$	$-1-10(0.08)^{1/2}$

We have already met the first two vectors in Section 4.4.

We see that we can preserve the first two states, if we start from a weighted combination of the latent vectors corresponding to λ_0 and λ_1. For instance, we might take the sum of the two vectors, and find

$$\begin{pmatrix}11\\2\\6\\4\end{pmatrix}\to\begin{pmatrix}9.7\\3.3\\8.6\\1.4\end{pmatrix}\to\begin{pmatrix}10.09\\2.91\\7.82\\2.18\end{pmatrix}\to\begin{pmatrix}9.973\\3.027\\8.054\\1.944\end{pmatrix}\quad\text{and so on}$$

In this case we have

$$\mathbf{R}^{(2)}=\begin{pmatrix}0.9&0.8&-0.1&-0.3\\0.1&0.2&0.1&0.3\\0.6&0&0.2&0.2\\0&0.4&0.1&0\end{pmatrix}$$

with characteristic equation

$$\begin{aligned}&\lambda^4-1.3\lambda^3+0.24\lambda^2+0.096\lambda-0.036\\&=(1-\lambda)(\lambda+0.3)(-\lambda^2+0.6\lambda-0.12)=0\end{aligned}\tag{4.20}$$

Once more, 1 and -0.3 are latent roots, and the corresponding latent vectors are given above.

If we tried to keep the first state alone constant, we would obtain a matrix with the characteristic equation

$$\lambda^4-1.4\lambda^3+0.3\lambda^2+0.084\lambda+0.016=0$$

which has, of course, the root 1, but not the root -0.3.

4.8

We might remark that it is easy enough to find a structure such that the total of the first two states, say, is kept constant during one step, but this does not mean that this total can be preserved in future as well. For instance, again with the matrix $\mathbf{P}_{18}$, we have

$$\begin{pmatrix}50\\100\\100\\0\end{pmatrix}\to\begin{pmatrix}115\\35\\50\\50\end{pmatrix}\quad\text{but then}\quad\to\begin{pmatrix}103.5\\38.5\\89.0\\19.0\end{pmatrix}$$

4.9

We look again at Example 11 in Section 2.13. We found there that the components of the latent vectors (except that corresponding to the latent root unity), for the same rank though for different ages, added up to zero. This offered an opportunity for constructing semi-stationary structures, which we did in Section 2.15, Example 13.

In Example 11 the rates of remaining in rank 1 during one year were

0.825 0.550 0.284 0.214 0.077

and if we wish the total in rank 1 to remain constant, those leaving this rank must be replaced by new entrants. It follows from the discussion in Section 2.1, leading to equation (2.4), that the difference equation for the new entrants has characteristic equation

$$(1-\lambda)(\lambda^5 + 0.825\lambda^4 + 0.454\lambda^3 + 0.129\lambda^2 + 0.027\lambda + 0.002) = 0 \tag{4.21}$$

Now the new entrants to rank 1 are, at the same time, the new entrants into the population, and we have seen (see the discussion in Section 2.13), that the difference equation for these has characteristic equation (2.13), or (2.18), which we repeat here for convenience

$$(1-\lambda)(\lambda^5 + 0.875\lambda^4 + 0.510\lambda^3 + 0.156\lambda^2 + 0.034\lambda + 0.003) = 0 \tag{4.22}$$

The solutions of the difference equations depend on the roots of their characteristic equations, and because we want equal solutions for the two difference equations, we look for common roots of equations (4.21) and (4.22).

The roots of equation (4.21) are

$$1 \quad -0.125 \quad -0.25 + iv \quad -0.25 - iv \quad -0.1 + 0.3i \quad -0.1 - 0.3i$$

where $v = 0.3225$, and those of equation (4.22) are

$$1 \quad -0.125 \quad -0.25 + iv \quad -0.25 - iv \quad -0.125 + iw \quad -0.125 - iw$$

where $v = 0.3225$, and $w = 0.3307$. The first four are common to equations (4.21) and (4.22).

If $\lambda_0, \ldots, \lambda_s$ are common roots of two difference equations for $n_0(t)$, then (we assume again that all roots are simple)

$$n_0(t) = a_0\lambda_0^t + \ldots + a_s\lambda_s^t \tag{4.23}$$

is a common solution. $a_0\lambda_0^t = a_0$ is the stationary number of entrants which keeps all ranks, and in fact all states, constant.

If we take

$$a_0 = 1000 \quad a_1 = 1 \quad a_2 = -70 + 60i \quad a_3 = -70 - 60i \quad a_4 = a_5 = 0$$

then

$$n_0(t) = 1000 - (-0.125)^t + (-70 + 60i)(-0.25 + 0.3225i)^t + (-70 - 60i)(-0.25 - 0.3225i)^t \tag{4.24}$$

These are the numbers of entrants

859, 996, 1025, 989, 1001, etc.

in Example 13, in Section 2.15.

4.10

In Example 13 not only the total of rank 1, but all rank totals were kept constant. We examine this point again, using difference equations and observing their solutions.

Those who survive in the population, but not in rank 1, may be called survivors in rank 2 and above, but they include also those who have just been promoted from rank 1 into rank 2. Their rates, which we shall call 'development rates', may exceed unity.

The development rates are obtained by subtracting equation (4.21) from equation (4.22), thus:

$$(1-\lambda)(0.050\lambda^4 + 0.056\lambda^3 + 0.027\lambda^2 + 0.007\lambda + 0.001) = 0$$

or (taking more significant numbers into account)

$$(1-\lambda)(\lambda^4 + 1.125\lambda^3 + 0.542\lambda^2 + 0.136\lambda + 0.010) = 0 \qquad (4.25)$$

This equation has those roots which are common to equations (4.21) and (4.22), and another root, –0.5 which is here irrelevant. The coefficients in the second factor on the left-hand side of equation (4.25) are the products of

1.125, 0.482, 0.251, 0.073,

the development rates in rank 2 and above. For instance

73 times 1.125 equals 60 + 22
(18 + 7) times 0.482 equals 8 + 4
(6 + 3) times 0.251 equals 0 + 2
(11 + 12) times 0.073 equals 1 + 1 (to the nearest integer).

4.11

In Example 13 the total of rank 2 alone was also kept constant. This is equivalent to saying that the combined ranks 1 and 2 were preserved. The survivors within these ranks are seen from the list in Section 2.13 to be

Age	Rank 1	Rank 2	Totals
0	1000	–	1000
1	825	50	875
2	454	41	495
3	129	18	147
4	27	3	30
5	2	0	2

The characteristic equation for the new entrants,

$$(1-\lambda)(\lambda^5 + 0.875\lambda^4 + 0.495\lambda^3 + 0.147\lambda^2 + 0.30\lambda + 0.002) = 0 \qquad (4.26)$$

has again those latent roots which were common to equations (4.21) and (4.22).

The difference between equations (4.22) and (4.26) gives by the ratios of its coefficients the development rates within the remaining rank 3 only. We refrain from numerical examples, because rounding errors would at this stage distort the results.

4.12

In the author's paper (Vajda, 1947), from which Example 13 is taken, the approach was in some sense the reverse to that adopted here. There it was asked if, for a given structure, transition rates, i.e. survival and promotion rates could be found to make that structure semi-stationary.

This question reduces to that of looking for polynomials which have common roots with one originally given, but smaller coefficients.

In the same paper promotion rates dependent on seniority within the rank were also treated, in a similar way.

4.13

A continuous model does not introduce any new principles, and we shall not deal with it here.

5

Changing Population Totals

5.1

Until now we have been concerned with populations whose total remained constant. Now we shall look at populations whose total might change from step to step. To begin with, we shall analyse the case of a constant rate of change, $1 + \alpha$. If α is positive, this means expansion, if it is negative, it means contraction. In any case $\alpha > -1$.

New entrants replace those members who are leaving, and they add α times the previous total, so that their numbers must be

$$\sum_{i=1}^{k} (w_i + \alpha) n_i(t) \tag{5.1}$$

This number cannot be negative, and so we obtain a lower bound for α, higher than -1, when $\mathbf{n}$ is given, viz.

$$\alpha \geqslant -\frac{\Sigma_{i=1}^{k} n_i w_i}{\Sigma_{i=1}^{k} n_i}$$

i.e.

$$1 + \alpha \geqslant \frac{\Sigma_{i=1}^{k} n_i \Sigma_{j=1}^{k} p_{ij}}{\Sigma_{i=1}^{k} n_i} \tag{5.2}$$

When $1 + \alpha$ equals this lower bound, then no new entrants are required to obtain the new total, viz. the previous one multiplied by $1 + \alpha$. At the next step the lower bound might have changed, though.

5.2

If the new entrants join the various states in proportions ρ_i, then

$$n_j(t+1) = (r_{1j} + \rho_j \alpha) n_1(t) + \ldots + (r_{kj} + \rho_j \alpha) n_k(t) \tag{5.3}$$

for $j = 1, \ldots, k$, where $r_{ij} = p_{ij} + \rho_j w_i$ as in equation (2.21).

We solve the system (5.3) by finding the roots of the characteristic equation

$$|\mathbf{R}(\rho,\alpha)-\lambda\mathbf{I}| = \begin{vmatrix} r_{11}+\rho_1\alpha-\lambda & r_{21}+\rho_1\alpha & \dots & r_{k1}+\rho_1\alpha \\ r_{12}+\rho_2\alpha & r_{22}+\rho_2\alpha-\lambda & \dots & r_{k2}+\rho_2\alpha \\ \vdots & \vdots & & \vdots \\ r_{1k}+\rho_k\alpha & r_{2k}+\rho_k\alpha & \dots & r_{kk}+\rho_k\alpha-\lambda \end{vmatrix} = 0 \tag{5.4}$$

Each column adds up to $1+\alpha-\lambda$, and therefore $1+\alpha$ is one of the roots. The other roots are independent of α, and they are the same as those of $\mathbf{R}$ defined in equation (2.23), where α was zero. To see this write the determinant as $(1+\alpha-\lambda)D$, where the first row of D consists only of ones. Then subtract this row $\rho_i\alpha$ times from the ith row, so that α disappears from D, and hence from the roots of $D=0$. The latent vectors are also those of the corresponding latent roots of equation (2.23).

5.3

If the latent roots of $\mathbf{R}(\rho,\alpha)$ are $\lambda_0=1+\alpha, \lambda_1, \dots, \lambda_{k-1}$ then

$$n_i(t) = a_0 c_{i0}(1+\alpha)^t + a_1 c_{i1}\lambda_1^t + \dots + a_{k-1}c_{i,k-1}\lambda_{k-1}^t \tag{5.5}$$

where $\mathbf{c}_j = [c_{1j}, \dots, c_{kj}]$ is the latent vector corresponding to λ_j. The constants $a_0, \dots, a_{k-1}$ depend on the original structure. (Compare the analogous argument in Section 2.3.)

5.4

As an illustration take again the transition matrix $\mathbf{P}_0$, and let $\rho_1=1$, i.e. all entrants join state 1. The latent roots of the system are

$$\lambda_0 = 1+\alpha \quad \lambda_1 = 0.2+\mathrm{i}(0.05)^{1/2} \quad \lambda_2 = 0.2-\mathrm{i}(0.05)^{1/2}$$

and the latent vectors are proportional to

$$\begin{matrix} 0.27+1.1\alpha+\alpha^2 & -0.02-0.1118\mathrm{i} & -0.02+0.1118\mathrm{i} \\ 0.25+0.4\alpha & -0.07+0.0894\mathrm{i} & -0.07-0.0894\mathrm{i} \\ 0.17+0.1\alpha & 0.09+0.0224\mathrm{i} & 0.09-0.0224\mathrm{i} \end{matrix}$$

For instance, when $\alpha=0.2$, then a latent root corresponding to λ_0 will be [53, 33, 19] and $\mathbf{n}(t)$ will be given by

$$\begin{aligned} n_1(t) &= 53(1.2)^t A + (-0.02-0.1118\mathrm{i})[0.2+\mathrm{i}(0.05)^{1/2}]^t B \\ &\quad + (-0.02+0.1118\mathrm{i})[0.2-\mathrm{i}(0.05)^{1/2}]^t C \\ n_2(t) &= 33(1.2)^t A + (-0.07+0.0894\mathrm{i})[0.2+\mathrm{i}(0.05)^{1/2}]^t B \\ &\quad + (-0.07-0.0894\mathrm{i})[0.2-\mathrm{i}(0.05)^{1/2}]^t C \\ n_3(t) &= 19(1.2)^t A + (0.09+0.0224\mathrm{i})[0.2+\mathrm{i}(0.05)^{1/2}]^t B \\ &\quad + (0.09-0.0224\mathrm{i})[0.2-\mathrm{i}(0.05)^{1/2}]^t C \end{aligned} \tag{5.6}$$

where A, B, and C are constants defined by the initial structure, at $t = 0$. (Compare with equations (2.31)–(2.33).)

If we start with [1000, 0, 0] and apply matrix

$$\mathbf{R}(\rho_i, 0.2) = \begin{pmatrix} 0.7 & 0.4 & 0.7 \\ 0.4 & 0.5 & 0.1 \\ 0.1 & 0.3 & 0.4 \end{pmatrix}$$

then we obtain, successively,

1000	700	720	861	1043	1256	1508	1810
0	400	490	556	654	782	938	1125
0	100	230	311	377	451	541	649
1000	1200	1440	1728	2074	2489	2987	3584

5.5

If the latent roots $\lambda_1, \ldots, \lambda_{k-1}$ have absolute values smaller than unity, then any initial structure will converge to $[a_0 c_{i0}(1 + \alpha)^t]$. If we start with $\mathbf{n}(0) = [a_0 c_{10}, \ldots, a_0 c_{k0}]$, then not only the total of the population, but also the total of each state will increase at the rate $(1 + \alpha)$. Expressed differently, the ratios of the totals of any two states will remain the same, after each step.

We call a structure with this property 'stable' with regard to given ρ and α.

Forbes (1970) calls a structure 'quasi-stationary' if the proportions of sizes of states remain constant. Though his definition does not state explicitly that the rate of expansion or contraction is the same at each step, this is an underlying assumption in his paper. It contains also a brief study of lower bounds on α.

5.6

For a stable population we have

$$(1 + \alpha)n_j = r_{1j}n_1 + \ldots + r_{kj}n_k + \alpha\rho_j \sum_{i=1}^{k} n_i \tag{5.7}$$

which can also be written

$$(1 + \alpha)n_j = p_{1j}n_1 + \ldots + p_{kj}n_k + \rho_j \sum_{i=1}^{k} (w_i + \alpha)n_i \tag{5.8}$$

The solution vector is clearly a latent vector of $\mathbf{R}(\rho, \alpha)$, corresponding to the latent root $1 + \alpha$.

It follows from equation (5.8) that we must have

$$(1 + \alpha)n_j \geqslant \sum_{i=1}^{k} n_i p_{ij} \quad \text{for all } j \tag{5.9}$$

i.e.

$$(1 + \alpha)n_j \geqslant \max_j \sum_{i=1}^{k} n_i p_{ij} \tag{5.10}$$

The lower limit in inequality (5.10) is that of α for which a given structure **n** can be stable, while that in inequality (5.2) was the lower limit of α at which the total of a given **n** can be changed in one step. It follows that the former lower limit can not be smaller than the latter. It follows also from the algebraic expressions, because clearly

$$\frac{\Sigma_i \Sigma_j n_i p_{ij}}{\Sigma_j n_j} \leqslant \max_j \left(\sum_i n_i p_{ij} / n_j \right)$$

5.7

It follows also from equation (5.8) that a condition for stability is $[(1+\alpha)\mathbf{I} - \mathbf{P}'] \geqslant 0$, so the region containing the stable structures for α_1 contains that for α_2 if $\alpha_1 > \alpha_2$. In particular, if α is positive, then the region of its stable structures will contain all stationary ones, viz. those for $\alpha = 0$.

5.8

The system (5.7) has a non-trivial solution, because one of its equations is redundant. If we add them, we obtain the identity

$$(1+\alpha)\sum_j n_j = (1+\alpha)\sum_j n_j$$

The n_j which solve equation (5.7) are proportional to the signed minors of the elements of any row of the matrix $\mathbf{R}(\rho, \alpha) - (1+\alpha)\mathbf{I}$.

For instance, if $\rho_1 = 1$, and hence all other ρ_i are zero, then $(-1)^i n_i$ will be proportional to the subdeterminants of the matrix

$$\begin{pmatrix} p_{12} & p_{22} - 1 - \alpha & \dots & p_{k2} \\ \vdots & \vdots & & \vdots \\ p_{1k} & p_{2k} & \dots & p_{kk} - 1 - \alpha \end{pmatrix}$$

If $(1+\alpha)$ is not a latent root of the transition matrix **P** as well, then the subdeterminants are, with alternating signs, proportional to the entries in the first column of $[\mathbf{P}' - (1+\alpha)\mathbf{I}]^{-1}$.

On the other hand, if $(1+\alpha)$ is a latent root of **P** (which is only possible if α is negative), then we see from equation (5.8) that the sum in the last term, i.e. the expression (5.1), is zero, and $[n_1, \dots, n_k]$ will be a latent vector corresponding to that latent root.

In such a case, and only then, no new entrants are required, and α will have the lower bound given by inequality (5.2).

This is, of course, only relevant if all n_i are non-negative and real, and if $1+\alpha$ is a real latent root. In fact, there exists always a non-negative latent root such that a corresponding latent vector is non-negative. (See Appendix I, Sections 1.12 and 1.13.)

5.9

$\mathbf{P}_0$ has one single real latent root, viz. 0.805, which means $\alpha = -0.195$. In this case

$$\begin{pmatrix} 0.3-0.805 & 0.1 & 0.2 \\ 0.4 & 0.5-0.805 & 0.1 \\ 0.1 & 0.3 & 0.4-0.805 \end{pmatrix} \begin{pmatrix} n_1 \\ n_2 \\ n_3 \end{pmatrix} = 0$$

has a solution

$$\underset{\overline{1000}}{\begin{pmatrix} 225 \\ 414 \\ 361 \end{pmatrix}} \text{ which transforms into } \underset{\overline{805}}{\begin{pmatrix} 181 \\ 333 \\ 291 \end{pmatrix}} \text{ without any new entrants.}$$

5.10

We add another example, using a transition matrix with three real roots. Let

$$\mathbf{P}_1 = \begin{pmatrix} 0.3 & 0.1 & 0.2 \\ 0 & 0.6 & 0.1 \\ 0 & 0 & 0.5 \end{pmatrix}$$

Its latent roots are evidently

0.3 0.6 0.5

and right-hand latent vectors of $\mathbf{P}_1'$ are

$$\begin{matrix} -6 & 0 & 0 \\ 2 & 0.5 & 0 \\ 5 & 0.5 & 1 \end{matrix}$$

The first of these is irrelevant. Those remaining are stable structures, without requiring new entrants:

$$\begin{pmatrix} 0 \\ 0.5 \\ 0.5 \end{pmatrix} \rightarrow \begin{pmatrix} 0 \\ 0.3 \\ 0.3 \end{pmatrix} = 0.6 \begin{pmatrix} 0 \\ 0.5 \\ 0.5 \end{pmatrix}$$

and

$$\begin{pmatrix} 0 \\ 0 \\ 1 \end{pmatrix} \rightarrow \begin{pmatrix} 0 \\ 0 \\ 0.5 \end{pmatrix} = 0.5 \begin{pmatrix} 0 \\ 0 \\ 1 \end{pmatrix}$$

In either case $1 + \alpha$ has the smallest possible value for the initial structure, and there is no initial structure for which $1 + \alpha < 0.5$

5.11

Returning to our example in Section 5.4, with $\mathbf{P}_0$, and $\alpha = 0.2$, (1.2 is not a latent root of $\mathbf{P}_0$), we have

$$(1.2\mathbf{I} - \mathbf{P}_0)^{-1} = \begin{pmatrix} 0.9 & -0.4 & -0.1 \\ -0.1 & 0.7 & -0.3 \\ -0.2 & -0.1 & 0.8 \end{pmatrix}^{-1}$$

$$= \begin{pmatrix} 1.305 & 0.812 & 0.468 \\ 0.344 & 1.723 & 0.688 \\ 0.369 & 0.419 & 1.453 \end{pmatrix} \tag{5.11}$$

The first row of the matrix in equation (5.11) gives a stable population when entries are only into state 1, thus:

$$\mathbf{S}_1^{(0.2)} = \underset{2585}{\begin{pmatrix} 1305 \\ 812 \\ 468 \end{pmatrix}} \to \begin{matrix} 566 + 1000 \\ 975 \\ 561 \end{matrix} = \underset{3102}{\begin{pmatrix} 1566 \\ 975 \\ 561 \end{pmatrix}} \to \begin{matrix} 679 + 1200 \\ 1170 \\ 673 \end{matrix} = \underset{3722}{\begin{pmatrix} 1879 \\ 1170 \\ 673 \end{pmatrix}} \text{ etc.}$$

With entries into the second, or into the third state, we get

$$\mathbf{S}_2^{(0.2)} = \underset{2755}{\begin{pmatrix} 344 \\ 1723 \\ 688 \end{pmatrix}} \to \begin{matrix} 413 \\ 1068 + 1000 = \\ 825 \end{matrix} \underset{3306}{\begin{pmatrix} 413 \\ 2068 \\ 825 \end{pmatrix}} \to \begin{matrix} 496 \\ 1282 + 1200 = \\ 991 \end{matrix} \underset{3969}{\begin{pmatrix} 496 \\ 2482 \\ 991 \end{pmatrix}} \text{ etc.}$$

and

$$\mathbf{S}_3^{(0.2)} = \underset{2241}{\begin{pmatrix} 369 \\ 419 \\ 1453 \end{pmatrix}} \to \begin{matrix} 443 \\ 502 \\ 744 + 1000 \end{matrix} = \underset{2689}{\begin{pmatrix} 443 \\ 502 \\ 1744 \end{pmatrix}} \to \begin{matrix} 532 \\ 603 \\ 892 + 1200 \end{matrix} = \underset{3227}{\begin{pmatrix} 532 \\ 603 \\ 2092 \end{pmatrix}} \text{ etc.}$$

The fact that the numbers of new entrants are, at each step, the same in each of the three cases can be explained in the same way as we explained the analogous result for stationary structures, in Section 3.5.

5.12

We denote by $\mathbf{S}_j^{(\alpha)}$ the stable distribution expanding at the rate $1 + \alpha$, with entries into state j only, Any structure in the convex hull of the $\mathbf{S}_j^{(\alpha)}$ is also stable, with the same α, and the required number of entrants into state j of the structure $\Sigma_{j=1}^{k} v_j \mathbf{S}_j^{(\alpha)}$, with $v_j \geqslant 0$, $\Sigma_j v_j = 1$ will be

$$\sum_{j=1}^{k} v_j \sum_{i=1}^{k} n_i^{(j)}(w_i + \alpha) \tag{5.12}$$

where $n_i^{(j)}$ is the membership of state i in $\mathbf{S}_j^{(\alpha)}$.

For instance, using once more $\mathbf{P}_0$ and $\alpha = 0.2$, let us take

$$\mathbf{S}_1^{(0.2)}/2 + \mathbf{S}_2^{(0.2)}/3 + \mathbf{S}_3^{(0.2)}/6 = \begin{pmatrix} 829 \\ 1050 \\ 705 \end{pmatrix}$$

$$\overline{2584}$$

This will transform into

$$\begin{matrix} 495 + 500 \\ 927 + 333 \\ 680 + 166 \end{matrix} = \begin{pmatrix} 995 \\ 1260 \\ 846 \end{pmatrix} = \begin{pmatrix} (1.2)829 \\ (1.2)1050 \\ (1.2)705 \end{pmatrix}$$

5.13

We have already mentioned that the lower limit for α in (5.2) depended on n. However, we might be interested in knowing a smallest α which depends on the transition matrix alone.

It is shown in Appendix I (Sections I.12 and I.13) that the smallest value of $1 + \alpha$ is a latent root of the transition matrix. It is also mentioned there that for irreducible matrices the latent root we are looking for is that of largest modulus, and that the corresponding latent vector is positive.

The matrix $\mathbf{P}_0$ is irreducible, and has only one latent root. The transition matrix $\mathbf{P}_1$, introduced in Section 5.10 is reducible. In such a case the smallest possible value of $1 + \alpha$ for stability is again a latent root, but not necessarily the largest. We have seen an example of this in Section 5.10, where the smallest possible value was 0.5, while the largest latent root was 0.6.

5.14

It is of interest to observe the effect of constant transition rates on a stable structure if an organization expands. Tables 15 and 16 give an idea of the dependence of the ratios of states for various α, with entries into state 1.

Table 15. Transition matrix $\mathbf{P}_0$

State \ α	0	0.01	0.025	0.05	0.10	0.15	0.20
1	0.392	0.398	0.408	0.424	0.453	0.480	0.505
2	0.362	0.360	0.356	0.350	0.337	0.325	0.314
3	0.246	0.242	0.236	0.226	0.210	0.195	0.181

Table 16. Transition matrix $\mathbf{P}_1$

State \ α	0	0.01	0.025	0.05	0.10	0.15	0.20
1	0.588	0.595	0.602	0.615	0.636	0.659	0.677
2	0.147	0.144	0.142	0.137	0.127	0.120	0.113
3	0.265	0.261	0.256	0.248	0.237	0.221	0.210

We notice that with increasing expansion rate the higher states contain decreasing portions of the total population. This means that promotion rates, which are appropriate for expanding populations will tend to make the structure top-heavy when the rate of expansion decreases, or expansion stops altogether. For a more detailed analysis see Young (1971).

5.15

So far, we have considered in this book cases where the total population was kept constant, or changed at a constant rate. We shall now consider different possibilities.

Models which analyse the effect of given input and transition rates have been called 'push models', and those where a required effect is given, and the appropriate input and transition rates depend on it, are 'pull models'. If the rates of a push model are only dependent on the present situation, the model is a 'Markov model', and if a pull model aims at retaining some feature, it is a 'renewal model'. Models can have aspects of both types. For instance, a stationary structure is at the same time a pull and a push model.

The scheme of Section 2.24 is clearly a pull model. We mention also that Grinold and Stanford (1974) call a Markov model with constant rates a 'fractional flow model'.

In the next Section we consider first push models, and then pull models.

5.16

Let the input at the end of step t be $ax^{t-1}\boldsymbol{\rho}$, where a and x are non-negative scalars, and the vectors $\boldsymbol{\rho}$ gives the distribution of new entrants over the various states.

Now we cannot use the earlier methods which assumed rates which were independent of time. Instead, we apply equation (I.16) from Appendix I.

Let the initial population be

$$\mathbf{n}(0) = \sum_{i=1}^{k} b_i \mathbf{v}_i \tag{5.13}$$

where the $\mathbf{v}_i$ are the left-hand latent vectors of the transition matrix $\mathbf{P}$ (and hence the right-hand latent vectors of $\mathbf{P}'$). Also, let

$$a\boldsymbol{\rho} = \sum_{i=1}^{k} a_i \mathbf{v}_i \tag{5.14}$$

Then, after the tth step, we shall have

$$(\mathbf{P})^t \mathbf{n}(0) = \sum_{i=1}^{k} b_i \mathbf{v}_i \lambda_i^t \tag{5.15}$$

left of the initial population, and of the inputs, including that at the end of t steps, there will still be left

$$(\mathbf{P}'^{t-1} + x\mathbf{P}'^{t-2} + \ldots + x^{t-1})a\boldsymbol{\rho}$$

$$= \sum_{i=1}^{k} a_i \mathbf{v}_i (\lambda_i^{t-1} + \lambda_i^{t-2}x + \ldots + \lambda_i x^{t-2} + x^{t-1})$$

$$= \sum_{i=1}^{k} a_i \mathbf{v}_i (\lambda_i^t - x^t)/(\lambda_i - x) \tag{5.16}$$

unless $x = \lambda_i$, a latent root of $\mathbf{P}$. In the latter case the ith term of the summation will be replaced by $a_i \mathbf{v}_i t \lambda_i^{t-1}$.

For illustration, we shall use the transition matrix from Section 1.21, viz.

$$\mathbf{P} = \begin{pmatrix} 0.590 & 0.036 & 0 \\ 0 & 0.214 & 0.187 \\ 0 & 0 & 0.276 \end{pmatrix}$$

with $\mathbf{w} = [0.374, 0.599, 0.724]$, latent roots

$$\lambda_1 = 0.590 \quad \lambda_2 = 0.214 \quad \lambda_3 = 0.276$$

and latent vectors (left-hand vectors of $\mathbf{P}$ = right-hand vectors of $\mathbf{P}'$)

$$\mathbf{v}_1 = \begin{pmatrix} 0.868 \\ 0.083 \\ 0.049 \end{pmatrix} \quad \mathbf{v}_2 = \begin{pmatrix} 0 \\ -0.496 \\ 1.496 \end{pmatrix} \quad \mathbf{v}_3 = \begin{pmatrix} 0 \\ 0 \\ 1 \end{pmatrix}$$

We shall also have occasion to use

$$(\mathbf{I} - \mathbf{P})^{-1} = \begin{pmatrix} 2.437 & 0.112 & 0.029 \\ 0 & 1.272 & 0.328 \\ 0 & 0 & 1.381 \end{pmatrix}$$

5.17

First, consider a case with constant input vector, i.e. $x = 1$. Then for $t \geqslant 1$

$$\mathbf{n}(t) = (\mathbf{P}')^t \mathbf{n}(0) + \sum_{\tau=1}^{t} (\mathbf{P}')^{t-\tau} a\boldsymbol{\rho} = (\mathbf{P}')^t \mathbf{n}(0) + \sum_{i=1}^{k} a_i \mathbf{v}_i (\lambda_i^t - 1)/(\lambda_i - 1) \tag{5.17}$$

With increasing t, $(\mathbf{P}')^t$ will vanish and $\mathbf{n}(t)$ converges to

$$\sum_{i=1}^{k} a_i \mathbf{v}_i/(1 - \lambda_i) \tag{5.18}$$

Let

$$\mathbf{n}(0) = \begin{pmatrix} 600 \\ 250 \\ 150 \end{pmatrix} = 691\mathbf{v}_1 - 388\mathbf{v}_2 + 697\mathbf{v}_3$$

and

$$a\boldsymbol{\rho} = \begin{pmatrix} 126 \\ 125 \\ 32 \end{pmatrix} = 146\mathbf{v}_1 - 228\mathbf{v}_2 + 366\mathbf{v}_3$$

Then

$$(\mathbf{P}')^t\mathbf{n}(0) = 691(0.590)^t \begin{pmatrix} 0.868 \\ 0.083 \\ 0.049 \end{pmatrix} - 388(0.214)^t \begin{pmatrix} 0 \\ -0.496 \\ 1.496 \end{pmatrix}$$

$$+ 697(0.276)^t \begin{pmatrix} 0 \\ 0 \\ 1 \end{pmatrix}$$

and

$$\sum_{\tau=1}^{t} (\mathbf{P}')^{t-\tau} a\boldsymbol{\rho} = [146(1 - 0.590^t)/0.410] \begin{pmatrix} 0.868 \\ 0.083 \\ 0.049 \end{pmatrix}$$

$$- [288(1 - 0.214^t)/0.786] \begin{pmatrix} 0 \\ -0.496 \\ 1.496 \end{pmatrix}$$

$$+ [366(1 - 0.276^t)/0.724] \begin{pmatrix} 0 \\ 0 \\ 1 \end{pmatrix}$$

The structure will develop as follows:

$$\underset{1000}{\begin{pmatrix} 600 \\ 250 \\ 150 \end{pmatrix}} \rightarrow \begin{matrix} 354 \\ 75 \\ 88 \end{matrix} + \begin{matrix} 126 \\ 125 \\ 32 \end{matrix} = \underset{800}{\begin{pmatrix} 480 \\ 200 \\ 120 \end{pmatrix}} \rightarrow \begin{matrix} 283 \\ 60 \\ 70 \end{matrix} + \begin{matrix} 126 \\ 125 \\ 32 \end{matrix} = \underset{696}{\begin{pmatrix} 409 \\ 185 \\ 102 \end{pmatrix}} \rightarrow \begin{matrix} 241 \\ 54 \\ 63 \end{matrix} + \begin{matrix} 126 \\ 125 \\ 32 \end{matrix}$$

$$= \underset{641}{\begin{pmatrix} 367 \\ 179 \\ 95 \end{pmatrix}} \rightarrow \begin{matrix} 217 \\ 52 \\ 60 \end{matrix} + \begin{matrix} 126 \\ 125 \\ 32 \end{matrix} = \underset{612}{\begin{pmatrix} 343 \\ 177 \\ 92 \end{pmatrix}} \rightarrow \begin{matrix} 202 \\ 50 \\ 58 \end{matrix} + \begin{matrix} 126 \\ 125 \\ 32 \end{matrix} = \underset{593}{\begin{pmatrix} 328 \\ 175 \\ 90 \end{pmatrix}} \rightarrow \begin{matrix} 194 \\ 49 \\ 58 \end{matrix} + \begin{matrix} 126 \\ 125 \\ 32 \end{matrix}$$

$$= \underset{584}{\begin{pmatrix} 320 \\ 174 \\ 90 \end{pmatrix}} \rightarrow \begin{matrix} 189 \\ 49 \\ 57 \end{matrix} + \begin{matrix} 126 \\ 125 \\ 32 \end{matrix} = \underset{578}{\begin{pmatrix} 315 \\ 174 \\ 89 \end{pmatrix}} \rightarrow \begin{matrix} 186 \\ 49 \\ 57 \end{matrix} + \begin{matrix} 126 \\ 125 \\ 32 \end{matrix} = \underset{575}{\begin{pmatrix} 312 \\ 174 \\ 89 \end{pmatrix}} \rightarrow \begin{matrix} 184 \\ 49 \\ 57 \end{matrix} + \begin{matrix} 126 \\ 125 \\ 32 \end{matrix}$$

$$= \underset{573}{\begin{pmatrix} 310 \\ 174 \\ 89 \end{pmatrix}} \text{ and so on}$$

With increasing t, $(\mathbf{P}')^t$ will vanish, and the structure converges to

$$(146/0.410)\begin{pmatrix}0.868\\0.083\\0.049\end{pmatrix} - (228/0.786)\begin{pmatrix}0\\-0.496\\1.496\end{pmatrix} + (366/0.724)\begin{pmatrix}0\\0\\1\end{pmatrix}$$

$$= \begin{matrix}309\\30+144\\17-434+506\end{matrix} = \begin{pmatrix}309\\174\\89\end{pmatrix}$$

$$\overline{572}$$

5.18

We could have obtained these same results by observing that the initial structure contains that stationary structure which is implied by new entrants [126, 125, 32], plus or minus another structure, which disappears in the course of time.

We see from $(\mathbf{I}-\mathbf{P})^{-1}$ that, with entries into the

first second third

state, the stationary structure is

$$\begin{pmatrix}2437a\\112a\\29a\end{pmatrix} \qquad \begin{pmatrix}0\\1272b\\328b\end{pmatrix} \qquad \begin{pmatrix}0\\0\\1381c\end{pmatrix}$$

requiring new entrants

$1000a$ $1000b$ $1000c$

so that, with entrants as above, we have

$a = 0.126$ $b = 0.125$ $c = 0.032$

and the stationary structure, with these numbers of entrants, is

$$\begin{pmatrix}390\\15\\3\end{pmatrix} + \begin{pmatrix}0\\159\\42\end{pmatrix} + \begin{pmatrix}0\\0\\44\end{pmatrix} = \begin{pmatrix}309\\174\\89\end{pmatrix}$$

Now

$$\begin{pmatrix}600\\250\\150\end{pmatrix} = \begin{pmatrix}309\\174\\89\end{pmatrix} + \begin{pmatrix}291\\76\\61\end{pmatrix}$$

and

$$\begin{pmatrix}291\\76\\61\end{pmatrix} = 0.335\mathbf{v}_1 - 0.097\mathbf{v}_2 + 0.190\mathbf{v}_3$$

After the next stage this portion develops into

$$\begin{matrix}171\\ 16 + 10\\ 9 - 31 + 53\end{matrix} \quad = \begin{pmatrix}171\\ 26\\ 31\end{pmatrix}$$

and adding

$$\begin{pmatrix}309\\ 174\\ 89\end{pmatrix}$$

we obtain

$$\begin{pmatrix}480\\ 200\\ 120\end{pmatrix} = \mathbf{n}(1) \text{ as above}$$

5.19

Now we turn to changing inputs.

Let again $\mathbf{n}(0) = [600, 250, 150]$, but this time let the input at the end of t steps be:

$$\text{(a)} \quad (0.8)^t \begin{pmatrix}126\\ 125\\ 32\end{pmatrix}; \qquad \text{or (b)} \quad (1.1)^t \begin{pmatrix}126\\ 126\\ 32\end{pmatrix}$$

Consider, then, first (a). The initial structure develops as follows:

$$\begin{array}{cccccccccc} \begin{pmatrix}600\\ 250\\ 150\end{pmatrix} & & \begin{matrix}354 & 126\\ 75 & +\ 125\\ 88 & 32\end{matrix} = & \begin{pmatrix}480\\ 200\\ 120\end{pmatrix} & \rightarrow & \begin{matrix}283 & 101\\ 60 & +\ 100\\ 70 & 26\end{matrix} = & \begin{pmatrix}384\\ 160\\ 96\end{pmatrix} & \rightarrow & \begin{matrix}227 & 80\\ 48 & +\ 80\\ 56 & 21\end{matrix} \\ \overline{1000} & & & \overline{800} & & & \overline{640} & & \end{array}$$

$$\begin{array}{cccccc} = & \begin{pmatrix}307\\ 120\\ 77\end{pmatrix} & \rightarrow & \begin{matrix}182 & 64\\ 38 & +\ 64\\ 45 & 17\end{matrix} = & \begin{pmatrix}246\\ 102\\ 62\end{pmatrix} \\ & \overline{512} & & & \overline{410} \end{array}$$

In this case the numbers of members in the states, and hence also the totals, are at each step multiplied by 0.8. This is so, because we have chosen those numbers of new entries which are appropriate for the stable population with $1 + \alpha = 0.8$. Now consider (b). This time the same initial structure as before develops as follows:

$$\begin{array}{ccccccccc} \begin{pmatrix}600\\ 250\\ 150\end{pmatrix} & \rightarrow & \begin{matrix}354 & 126\\ 75 & +\ 125\\ 88 & 32\end{matrix} = & \begin{pmatrix}480\\ 200\\ 120\end{pmatrix} & \rightarrow & \begin{matrix}283 & 139\\ 60 & +\ 138\\ 70 & 35\end{matrix} = & \begin{pmatrix}422\\ 198\\ 105\end{pmatrix} & \rightarrow & \begin{matrix}249 & 153\\ 58 & +\ 152\\ 67 & 39\end{matrix} \\ \overline{1000} & & & \overline{800} & & & \overline{725} & & \end{array}$$

$$= \begin{pmatrix} 402 \\ 210 \\ 106 \end{pmatrix} \rightarrow \begin{matrix} 237 & 168 \\ 59 + 167 = \\ 69 & 43 \end{matrix} \begin{pmatrix} 405 \\ 226 \\ 112 \end{pmatrix} \rightarrow \begin{matrix} 239 & 185 \\ 63 + 184 = \\ 73 & 47 \end{matrix} \begin{pmatrix} 424 \\ 247 \\ 120 \end{pmatrix} \rightarrow \begin{matrix} 250 & 203 \\ 68 + 201 \\ 79 & 52 \end{matrix}$$

$$\quad 718 \qquad\qquad\qquad 743 \qquad\qquad\qquad 791$$

$$= \begin{pmatrix} 453 \\ 269 \\ 131 \end{pmatrix} \rightarrow \begin{matrix} 267 & 223 \\ 74 + 221 = \\ 86 & 57 \end{matrix} \begin{pmatrix} 490 \\ 295 \\ 143 \end{pmatrix} \rightarrow \begin{matrix} 289 & 245 \\ 81 + 243 = \\ 95 & 63 \end{matrix} \begin{pmatrix} 534 \\ 324 \\ 158 \end{pmatrix} \rightarrow \begin{matrix} 315 & 270 \\ 89 + 267 \\ 104 & 69 \end{matrix}$$

$$\quad 853 \qquad\qquad\qquad 928 \qquad\qquad\qquad 1016$$

$$= \begin{pmatrix} 585 \\ 356 \\ 173 \end{pmatrix} \text{ and so on}$$

$$\quad 1114$$

After reductions to begin with, the totals tend to increase by a factor of 1.1.

5.20

We consider now a pull model, where the development of the size rather than that of the input is given. The latter must then make up not only for the wastage, but also for the required increase (or be adjusted for the decrease) of the size of the population.

We can use formulae of the type (5.17), replacing $\mathbf{P}'$ by a matrix $\mathbf{R}(\rho)$ to take account of the distribution of the new entries into the various states.

For instance, take again the transition matrix $\mathbf{P}$ of Section 5.16, and $\boldsymbol{\rho} = [0.567, 0.333, 0.100]$. Then

$$\mathbf{R}(\rho) = \begin{pmatrix} 0.590 + (0.374)(0.567) & (0.599)(0.567) & (0.724)(0.567) \\ 0.036 + (0.374)(0.333) & 0.214 + (0.599)(0.333) & (0.724)(0.333) \\ (0.374)(0.100) & 0.187 + (0.599)(0.100) & 0.267 + (0.724)(0.100) \end{pmatrix}$$

$$= \begin{pmatrix} 0.802 & 0.340 & 0.411 \\ 0.161 & 0.413 & 0.241 \\ 0.037 & 0.247 & 0.348 \end{pmatrix}$$

The latent roots of $\mathbf{R}(\rho)$ are

$$\lambda_0 = 1 \qquad \lambda_1 = 0.416 \qquad \lambda_2 = 0.147$$

with latent vectors proportional to

$\mathbf{v}_0$	$\mathbf{v}_1$	$\mathbf{v}_3$
649	−6	−6
229	2	−24
122	4	30

5.21

Consider, first, a constant vector addition, $c\boldsymbol{\rho} = \Sigma_{i=1}^{k} c_i \mathbf{v}_i$. Then, for $t \geqslant 1$,

$$\mathbf{n}(t) = \mathbf{R}^t\mathbf{n}(0) + \sum_{\tau=1}^{k} \mathbf{R}^{t-\tau}c\boldsymbol{\rho} = \mathbf{R}^t\mathbf{n}(0) + \sum_{i=0}^{k-1} c_i\mathbf{v}_i(\lambda_i^t - 1)/(\lambda_i - 1) \tag{5.19}$$

If, for example,

$$\mathbf{n}(0) = [643, 283, 74] = \mathbf{v}_0 + 3\mathbf{v}_1 - 2\mathbf{v}_2$$

and

$$c\boldsymbol{\rho} = [28, 17, 5] = 0.050\mathbf{v}_0 + 0.898\mathbf{v}_1 - 0.156\mathbf{v}_2$$

then

$$\mathbf{R}(\rho)^t\mathbf{n}(0) = \begin{pmatrix}649\\229\\122\end{pmatrix} + 3(0.416)^t \begin{pmatrix}-6\\2\\4\end{pmatrix} - 2(0.147)^t \begin{pmatrix}-6\\-24\\30\end{pmatrix}$$

and

$$\sum_{\tau=1}^{t} \mathbf{R}(\rho)^{t-\tau}c\boldsymbol{\rho} = 0.050t \begin{pmatrix}649\\229\\122\end{pmatrix} + [0.898(1 - 0.416^t)/0.584] \begin{pmatrix}-6\\2\\4\end{pmatrix}$$

$$+ [(-0.156)(1 - 0.147^t)/0.853] \begin{pmatrix}-6\\-24\\30\end{pmatrix}$$

(1 is a latent root, hence the form of the first term.) The initial structure develops as follows:

$$\underset{1000}{\begin{pmatrix}643\\283\\74\end{pmatrix}} \rightarrow \begin{matrix}642\\283\\120\end{matrix} + \begin{matrix}28\\17\\5\end{matrix} = \underset{1050}{\begin{pmatrix}670\\255\\125\end{pmatrix}} \rightarrow \begin{matrix}676\\243\\131\end{matrix} + \begin{matrix}28\\17\\5\end{matrix} = \underset{1100}{\begin{pmatrix}704\\260\\136\end{pmatrix}} \rightarrow \begin{matrix}709\\253\\138\end{matrix} + \begin{matrix}28\\17\\5\end{matrix}$$

$$= \underset{1150}{\begin{pmatrix}737\\270\\143\end{pmatrix}} \text{ and so on}$$

5.22

Now let the increase of the total population after t years equal $c\boldsymbol{\rho}y^{t-1}$. Then

$$\mathbf{n}(t) = \mathbf{R}(\rho)^t\mathbf{n}(0) + \sum_{i=0}^{k-1} c_i\mathbf{v}_i(\lambda_i^t - y^t)/(\lambda_i - y) \tag{5.20}$$

unless $\lambda_i = y$, when the ith term of the summation is replaced by $c_i\mathbf{v}_i t\lambda_i^{t-1}$.

For instance, if once more $\mathbf{n}(0) = [643, 283, 74]$ and $c\boldsymbol{\rho} = [28, 17, 5]$, and if $y = 1.05$, then

$$\mathbf{n}(t) = \mathbf{R}(\rho)^t\mathbf{n}(0) + [0.050(1.05^t - 1)/0.05] \begin{pmatrix} 649 \\ 229 \\ 122 \end{pmatrix}$$

$$+ [0.898(1.05^t - 0.416^t)/0.634] \begin{pmatrix} -6 \\ 2 \\ 4 \end{pmatrix}$$

$$- [0.156(1.05^t - 0.147^t)/0.803] \begin{pmatrix} -6 \\ -24 \\ 30 \end{pmatrix}$$

The structures develop as follows:

$$\underset{1000}{\begin{pmatrix} 643 \\ 283 \\ 74 \end{pmatrix}} \rightarrow \begin{matrix} 642 \\ 238 \\ 120 \end{matrix} + \begin{matrix} 28 \\ 17 \\ 5 \end{matrix} = \underset{1050}{\begin{pmatrix} 670 \\ 255 \\ 125 \end{pmatrix}} \rightarrow \begin{matrix} 676 \\ 243 \\ 131 \end{matrix} + \begin{matrix} 29 \\ 18 \\ 5 \end{matrix} = \underset{1102}{\begin{pmatrix} 705 \\ 261 \\ 136 \end{pmatrix}} \rightarrow \begin{matrix} 710 \\ 254 \\ 138 \end{matrix} + \begin{matrix} 31 \\ 19 \\ 5 \end{matrix}$$

$$= \underset{1157}{\begin{pmatrix} 741 \\ 273 \\ 143 \end{pmatrix}} \rightarrow \begin{matrix} 746 \\ 266 \\ 145 \end{matrix} + \begin{matrix} 33 \\ 20 \\ 6 \end{matrix} = \underset{1216}{\begin{pmatrix} 779 \\ 286 \\ 151 \end{pmatrix}} \text{ and so on}$$

We look also at another example, with $y < 1$, say $y = 0.5$. Then, with the same assumptions about $\mathbf{n}(0)$ and $c\boldsymbol{\rho}$ as in the previous case, the structures develop as follows:

$$\underset{1000}{\begin{pmatrix} 643 \\ 283 \\ 74 \end{pmatrix}} \rightarrow \begin{matrix} 642 \\ 238 \\ 120 \end{matrix} + \begin{matrix} 28 \\ 17 \\ 5 \end{matrix} = \underset{1050}{\begin{pmatrix} 670 \\ 255 \\ 125 \end{pmatrix}} \rightarrow \begin{matrix} 676 \\ 243 \\ 131 \end{matrix} + \begin{matrix} 14 \\ 9 \\ 2 \end{matrix} = \underset{1075}{\begin{pmatrix} 690 \\ 252 \\ 133 \end{pmatrix}} \rightarrow \begin{matrix} 694 \\ 247 \\ 134 \end{matrix} + \begin{matrix} 7 \\ 4 \\ 1 \end{matrix}$$

$$= \underset{1087}{\begin{pmatrix} 701 \\ 251 \\ 135 \end{pmatrix}} \rightarrow \begin{matrix} 703 \\ 249 \\ 135 \end{matrix} + \begin{matrix} 3 \\ 2 \\ 1 \end{matrix} = \underset{1093}{\begin{pmatrix} 706 \\ 251 \\ 136 \end{pmatrix}} \text{ and so on}$$

When y is smaller than 1, then the population remains finite, and its total approaches

$$\mathbf{n}(0)'\mathbf{e} + [c\boldsymbol{\rho}/(1-y)]'\mathbf{e}$$

5.23

The case of constant increase in size is dealt with in a similar manner by Young and Almond (1961). Bartholomew (1973, pp. 79ff.) treats more general cases in greater detail. He analyses, in particular, the speed with which limiting structures are being approached.

We mention also, without giving details, the existence of non-linear models, where the rate of leaving changes. This will, for instance, happen when members join an organization which has in the past enjoyed high promotion rates, and then find that these rates had to be abandoned, making membership of the organization less attractive than they had thought it to be. (Cf. Young (1971), and the more recent paper by Vassiliou (1976).)

5.24

We mention here a generalization of the insistence on a constant population, which also leads to changing totals. We consider the requirement of keeping a weighted sum of the numbers in the various states constant. The weights may, for instance, be the efficiency of some state or rank, or its cost, or some other parameter. We shall call the weighted total the 'efficiency' of the structure.

Let the weight of $n_i(t)$ be denoted by f_i, positive and independent of time t. We shall denote the vector $[f_1, \ldots, f_k]$ by $\mathbf{f}$.

The weighted total which we want to keep constant is then $\mathbf{n}(t)'\mathbf{f}$, and after transition, but before recruitment, we have

$$\begin{aligned}&\sum_{i=1}^{k} [p_{1i}n_1(t) + \ldots + p_{ki}n_k(t)]\,\mathbf{f}_i \\ &= (p_{11}f_1 + \ldots + p_{1k}f_k)n_1(t) + \ldots + (p_{k1}f_1 + \ldots + p_{kk}f_k)n_k(t) \qquad (5.21)\\ &= \mathbf{n}(t)'\mathbf{Pf}\end{aligned}$$

To keep $\mathbf{n}(t)'\mathbf{f}$ constant, we have to recruit $\mathbf{n}(t)'(\mathbf{I}-\mathbf{P})\mathbf{f}$.

If $u_i(t)$ new entrants into state i have weight $f_iu_i(t)$, then we make

$$u_i(t) = \rho_i\mathbf{n}(t)'(\mathbf{I}-\mathbf{P})\mathbf{f}/f_i \qquad (5.22)$$

and thus

$$\sum_{i=1}^{k} u_i(t)f_i = \mathbf{n}(t)'(\mathbf{I}-\mathbf{P})\mathbf{f} \qquad (5.23)$$

as required.

Now

$$\mathbf{n}(t)'(\mathbf{I}-\mathbf{P})\mathbf{f} = n_1(t)F_1 + \ldots + n_kF_k \qquad (5.24)$$

where

$$F_i = f_i - \sum_{j=1}^{k} p_{ij}f_j \qquad (5.25)$$

The transition matrix, including provision for new entrants (analogous to $\mathbf{R}(\rho)$ for constant populations) is therefore

$$\mathbf{R}(F) = \begin{pmatrix} p_{11} + \rho_1 F_1/f_1 & p_{21} + \rho_1 F_2/f_1 & \ldots & p_{k1} + \rho_1 F_k/f_1 \\ p_{12} + \rho_2 F_1/f_2 & p_{22} + \rho_2 F_2/f_2 & \ldots & p_{k2} + \rho_2 F_k/f_2 \\ \vdots & \vdots & & \vdots \\ p_{1k} + \rho_k F_1/f_k & p_{2k} + \rho_k F_2/f_k & \ldots & p_{kk} + \rho_k F_k/f_k \end{pmatrix} \tag{5.26}$$

5.25

We prove now that 1 is a latent root of this matrix. Multiply the jth row of $\mathbf{R}(F) - \mathbf{I}\lambda$ by f_j, and add for $j = 1, 2, \ldots, k$. This produces a row vector, whose ith component is

$$-\lambda f_i + \sum_{j=1}^{k} p_{ij} f_j + F_i = -\lambda f_i + f_i \tag{5.27}$$

and this is zero for $\lambda = 1$.

If $\mathbf{n}$ is a stationary vector for $\mathbf{R}(\rho)$, then clearly not only $\mathbf{n}(t)'\mathbf{e}$, but also $\mathbf{n}(t)'\mathbf{f}$ remains constant, and it follows that $\mathbf{n}$ is a latent vector of $\mathbf{R}(F)$ corresponding to the latent root 1. Formally, this follows from the fact that

$$(\rho_i/f_i)(n_1 F_1 + \ldots + n_k F_k) = 0 \tag{5.28}$$

because

$$\sum_{i=1}^{k} n_i F_i = \sum_{i=1}^{k} n_i f_i - \sum_{i=1}^{k} \sum_{j=1}^{k} p_{ij} f_j$$

$$= \sum_{i=1}^{k} f_i \left(n_i - \sum_{j=1}^{k} n_j p_{ji} \right) = 0 \tag{5.29}$$

when $\mathbf{n}$ is stationary.

5.26

As an example, take $\mathbf{f} = [1, 2, 4]$, and the transition matrix $\mathbf{P}_0$. Then

$$(\mathbf{I} - \mathbf{P})\mathbf{f} = [-0.5, -0.3, 2.0] \tag{5.30}$$

and, when $\rho_1 = 1$,

$$\mathbf{R}(F) = \begin{pmatrix} -0.2 & -0.2 & 2.2 \\ 0.4 & 0.5 & 0.1 \\ 0.1 & 0.3 & 0.4 \end{pmatrix}$$

The characteristic equation of $\mathbf{R}(F)$ is

$$(\lambda - 1)(\lambda^2 + 0.2\lambda + 0.15) = 0$$

Because the latent roots apart from 1 have absolute values less than unity, any structure will converge to a latent vector corresponding to the latent root 1.

If we start with [500, 300, 200], we have the following development:

	500	280	354	364	352	352	354	354	
	300	370	319	324	330	328	327	327	and so on
	200	220	227	222	222	223	223	223	
n′e	1000	870	900	910	904	903	904	904	
n′f	1900	1900	1900	1900	1900	1900	1900	1900	

The last structure in this list is stationary. It is, in fact, 0.904 times [392, 362, 246].

5.27

We have seen at the beginning of this chapter that the formulae for stable structures are derivable from those for stationary structures by providing not only for the replacement of wastage, but also for expansion. This approach can also be used for the continuous case. We mention here merely one example, referring to Section 3.8.

When, with the other assumptions as in that section, we consider not a stationary population, but a stable one with expansion rate α, then we obtain again formula (3.13), but with μ_x replaced by $\mu_x + \alpha$. This formula is given in Keenay, Morgan and Ray (1974), who call the stable population being one of 'hypothetical age' structure.

PART II

6

Introduction, Lemma

6.1

In the first part of this book we were dealing with long-term aspects of the development of a population structure, when transition rates between states are given. In this second part we shall consider short-term aspects. We shall investigate which structures can be obtained from a given structure, after a finite number of steps, and we shall not only treat the case when the transition rates are given but we shall also ask which transition rates are required to obtain a required structure.

To begin with, we assume the transfer and loss rates given, independent of time. They act at discrete time intervals, say one year, and control is excercised by allocating new entrants appropriately to the various states. We shall not always assume that all new entrants join the same state, or that they are at each step distributed among the states in the same proportions. This distinguishes our approach from that in Part I.

We shall assume that the number of new entrants is always non-negative, in other words, we exclude the possibility of making people redundant, in order to obtain some required structure.

6.2

Our analysis will be based on the following formulae.

Let the original structure be expressed by the vector

$$\mathbf{n}(0) = [n_1(0), \ldots, n_k(0)] \qquad (6.1)$$

where $\mathbf{n}(0)'\mathbf{e} = 1$, and $\mathbf{e}$ is the vector whose every component is unity.

The structure attained after t steps is

$$\mathbf{n}(t) = [n_1(t), \ldots, n_k(t)] \qquad (6.2)$$

We denote the number of new entrants after t steps into state i by $u_i(t-1)$, and the vector

$$[u_1(t-1), \ldots, u_k(t-1)] \qquad (6.3)$$

by $\mathbf{u}(t-1)$.

If the transition matrix is (p_{ij}), where p_{ij} is the rate of transition from state i to state j, and is independent of time, then

$$\mathbf{n}(t) = (\mathbf{P}')^t\mathbf{n}(0) + (\mathbf{P}')^{t-1}\mathbf{u}(0) + \ldots + \mathbf{P}'\mathbf{u}(t-2) + \mathbf{u}(t-1) \tag{6.4}$$

In order to keep the total membership constant, i.e. to have $\mathbf{n}(t)'\mathbf{e} = 1$ for all t, we must have

$$\mathbf{u}(0)'\mathbf{e} = \mathbf{n}(0)'(\mathbf{I} - \mathbf{P})\mathbf{e} \tag{6.5}$$

and

$$\mathbf{u}(t)'\mathbf{e} = \mathbf{n}(t)'(\mathbf{I} - \mathbf{P})\mathbf{e} = [\mathbf{n}(0)'\mathbf{P}^t + \mathbf{u}(0)'\mathbf{P}^{t-1} + \ldots + \mathbf{u}(t-1)]\,(\mathbf{I} - \mathbf{P})\mathbf{e} \tag{6.6}$$

6.3

We recall a few definitions from Part I.

We denote $(\mathbf{I} - \mathbf{P})\mathbf{e}$ by $\mathbf{w} = [w_1, \ldots, w_k]$, as in equation (2.19), $p_{ij} + \rho_j w_i$ by r_{ij}, as in equation (2.21), where ρ_j is the proportion of new entrants into state j, and we define, as in equation (2.23)

$$\mathbf{R}(\rho) = \begin{pmatrix} r_{11} & \ldots & r_{k1} \\ \vdots & & \vdots \\ r_{1k} & \ldots & r_{kk} \end{pmatrix}$$

which can be written

$$\rho_1 \begin{pmatrix} p_{11} + w_1 & p_{21} + w_2 & \ldots & p_{k1} + w_k \\ p_{12} & p_{22} & \ldots & p_{k2} \\ \vdots & \vdots & & \vdots \\ p_{1k} & p_{2k} & \ldots & p_{kk} \end{pmatrix}$$

$$+ \ldots + \rho_k \begin{pmatrix} p_{11} & p_{21} & \ldots & p_{k1} \\ p_{12} & p_{22} & \ldots & p_{k2} \\ \vdots & \vdots & & \vdots \\ p_{1k} + w_1 & p_{2k} + w_2 & \ldots & p_{kk} + w_k \end{pmatrix} = \sum_{i=1}^{k} \rho_i \mathbf{P}'_{(i)} \text{ say} \tag{6.7}$$

The last line defines $\mathbf{P}_{(i)}$.

6.4

In what follows we shall make use of the following Lemma.

Let the vectors $\mathbf{n}_j = [n_{j1}, \ldots, n_{jk}]$ $(j = 1, \ldots, m)$ be given, and let the vector $\mathbf{n} = [n_1, \ldots, n_k]$ be in the convex hull of the $\mathbf{n}_j$, i.e.

$$\mathbf{n} = \sigma_1\mathbf{n}_1 + \ldots + \sigma_m\mathbf{n}_m, \quad \sigma_1 + \ldots + \sigma_m = 1 \quad \text{all } \sigma_j \geqslant 0 \tag{6.8}$$

Then

(i) $\mathbf{R}(\rho)\mathbf{n}$ is in the convex hull of

$$\mathbf{P}'_{(i)}\mathbf{n}_j \quad (i = 1, \ldots, k; j = 1, \ldots, m) \tag{6.9}$$

(ii) every point in the convex hull of $\mathbf{P}'_{(i)}\mathbf{n}_j$ equals $\mathbf{R}(\rho)\mathbf{y}$ where $\mathbf{y}$ is some vector in the convex hull of $\mathbf{n}_1, \ldots, \mathbf{n}_m$, and $\boldsymbol{\rho}$ is some non-negative vector, with its components adding up to unity.

Proof of (i)

$$\mathbf{R}(\rho)\mathbf{n} = \mathbf{R}(\rho)\sum_{j=1}^{m} \sigma_j\mathbf{n}_j = \sum_{j=1}^{m} \sigma_j\mathbf{R}(\rho)\mathbf{n}_j = \sum_{i=1}^{k} \rho_i \sum_{j=1}^{m} \sigma_j\mathbf{P}'_{(i)}\mathbf{n}_j \tag{6.10}$$

and

$$\sum_{i=1}^{k}\sum_{j=1}^{m} \rho_i\sigma_j = 1 \qquad \rho_i\sigma_j \geqslant 0 \quad (\text{all } i, \text{all } j) \tag{6.11}$$

Proof of (ii)

Let

$$z = \sum_{i=1}^{k}\sum_{j=1}^{m} c_{ij}\mathbf{P}'_{(i)}\mathbf{n}_j \qquad c_{ij} \geqslant 0 \quad (\text{all } i, \text{all } j), \qquad \sum_{i=1}^{k}\sum_{j=1}^{m} c_{ij} = 1 \tag{6.12}$$

We have to find $\rho_i \geqslant 0$ $(i = 1, \ldots, k)$, and $\sigma_j \geqslant 0$ $(j = 1, \ldots, m)$ such that

$$\mathbf{R}(\rho)\sum_{j=1}^{m} \sigma_j\mathbf{n}_j = \mathbf{z} \tag{6.13}$$

and $\Sigma_i\rho_i = \Sigma_j\sigma_j = 1$.

Write

$$\mathbf{P}'_{(i)} = \mathbf{P}' + \begin{pmatrix} 0 & \ldots & 0 \\ \vdots & & \vdots \\ w_1 & \ldots & w_k \\ \vdots & & \vdots \\ 0 & \ldots & 0 \end{pmatrix} = \mathbf{P}' + \mathbf{W}_{(i)} \text{ say} \tag{6.14}$$

where only the ith row of the matrix $\mathbf{W}_{(i)}$ differs from a row of zeros, and the ith row equals $\mathbf{w}'$. Then we must find ρ_i and σ_j to satisfy

$$\left(\mathbf{P}' + \sum_{i=1}^{k} \rho_i\mathbf{W}_{(i)}\right)\sum_{j=1}^{m} \sigma_j\mathbf{n}_j = \sum_{i=1}^{k}\sum_{j=1}^{m} c_{ij}(\mathbf{P}' + \mathbf{W}_{(i)})\mathbf{n}_j \tag{6.15}$$

Equation (6.15) can be satisfied by making

$$\sigma_j = \sum_{i=1}^{k} c_{ij} (j = 1, \ldots, m) \qquad \text{and hence} \qquad \sum_{j=1}^{m} \sigma_j = 1$$

and

$$\left(\sum_{i=1}^{k} \rho_i \mathbf{W}_{(i)}\right) \sum_{i=1}^{k} \sum_{j=1}^{m} c_{ij}\mathbf{n}_j = \sum_{i=1}^{k} \sum_{j=1}^{m} c_{ij}\mathbf{W}_{(i)}\mathbf{n}_j \tag{6.16}$$

i.e., for all i

$$\rho_i \mathbf{W}_{(i)} \sum_{i=1}^{k} \sum_{j=1}^{m} c_{ij}\mathbf{n}_j = \sum_{j=1}^{m} c_{ij}\mathbf{W}_{(i)}\mathbf{n}_j \tag{6.17}$$

By the definition of $\mathbf{W}_{(i)}$ this means

$$\rho_i = \left(\sum_{j=1}^{m} c_{ij}(w_1 n_{j1} + \ldots + w_k n_{jk})\right)\left(\sum_{i=1}^{k} \sum_{j=1}^{m} c_{ij}(w_1 n_{j1} + \ldots + w_k n_{jk})\right)^{-1} \tag{6.18}$$

and $\Sigma_{i=1}^{k} \rho_i = 1$.

If for some i_0, j_0 we have $c_{i_0 j_0} = 1$, then $\sigma_{j_0} = \rho_{i_0} = 1$.

6.5

Example 20

$$\mathbf{n}_1 = \begin{pmatrix} 0.5 \\ 0.1 \\ 0.4 \end{pmatrix} \qquad \mathbf{n}_2 = \begin{pmatrix} 0.2 \\ 0.6 \\ 0.2 \end{pmatrix}$$

We use again the transition matrix $\mathbf{P}_0$, so that

$$\mathbf{P}'_{(1)} = \begin{pmatrix} 0.5 & 0.2 & 0.5 \\ 0.4 & 0.5 & 0.1 \\ 0.1 & 0.3 & 0.4 \end{pmatrix}$$

$$\mathbf{P}'_{(2)} = \begin{pmatrix} 0.3 & 0.1 & 0.2 \\ 0.6 & 0.6 & 0.4 \\ 0.1 & 0.3 & 0.4 \end{pmatrix}$$

$$\mathbf{P}'_{(3)} = \begin{pmatrix} 0.3 & 0.1 & 0.2 \\ 0.4 & 0.5 & 0.1 \\ 0.3 & 0.4 & 0.7 \end{pmatrix}$$

and therefore

$$\mathbf{P}'_{(1)}\mathbf{n}_1 = \begin{pmatrix} 0.47 \\ 0.29 \\ 0.24 \end{pmatrix} \qquad \mathbf{P}'_{(1)}\mathbf{n}_2 = \begin{pmatrix} 0.32 \\ 0.40 \\ 0.28 \end{pmatrix}$$

$$\mathbf{P}'_{(2)}\mathbf{n}_1 = \begin{pmatrix} 0.24 \\ 0.52 \\ 0.24 \end{pmatrix} \qquad \mathbf{P}'_{(2)}\mathbf{n}_2 = \begin{pmatrix} 0.16 \\ 0.56 \\ 0.28 \end{pmatrix}$$

$$\mathbf{P}'_{(3)}\mathbf{n}_1 = \begin{pmatrix} 0.24 \\ 0.29 \\ 0.47 \end{pmatrix} \qquad \mathbf{P}'_{(3)}\mathbf{n}_2 = \begin{pmatrix} 0.16 \\ 0.40 \\ 0.44 \end{pmatrix}$$

(i) Let $\sigma_1 = 0.6$, $\sigma_2 = 0.4$, then

$$\mathbf{n} = \begin{pmatrix} 0.38 \\ 0.30 \\ 0.32 \end{pmatrix}$$

Also, let $\rho_1 = 0.25$, $\rho_2 = 0.50$, $\rho_3 = 0.25$, so that

$$\mathbf{R}(\rho)\mathbf{n} = \begin{pmatrix} 0.35 & 0.125 & 0.275 \\ 0.50 & 0.550 & 0.250 \\ 0.15 & 0.325 & 0.475 \end{pmatrix} \begin{pmatrix} 0.38 \\ 0.30 \\ 0.32 \end{pmatrix} = \begin{pmatrix} 0.2585 \\ 0.4350 \\ 0.3065 \end{pmatrix}$$

The last vector is indeed in the convex hull of the $\mathbf{P}'_{(i)}\mathbf{n}_j$, because it equals

$$0.15 \begin{pmatrix} 0.47 \\ 0.29 \\ 0.24 \end{pmatrix} + 0.30 \begin{pmatrix} 0.24 \\ 0.52 \\ 0.24 \end{pmatrix} + 0.15 \begin{pmatrix} 0.24 \\ 0.29 \\ 0.47 \end{pmatrix}$$

$$+ 0.10 \begin{pmatrix} 0.32 \\ 0.40 \\ 0.28 \end{pmatrix} + 0.20 \begin{pmatrix} 0.16 \\ 0.56 \\ 0.28 \end{pmatrix} + 0.10 \begin{pmatrix} 0.16 \\ 0.40 \\ 0.44 \end{pmatrix}$$

(ii) Let

$$(c_{ij}) = \begin{pmatrix} 0.15 & 0.10 \\ 0.30 & 0.20 \\ 0.15 & 0.10 \end{pmatrix}$$

so that

$$\sum_{i=1}^{k} \sum_{j=1}^{m} c_{ij}\mathbf{P}'_{(i)}\mathbf{n}_j = \begin{pmatrix} 0.2585 \\ 0.4350 \\ 0.3065 \end{pmatrix}$$

We obtain

$$\sigma_1 = 0.15 + 0.30 + 0.15 = 0.6$$

$$\sigma_2 = 0.10 + 0.20 + 0.10 = 0.4$$

and

$$\rho_1 = 0.0505/0.2020 = 0.25$$

$$\rho_2 = 0.1010/0.2020 = 0.50$$

$$\rho_3 = 0.0505/0.2020 = 0.25$$

7

Attainable Structures

7.1

We derive now various consequences of the lemma in Section 6.4. Any point $\mathbf{n} = [n_1, \ldots, n_k]$ equals $n_1\mathbf{i}_{(1)} + \ldots + n_k\mathbf{i}_{(k)}$, where $\mathbf{i}_{(j)}$ is the jth column of the identity matrix. Hence any point into which $\mathbf{n}$ can be transformed in one step will be in the convex hull of $\mathbf{P}'_{(i)}\mathbf{i}_{(j)} (i, j = 1, \ldots, k)$. Also any point in this convex hull can be attained in one step from some other point, while no point outside that convex hull can be attained from any other point in one step.

For instance, using again the transition matrix $\mathbf{P}_0$, we have

$$\mathbf{P}'_{(i)}\mathbf{i}_{(j)}$$

	$i = 1$	$i = 2$	$i = 3$
$j = 1$	[0.5, 0.4, 0.1] *	[0.3, 0.6, 0.1] *	[0.3, 0.4, 0.3]
$j = 2$	[0.2, 0.5, 0.3]	[0.1, 0.6, 0.3] *	[0.1, 0.5, 0.4] *
$j = 3$	[0.5, 0.1, 0.4] *	[0.2, 0.4, 0.4]	[0.2, 0.1, 0.7] *

Each of these structures is obtained from $\mathbf{i}_{(j)}$ by recruiting only into state i. The numbers of recruits are, of course, $w_1, \ldots, w_k$ for $j = 1, \ldots, k$ respectively. Not all the $\mathbf{P}'_{(i)}\mathbf{i}_{(j)}$ are vertices of their convex hull in n-space. Those which are are marked with an asterisk.

The structures which are at all attainable from somewhere, after some number of steps, must clearly be attainable from somewhere after just one step. Those not in the convex hull just described are, therefore, not attainable after any number of steps, from anywhere.

7.2

It might be helpful if we gave here a geometric description of the procedure of attaining a point from $\mathbf{i}_{(j)}$. For the sake of simplicity, we illustrate this for $k = 2$.

Let the transition matrix be

$$\begin{pmatrix} p_{11} & p_{12} \\ p_{21} & p_{22} \end{pmatrix} \quad \text{hence} \quad \mathbf{w} = \begin{pmatrix} 1 - p_{11} - p_{12} \\ 1 - p_{21} - p_{22} \end{pmatrix}$$

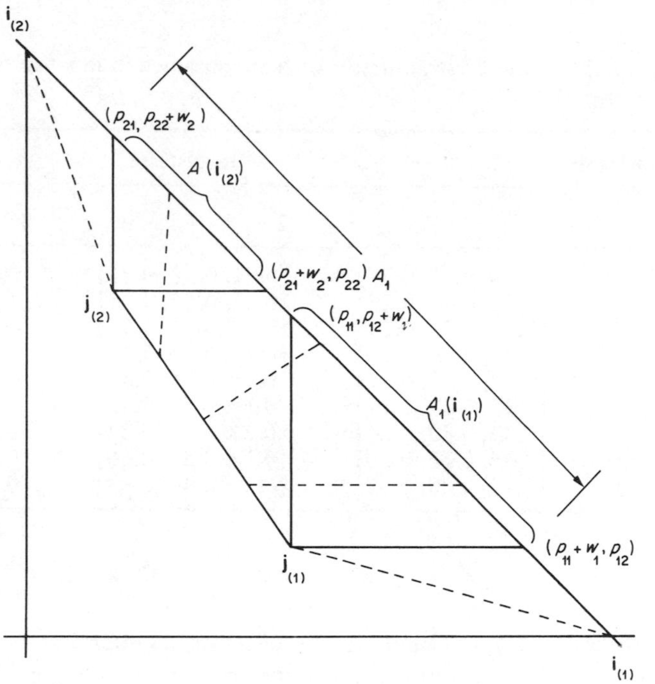

Figure 3

The point $\mathbf{i}_{(1)} = [1, 0]$ will be transformed into $\mathbf{j}_1 = [p_{11}, p_{12}]$, and the point $\mathbf{i}_{(2)} = [0, 1]$ into $\mathbf{j}_2 = [p_{21}, p_{22}]$ (see Figure 3). Any point $a_1\mathbf{i}_{(1)} + a_2\mathbf{i}_{(2)}$, with $a_1 + a_2 = 1$, transforms into $a_1\mathbf{j}_1 + a_2\mathbf{j}_2$, so that the straight line segment $(\mathbf{i}_{(1)}, \mathbf{i}_{(2)})$ transforms into the straight line segment (j_1, j_2).

The points of $A_1(\mathbf{i}_{(j)})$ are those on the line segment from $[p_{j1}, p_{j2} + w_j]$ to $[p_{j1} + w_j, p_{j2}]$, and A_1 is the convex hull of these points. In Figure 3 these are the points between $[p_{21}, p_{22} + w_2]$ and $[p_{11} + w_1, p_{12}]$. It is clear from the figure that with varying values of the p_{ij}, the sets $A_1(\mathbf{i}_{(j)}), j = 1, 2$ might, but need not overlap. (For the notation, see Section 7.5.)

7.3

We shall now determine which structures are attainable after two steps, starting from some structure. In one step they are attainable from one of those structures which are, themselves, attainable from some structure in one step.

We have therefore, by our lemma, to take all those attainable from any of the $\mathbf{i}_{(j)}$, by recruiting into one single state (there will be k^2 of these) and then to see which structures are obtainable from the latter, again by recruiting into a single state. We obtain thus k^3 structures, and their convex hull will contain all those, and only those structures attainable in two steps from somewhere.

Again, not all these vectors will be vertices of their convex hull.

7.4

We give here a list of the 27 structures which are obtained in this manner using the transition matrix $\mathbf{P_0}$.

From $\mathbf{P}'_{(i)}\mathbf{i}_{(j)}$		New entrants at second step	into states		
i	j		1	2	3
1	1	0.17	[0.38, 0.41, 0.21]*	[0.21, 0.58, 0.21]*	[0.21, 0.41, 0.38]
2	1	0.15	[0.32, 0.43, 0.25]	[0.17, 0.58, 0.25]*	[0.17, 0.43, 0.40]
3	1	0.19	[0.38, 0.35, 0.27]	[0.19, 0.54, 0.27]	[0.19, 0.35, 0.46]
1	2	0.18	[0.35, 0.36, 0.29]	[0.17, 0.54, 0.29]	[0.17, 0.36, 0.47]
2	2	0.17	[0.32, 0.37, 0.31]	[0.15, 0.54, 0.31]*	[0.15, 0.37, 0.48]*
3	2	0.19	[0.35, 0.33, 0.32]	[0.16, 0.52, 0.32]	[0.16, 0.33, 0.51]*
1	3	0.23	[0.47, 0.29, 0.24]*	[0.24, 0.52, 0.24]	[0.24, 0.29, 0.47]
2	3	0.20	[0.38, 0.32, 0.30]	[0.18, 0.52, 0.30]	[0.18, 0.32, 0.50]
3	3	0.26	[0.47, 0.20, 0.33]*	[0.21, 0.46, 0.33]	[0.21, 0.20, 0.59]*

*vertices of the convex hull.

7.5

Following Davies (1973), we denote the set of structures attainable from somewhere in t steps by A_t, and the set of those attainable from the structure **n** after t steps by

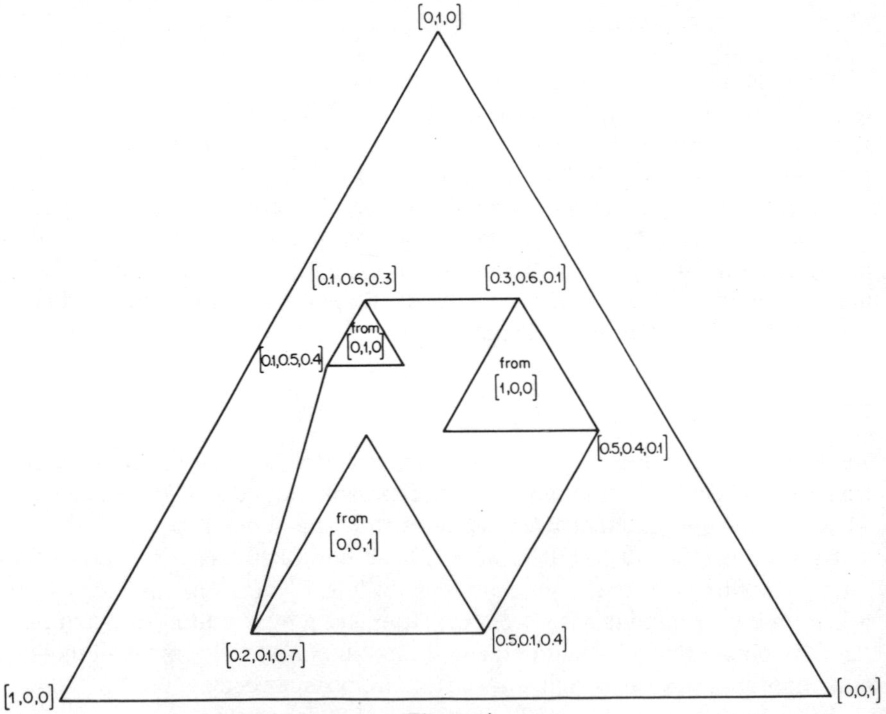

Figure 4

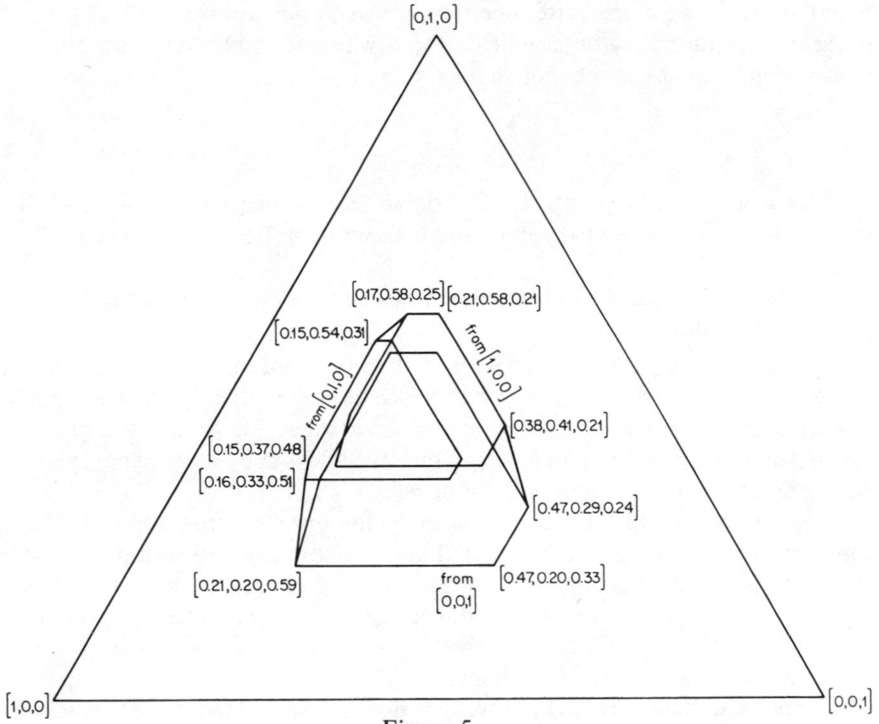

Figure 5

$A_t(\mathbf{n})$. A_t is the convex hull of (the vertices of) the sets $A_t(\mathbf{i}_{(1)}), A_t(\mathbf{i}_{(2)}), \ldots, A_t(\mathbf{i}_{(k)})$.

The sets $A_t(\mathbf{n})$ are closed and polyhedral for all $\mathbf{n}$ and all t, and so are the sets A_t for all t.

Figures 4 and 5 show, in barycentric coordinates, the regions $A_t(\mathbf{n})$ for $k = 3$, $\mathbf{n} = \mathbf{i}_{(i)}$, $i = 1, 2, 3$ and their convex hulls, for $t = 1$ and 2 respectively.

7.6

A_0 is the convex hull of all possible structures, $\mathbf{n}$, merely restricted to satisfy $\mathbf{n}'\mathbf{e} = 1$.

If s exceeds t, then clearly A_s will be contained in A_t. It does not follow, though, that A_{t+1} is strictly contained in A_t, as it happens to be in our example.

This is not so, for instance, when the transition matrix is

$$\begin{pmatrix} 0 & p_{12} & p_{13} & \ldots & p_{1k} \\ 0 & 0 & p_{23} & \ldots & p_{2k} \\ \vdots & \vdots & \vdots & & \vdots \\ 0 & 0 & 0 & \ldots & 0 \end{pmatrix}$$

With this matrix we obtain, after one step, from $\mathbf{i}_{(k)}$ the vector $[u_1(0), \ldots, u_k(0)]$, so that any vector can be obtained from 'somewhere', notably from $\mathbf{i}_{(k)}$. This remains true after any number of steps.

7.7

The intersection of all $A_t (t = 0, 1, \ldots)$ contains all stationary structures, and all the re-attainable ones (see next chapter), and is therefore not empty when $(\mathbf{I} - \mathbf{P})^{-1}$ exists.

Because A_t contains A_{t+1}, it seems reasonable to denote the set of points in the intersection of all A_t by A_∞.

Any point $\mathbf{v}$ in A_∞ will (a) transform after recruitment into a point of this same set, because the new point is reached after one more step then the first is reached, and so again after any number of steps from somewhere. Because of this property Grinold and Stanford (1976) call A_∞ (which they denote by L) a 'trapping set': having reached a point in it, it will not be left.

Also, (b) any point in A_∞ can be reached, after one step, from some point in the same set. If this were not so, then it could only be attained in one step from one or more points outside A_∞. Any one of these points, $\mathbf{a}_i$ say, lies in the intersection of $A_0, A_1, \ldots, A_{q_i} (q_i \geqslant 0$, finite). Let the largest of the q_i be q. Then the point $\mathbf{v}$ in A_∞ could not be reached after a number t of steps when $t > q + 1$. This contradicts the definition of A_∞ to which $\mathbf{v}$ belongs.

Grinold and Stanford (1976) prove that if $\mathbf{w}$ is positive then A_∞ is the unique closed non-empty set of structures $\mathbf{n} \geqslant 0$, $\mathbf{n}'\mathbf{e} = 1$, which satisfy (a) and (b). Furthermore, under the same condition, any $\mathbf{n}$ in the interior of A_∞ is re-attainable after a finite number of steps.

We cannot say, in general, how long it will take to reach a given point from another point, if at all. However, we know that any stationary point can be attained asymptotically. About points in the interior of the region of stationary points we can say more. These are the structures which need a positive number of new entrants into all states, i.e. those $\mathbf{n}$ for which

$$n_j - \sum_{i=1}^{k} p_{ij} n_i = a_j \quad \text{say}$$

is strictly positive for all j.

We show now that such a structure can be attained, in a finite number of steps, from any other structure with the same total membership.

The structure $\mathbf{n}$ can be reached in one single step from a structure $\mathbf{x}$ such that

$$n_j - \sum_{i=1}^{k} p_{ij} x_i \geqslant 0 \quad \text{for all } j$$

and this can be written

$$a_j + \sum_{i=1}^{k} p_{ij}(n_i - x_i) \geqslant 0 \quad \text{for all } j$$

We want also

$$(\mathbf{n}-\mathbf{x})'\mathbf{e}=0$$

This system is certainly not inconsistent; one solution is $\mathbf{x}=\mathbf{n}$. Since a_j is strictly positive, there will be a neighbourhood of **n** containing all those $\mathbf{x} \geqslant 0$ which satisfy the system.

Starting from any structure y we can approach **n** asymptotically using the proportion $a_1 : \ldots : a_k$ of new entrants into the various states. After a finite number of steps we shall have entered the neighbourhood just mentioned, and at the next step we can reach **n** by appropriate recruiting, which might not, at this last step, be in proportions $a_1 : \ldots : a_k$.

This argument cannot be applied to a point on the boundary of, or outside, the region of stationary points, because $a_j > 0$ was a crucial point in our proof.

7.8

We ask now how $A_t(\mathbf{n})$ relates to **n**. After one step, **n** can be transformed into any vector in the convex hull of $\mathbf{P}'_{(i)}\mathbf{n}$, i.e. into

$$\begin{pmatrix} p_{11}n_1 + & \ldots & + p_{k1}n_k + u_1 \\ \vdots & & \vdots \quad \vdots \\ p_{1k}n_1 + & \ldots & + p_{kk}n_k + u_k \end{pmatrix} \tag{7.1}$$

where the new entrants into state i number

$$u_i = \rho_i(w_1 n_1 + \ldots + w_k n_k) \tag{7.2}$$

the ρ_i being non-negative values adding up to unity.

The vertices of the convex hull, i.e. of $A_1(\mathbf{n})$, are given by $\rho_i = 1$ $(i = 1, \ldots, k)$, i.e. by structures obtained by recruiting into one single state only.

Example 21

For instance, using $\mathbf{P}_0$, we find that $[0.32, 0.43, 0.25]$ can be transformed into

$$\begin{matrix} 0.189 + 0.182\rho_1 & & 0.371\rho_1 + 0.189\rho_2 + 0.189\rho_3 \\ 0.368 + 0.182\rho_2 & = & 0.368\rho_1 + 0.550\rho_2 + 0.368\rho_3 \\ 0.261 + 0.182\rho_3 & & 0.261\rho_1 + 0.261\rho_2 + 0.443\rho_3 \end{matrix} \tag{7.3}$$

By the same argument, the convex region $A_t(\mathbf{n})$ will be the convex hull of those structures which are attained by recruiting at each step into one single state, but not neccesarily into the same state at each step. Not all these structures need be vertices, though.

The proportions of new entrants joining the various states need not be the same at each step. This differs from our assumptions in Part I, where ρ_i was independent of t (See Section 2.17).

7.9

In Example 21 the vertices of $A_1([0.32, 0.43, 0.25])$ are $[0.371, 0.368, 0.261]$, $[0.189, 0.550, 0.261]$, $[0.189, 0.368, 0.443]$ and $A_2([0.32, 0.43, 0.25])$ is given by the vectors

0.3896	0.2003	0.2003	0.3350	0.1639	0.1639	0.3896	0.1821	0.1821
0.3585	0.5478	0.3585	0.3767	0.5478	0.3767	0.3039	0.5114	0.3039
0.2519	0.2519	0.4412	0.2883	0.2883	0.4594	0.3065	0.3065	0.5140
*	*			*	*	*		*
$\mathbf{v}_{11}$	$\mathbf{v}_{12}$	$\mathbf{v}_{13}$	$\mathbf{v}_{21}$	$\mathbf{v}_{22}$	$\mathbf{v}_{23}$	$\mathbf{v}_{31}$	$\mathbf{v}_{32}$	$\mathbf{v}_{33}$

We have denoted these vectors in such a way that their subscripts indicate the states into which entries take place, at the first, and then at the second step. The vertices of the convex hull are again marked by asterisks.

We notice that $A_1(\mathbf{n})$ and $A_2(\mathbf{n})$ overlap again.

The required numbers of new entrants can be worked out step by step. For instance, if we ask how to obtain $\mathbf{v}_{11}$, starting from $[0.32, 0.43, 0.25]$, we notice that

$$w = 0.2(0.32) + 0.1(0.43) + 0.3(0.25) = 0.182$$

and this number must enter the first state. Thus

$$\begin{pmatrix} 0.32 \\ 0.43 \\ 0.25 \end{pmatrix} \to \begin{matrix} 0.189 + 0.182 \\ 0.368 \\ 0.261 \end{matrix} = \begin{pmatrix} 0.371 \\ 0.368 \\ 0.261 \end{pmatrix}$$

Then

$$w = 0.2(0.371) + 0.1(0.368) + 0.3(0.261) = 0.1893$$

and

$$\begin{pmatrix} 0.371 \\ 0.368 \\ 0.261 \end{pmatrix} \to \begin{matrix} 0.2003 + 0.1893 \\ 0.3585 \\ 0.2519 \end{matrix} = \begin{pmatrix} 0.3896 \\ 0.3585 \\ 0.2519 \end{pmatrix}$$

By an analogous procedure we find that to obtain

$\mathbf{v}_{11}$ $\mathbf{v}_{12}$ $\mathbf{v}_{13}$ $\mathbf{v}_{21}$ $\mathbf{v}_{22}$ $\mathbf{v}_{23}$ $\mathbf{v}_{31}$ $\mathbf{v}_{32}$ $\mathbf{v}_{33}$

we need the following numbers of new entrants:

$u_1(0)$	0.182	0.182	0.182						
$u_2(0)$				0.182	0.182	0.182			
$u_3(0)$							0.182	0.182	0.182
$u_1(1)$	0.1893			0.1711			0.2075		
$u_2(1)$		0.1893			0.1711			0.2075	
$u_3(1)$			0.1893			0.1711			0.2075

Any further recruitment, after 3, 4, . . . steps could be computed in the same way.

7.10

The method by which we have found the regions $A_t(\mathbf{n})$ presumed that we pass successively through all previous stages to obtain the answer for the tth step. We introduce now a method which does not require this sequential procedure, but enables us to determine the result after t steps directly. For this purpose it is necessary that we know all powers of the transition matrix up to the tth power.

The procedure is based on principles of linear programming (Appendix II), and it will, incidentally, also throw some light on the reason why not all structures obtained in our example are vertices of their convex hull.

We exhibit the method by showing how to obtain $\mathbf{v}_{11}, \ldots, \mathbf{v}_{33}$ of Example 21.

We denote $\mathbf{n}(0)$ by $\mathbf{n}$ and $\mathbf{n}(2)$ by $\bar{\mathbf{n}}$, and we base our analysis on the relationship

$$\bar{\mathbf{n}} = (\mathbf{P}')^2\mathbf{n} + \mathbf{P}'\mathbf{u}(0) + \mathbf{u}(1) \tag{7.4}$$

and

$$\mathbf{u}(0)'\mathbf{e} = \mathbf{n}'\mathbf{w} \quad \mathbf{u}(1)'\mathbf{e} = \mathbf{n}'\mathbf{P}\mathbf{w} + \mathbf{u}(0)'\mathbf{w} \tag{7.5}$$

(special cases of (6.4) to (6.6)),

$$\mathbf{u}(0) \geqslant 0 \quad \mathbf{u}(1) \geqslant 0 \quad \bar{\mathbf{n}} \geqslant 0$$

where $\mathbf{n}$ is given, and $\bar{\mathbf{n}}$, $\mathbf{u}(0)$ and $\mathbf{u}(1)$ are the unknowns.

Equations (7.4) and (7.5) are satisfied by an infinity of vectors. Since the relationships are linear, the vectors $[\bar{\mathbf{n}}, \mathbf{u}(0), \mathbf{u}(1)]$ form a polygonal set, nine-dimensional in this case. We are looking for its vertices.

Now

$$(\mathbf{P}_0')^2 = \begin{pmatrix} 0.15 & 0.14 & 0.15 \\ 0.33 & 0.32 & 0.17 \\ 0.19 & 0.28 & 0.21 \end{pmatrix} \tag{7.6}$$

and with $\mathbf{n} = [0.32, 0.43, 0.25]$ we have to solve

$$\bar{n}_1 - 0.3u_1(0) - 0.1u_2(0) - 0.2u_3(0) - u_1(1) = 0.1457 \tag{7.7}$$
$$(\text{i.e. } 0.15n_1 + 0.14n_2 + 0.15n_3)$$

$$\bar{n}_2 - 0.4u_1(0) - 0.5u_2(0) - 0.1u_3(0) - u_2(1) = 0.2857 \tag{7.8}$$
$$(\text{i.e. } 0.33n_1 + 0.32n_2 + 0.17n_3)$$

$$\bar{n}_3 - 0.1u_1(0) - 0.3u_2(0) - 0.4u_3(0) - u_3(1) = 0.2337 \tag{7.9}$$
$$(\text{i.e. } 0.19n_1 + 0.28n_2 + 0.21n_3)$$

$$u_1(0) + \quad u_2(0) + \quad u_3(0) = 0.1820 \tag{7.10}$$
$$(\text{i.e. } 0.2n_1 + 0.1n_2 + 0.3n_3)$$

$$-0.2u_1(0) - 0.1u_2(0) - 0.3u_3(0) + u_1(1) + u_2(1) + u_3(1) = 0.1529$$
$$(\text{i.e. } 0.13n_1 + 0.16n_2 + 0.17n_3) \tag{7.11}$$

In tableau form, with s_1 and s_2 as artificial variables, this reads

	$u_1(0)$	$u_2(0)$	$u_3(0)$	$u_1(1)$	$u_2(1)$	$u_3(1)$	
$\bar{n}_1$	−0.3	−0.1	−0.2	−0.1	0	0	0.1457
$\bar{n}_2$	−0.4	−0.5	−0.1	0	−1.0	0	0.2857
$\bar{n}_3$	−0.1	−0.3	−0.4	0	0	−1.0	0.2337
s_1	1.0*	1.0	1.0	0	0	0	0.1820
s_2	−0.2	−0.1	−0.3	1.0*	1.0	1.0	0.1529

After dropping s_1 and s_2 (the pivots are indicated by asterisks) we obtain

	$u_2(0)$	$u_3(0)$	$u_2(1)$	$u_3(1)$	
$\bar{n}_1$	0.3	0	1.0	1.0	0.3896
$\bar{n}_2$	−0.1	0.3	−1.0	0	0.3585
$\bar{n}_3$	−0.2	−0.3	0	−1.0	0.2519
$u_1(0)$	1.0	1.0	0	0	0.1820
$u_1(1)$	0.1	−0.1	1.0	1.0	0.1893

The result is, of course, $\mathbf{v}_{11}$, and the rates of new entrants are also exhibited. The complete answer is [0.3896, 0.3585, 0.2519, 0.1820, 0, 0, 0.1893, 0, 0] a vertex in nine-dimensional space of the region of all $[\bar{\mathbf{n}}, \mathbf{u}(0), \mathbf{u}(1)]$ which solve equations (7.7)–(7.11).

Our result above is not the only vertex solving the set (7.7)–(7.11). For instance, if we exchange $u_1(0)$ and $u_2(0)$, which we can do because 0.1826/1.0 is smaller than either 0.3896/0.3 or 0.1893/0.1, then we have the tableau

	$u_1(0)$	$u_3(0)$	$u_2(1)$	$u_3(1)$	
$\bar{n}_1$	−0.3	−0.3	1.0	1.0	0.3350
$\bar{n}_2$	0.1	0.4	−1.0	0	0.3767
$\bar{n}_3$	0.2	−0.1	0	−1.0	0.2883
$u_2(0)$	1.0	1.0	0	0	0.1820
$u_1(1)$	−0.1	−0.2	1.0	1.0	0.1711

We recognize $\mathbf{v}_{21}$, and the rates of new entrants necessary to keep the totals constant.

In this manner we can obtain all vertices in $(\bar{\mathbf{n}}, \mathbf{u}(0), \mathbf{u}(1))$-space, each having as first three components $[\bar{n}_1, \bar{n}_2, \bar{n}_3]$ one of the vectors $\mathbf{v}_{ij}$. The latter are thus projections of the nine-dimensional vertices onto the three-dimensional $\bar{\mathbf{n}}$-space, and it is understandable that not all $\mathbf{v}_{ij}$ are vertices of the projection.

7.11

We have just seen how we can obtain the region $A_t(\mathbf{n})$, i.e. that of the structures which can be obtained from $\mathbf{n}$ after t steps. If we then wish to know whether a given structure $\bar{\mathbf{n}}(t)$ can be obtained from a given $\mathbf{n}(0)$ in t steps, then we have to ascertain if $\mathbf{n}(t)$, expressed as a linear combination of the vertices of $A_t(\mathbf{n}(0))$ has only non-negative coefficients.

In the case of one step this is easily answered. If all of

$$n_i(1) - (p_{1i}n_1 + \ldots + p_{ki}n_k) \quad (i = 1, \ldots, k) \tag{7.12}$$

are non-negative, then these are the values of $u_i(0)$.

In the case of more steps, even if we ascertained that $\mathbf{n}(t)$ is attainable, by investigating the region of $A_t(\mathbf{n}(0))$, this would not give us immediately the recruiting rates, and it is convenient to apply again the simplex technique of linear programming.

7.12

Example 22

We illustrate the procedure for $t = 2$ by Example 21 in Section 7.8, but this time $\bar{\mathbf{n}}(2)$ is also given. Let it be

$$\bar{\mathbf{n}}(2) = [0.37, 0.37, 0.26]$$

We write now equations (7.7)–(7.10) as follows (in tableau form):

	$u_1(0)$	$u_2(0)$	$u_3(0)$		
$u_1(1)$	0.3	0.1	0.2	0.2243	(i.e. 0.37 – 0.1457)
$u_2(1)$	0.4	0.5	0.1	0.0843	(i.e. 0.37 – 0.2857)
$u_3(1)$	0.1	0.3	0.4	0.0263	(i.e. 0.26 – 0.2337)
s_1	1.0*	1.0	1.0	0.1820	

Only one artificial variable is required this time, because equation (7.11) is automatically satisfied by choosing $\bar{\mathbf{n}}(2)$ such that its components add up to unity.

Dropping s_1 by using the pivot marked by an asterisk, we have

(a)	$u_2(0)$	$u_3(0)$	
$u_1(1)$	–0.2	–0.1	0.1697
$u_2(1)$	0.1	–0.3	0.0115
$u_3(1)$	0.2	0.3	0.0081
$u_1(0)$	1.0	1.0	0.1820

We have found one vertex in $[\mathbf{u}(0), \mathbf{u}(1)]$-space. Our result means that we can get from $\mathbf{n}(0)$ to $\mathbf{n}(2)$ as follows:

$$\begin{pmatrix} 0.32 \\ 0.43 \\ 0.25 \end{pmatrix} \rightarrow \begin{matrix} 0.189 + 0.182 \\ 0.368 \\ 0.261 \end{matrix} = \begin{pmatrix} 0.371 \\ 0.368 \\ 0.261 \end{pmatrix} \rightarrow \begin{matrix} 0.2003 + 0.1697 \\ 0.3585 + 0.0115 \\ 0.2519 + 0.0081 \end{matrix} = \begin{pmatrix} 0.37 \\ 0.37 \\ 0.26 \end{pmatrix}$$

There are two more vertices, viz.

(b)	$u_3(1)$	$u_3(0)$	
$u_1(1)$	1.0	0.2	0.1778
$u_2(1)$	−0.5	−0.45	0.0075
$u_2(0)$	5.0	1.5	0.0405
$u_1(0)$	−5.0	−0.5	0.1415

and

(c)	$u_2(0)$	$u_3(1)$	
$u_1(1)$	−2/15	1/3	0.1724
$u_2(1)$	3/10	1	0.0196
$u_3(0)$	2/3	10/3	0.0270
$u_1(0)$	1/3	−10/3	0.1550

which means, respectively

$$\begin{pmatrix}0.32\\0.43\\0.25\end{pmatrix} \to \begin{array}{l}0.189+0.1415\\0.368+0.0405\\0.261\end{array} = \begin{pmatrix}0.3305\\0.4085\\0.2610\end{pmatrix} \to \begin{array}{l}0.1922+0.1778\\0.3625+0.0075\\0.2600\end{array} = \begin{pmatrix}0.37\\0.37\\0.26\end{pmatrix}$$

and

$$\begin{pmatrix}0.32\\0.43\\0.25\end{pmatrix} \to \begin{array}{l}0.189+0.1550\\0.368\\0.261+0.0270\end{array} = \begin{pmatrix}0.3440\\0.3680\\0.2880\end{pmatrix} \to \begin{array}{l}0.1976+0.1724\\0.3504+0.0196\\0.2600\end{array} = \begin{pmatrix}0.37\\0.37\\0.26\end{pmatrix}$$

7.13

We have just seen that $\bar{\mathbf{n}} = [0.37, 0.37, 0.26]$ is attainable from $[0.32, 0.43, 0.25]$ in two steps. Therefore $\bar{\mathbf{n}}$ lies in the convex hull of those vertices $\mathbf{v}_{ij}$ which were derived in Section 7.9. Hence it can be expressed as a linear combination of various triangles whose vertices are three of the $\mathbf{v}_{ij}$.

For instance, we have

$$\bar{\mathbf{n}} = 0.896\mathbf{v}_{11} + 0.061\mathbf{v}_{12} + 0.043\mathbf{v}_{13} \tag{7.13}$$

$$= 0.738\mathbf{v}_{11} + 0.040\mathbf{v}_{12} + 0.222\mathbf{v}_{21} \tag{7.14}$$

$$= 0.852\mathbf{v}_{11} + 0.054\mathbf{v}_{31} + 0.094\mathbf{v}_{32} \tag{7.15}$$

$$= 0.807\mathbf{v}_{11} + 0.134\mathbf{v}_{21} + 0.059\mathbf{v}_{32} \tag{7.16}$$

The corresponding rates of new entrants can be derived from those in the list at the end of Section 7.9. For instance, regarding equation (7.13), we have

$$u_1(0) = 0.896(0.182) + 0.061(0.182) + 0.043(0.182) = 0.182$$

$$u_1(1) = 0.896(0.1893) = 0.1697$$

$$u_1(2) = 0.061(0.1893) = 0.0115$$

$$u_1(3) = 0.043(0.1893) = 0.0081$$

These are the values in tableau (a) in Section 7.12.

The correspondence is not accidental. In equation (7.13) $\bar{\mathbf{n}}$ is made up of $\mathbf{v}_{11}$ (with entries first, and again at the second step, into state 1), $\mathbf{v}_{12}$ (with entries first into state 1, then into state 2), and $\mathbf{v}_{13}$ (with entries first into state 1, and then into state 3). Hence in their combination $u_1(0), u_1(1), u_2(1), u_3(1)$ are positive, i.e. basic variables in a tableau which described a vertex in $(\mathbf{u}(0), \mathbf{u}(1))$-space.

By an analogous argument we find a correspondence between equation (7.14) and tableau (b), and also between equation (7.15) and tableau (c).

If we scrutinize equation (7.16), then we find that more than four of the $u_i(0)$ and $u_j(1)$ are positive, since $\mathbf{v}_{11}$, $\mathbf{v}_{21}$ and $\mathbf{v}_{32}$ imply positive entries $u_1(0), u_2(0)$, $u_3(0)$ and also $u_1(1)$ and $u_2(1)$, thus:

$$\begin{pmatrix}0.32\\0.43\\0.25\end{pmatrix} \to \begin{matrix}0.189+0.147\\0.368+0.024\\0.261+0.011\end{matrix} = \begin{pmatrix}0.338\\0.392\\0.272\end{pmatrix} \to \begin{matrix}0.195+0.175\\0.359+0.011\\0.260\end{matrix} = \begin{pmatrix}0.37\\0.37\\0.26\end{pmatrix}$$

This does not correspond to a vertex in $(\mathbf{u}(0), \mathbf{u}(1))$-space but to the combination 0.59(b) + 0.41(c).

7.14

We have seen how to find the region of those structures which can be obtained, from some given structure, in one, two, . . . steps. This suggests the question of finding those structures from which a given structure $\bar{\mathbf{n}}$ can be obtained in t steps.

We denote, again following Davies (1973), the set of those structures by $B_t(\bar{\mathbf{n}})$. Of course, the given structure $\bar{\mathbf{n}}$ may not be attainable from anywhere in t steps. If this is the case, then our method of solution will disclose this fact.

The structures in $B_1(\bar{\mathbf{n}})$ can again be found by an application of the simplex method of linear programming. We are looking for vectors $\mathbf{n}$ such that $\mathbf{n}'\mathbf{e} = \bar{\mathbf{n}}'\mathbf{e}$, and

$$p_{1i}n_1 + \ldots + p_{ki}n_k + u_i = \bar{n}_i \tag{7.16}$$

$$n_j, u_i \geqslant 0 \quad (i, j = 1, \ldots, k) \tag{7.17}$$

The set (7.16) can be written

$$\mathbf{n}'\mathbf{w} = \mathbf{u}'\mathbf{e} \tag{7.18}$$

For instance, if we choose $\bar{\mathbf{n}} = [0.37, 0.37, 0.26]$, then we solve

$$\begin{aligned}
0.3n_1 + 0.1n_2 + 0.2n_3 + u_1 &= 0.37\\
0.4n_1 + 0.5n_2 + 0.1n_3 + u_2 &= 0.37\\
0.1n_3 + 0.3n_2 + 0.4n_3 + u_3 &= 0.26\\
n_1 + n_2 + n_3 &= 1.00\\
n_1, n_2, n_3, u_1, u_2, u_3 &\geqslant 0
\end{aligned}$$

We have used this case as an example in Appendix II, Section II.2 and we have found the solution

$$\begin{aligned}
n_1 &= 0.9\rho_1 + 0.467\rho_2 + 0.322\rho_3\\
n_2 &= 0.433\rho_3\\
n_3 &= 0.1\rho_1 + 0.533\rho_2 + 0.245\rho_3
\end{aligned}$$

$$u_1 = 0.08\rho_1 + 0.123\rho_2 + 0.181\rho_3 \tag{7.19}$$
$$u_2 = \qquad 0.130\rho_2$$
$$u_3 = 0.13\rho_1$$
$$\rho_1 + \rho_2 + \rho_3 = 1 \quad \rho_1, \rho_2, \rho_3 \geqslant 0$$

Any of the $\rho_i = 1$ (and hence the others are equal to zero) produces a vertex in a polyhedron in $(\mathbf{n}, \mathbf{u})$-space. If we are interested in $B_1(\bar{\mathbf{n}})$, then we project this polyhedron onto three-dimensional $\mathbf{n}$-space. The projection is again a polyhedron – in this case with vertices

$$\mathbf{v}_1 = \begin{pmatrix} 0.9 \\ 0 \\ 0.1 \end{pmatrix} \quad \mathbf{v}_2 = \begin{pmatrix} 0.467 \\ 0 \\ 0.533 \end{pmatrix} \quad \mathbf{v}_3 = \begin{pmatrix} 0.322 \\ 0.433 \\ 0.245 \end{pmatrix}$$

[0.37, 0.37, 0.26] can be obtained, in one step, from any structure in this triangle, (and from none outside it,) with non-negative u_i.

For instance,

$$0.087\mathbf{v}_1 + 0.130\mathbf{v}_2 + 0.783\mathbf{v}_3 = [0.391, 0.339, 0.270]$$

and starting from the latter, we have

$$\begin{pmatrix} 0.391 \\ 0.339 \\ 0.270 \end{pmatrix} \rightarrow \begin{matrix} 0.209 + 0.087(0.08) + 0.130(0.123) + 0.783(0.181) = \\ 0.353 + 0.087(0) \quad + 0.130(0.130) + 0.783(0) \quad = \\ 0.249 + 0.087(0.13) + 0.130(0) \quad + 0.783(0) \quad = \end{matrix} \begin{pmatrix} 0.37 \\ 0.37 \\ 0.26 \end{pmatrix}$$

The additions are, of course, the coefficients of the ρ_i in equation (7.19), multiplied by the corresponding weights of $\mathbf{v}_1$, $\mathbf{v}_2$, and $\mathbf{v}_3$.

On the other hand,

$$[0.32, 0.43, 0.25] = -0.0077\mathbf{v}_1 + 0.0154\mathbf{v}_2 + 0.09923\mathbf{v}_3$$

and hence this vector does not lie in $B_1([0.37, 0.37, 0.26])$. Indeed, [0.37, 0.37, 0.26] does not lie in $A_1([0.32, 0.43, 0.25])$ given in Section 7.6.

7.15

It might be of interest to insert here an example in which $R_1(\mathbf{n})$ is empty, and to show how this is found out.

We choose a structure outside A_1, i.e. one which cannot be obtained from anywhere in one step with the transition matrix $\mathbf{P}_0$. Take

$$\begin{pmatrix} 0.35 \\ 0.60 \\ 0.05 \end{pmatrix} = -0.25 \begin{pmatrix} 0.1 \\ 0.6 \\ 0.3 \end{pmatrix} + 1.25 \begin{pmatrix} 0.3 \\ 0.6 \\ 0.1 \end{pmatrix}$$

We now try to solve this problem in tableau form

	n_1	n_2	n_3	
u_1	0.3	0.1	0.2	0.35
u_2	0.4	0.5	0.1	0.60
u_3	0.1	0.3	0.4	0.05
s	1.0*	1.0	1.0	1.00

and obtain at the next iteration

	n_2	n_3	
u_1	−0.2	−0.1	0.05
u_2	0.1	−0.3	0.20
u_3	0.2	0.3	−0.05
n_1	1.0	1.0	1.00

We find that no (non-negative) solution exists, since the third row, which means

$$u_3 + 0.2n_2 + 0.3n_3 = -0.05$$

cannot have a solution for non-negative u_3, n_2, n_3.

7.16

We have seen in Section 7.1 that the region of those structures which are attainable from somewhere in one step, i.e. A_1, is the convex hull of $\mathbf{P}'_{(i)}\mathbf{i}_{(j)}$. If we express a vector $\bar{\mathbf{n}}$ as a weighted average of the $\mathbf{P}'_{(i)}\mathbf{i}_{(j)}$, then the lemma in Chapter 6 shows how to find a vector $\mathbf{n}$ from which $\bar{\mathbf{n}}$ can be attained in one step.

Now any structure, say $\mathbf{n} = [0.37, 0.37, 0.26]$, can be expressed in various ways as a weighted average of $\mathbf{P}'_{(i)}\mathbf{i}_{(j)}$. For instance, $\mathbf{n}$ equals

$$0.54\mathbf{P}'_{(2)}\mathbf{i}_{(1)} + 0.386\mathbf{P}'_{(1)}\mathbf{i}_{(3)} + 0.073\mathbf{P}'_{(3)}\mathbf{i}_{(3)} \tag{7.20}$$

and also

$$0.343\mathbf{P}'_{(1)}\mathbf{i}_{(1)} + 0.038\mathbf{P}'_{(1)}\mathbf{i}_{(3)} + 0.557\mathbf{P}'_{(3)}\mathbf{i}_{(1)} + 0.062\mathbf{P}'_{(3)}\mathbf{i}_{(3)} \tag{7.21}$$

The coefficients are the c_{ij} of the lemma. Finding the σ_j of that lemma, we have a possible source for $\bar{\mathbf{n}}$.

Equation (7.20) leads to

$$0.541\mathbf{i}_{(1)} + (0.386 + 0.073)\mathbf{i}_{(3)} = [0.541, 0, 0.359]$$

and equation (7.21) leads to

$$\begin{pmatrix} 0.343 + 0.557 \\ 0 \\ 0.038 + 0.062 \end{pmatrix} = \begin{pmatrix} 0.9 \\ 0 \\ 0.1 \end{pmatrix}$$

The first of these vectors is not a vertex $\mathbf{v}_i$, while the second is identical with $\mathbf{v}_1$.

7.17

If we apply this argument to a vertex of A_t, then we find that the source from which that vertex can be obtained in t steps is unique. On the other hand, let us consider [0.3, 0.4, 0.3] which lies in A_1. It can be obtained from $\mathbf{i}_{(1)}$, though it is not a vertex of A_1. It equals

$$0.445\mathbf{P}'_{(1)}\mathbf{i}_{(1)} + 0.333\mathbf{P}'_{(2)}\mathbf{i}_{(2)} + 0.222\mathbf{P}'_{(3)}\mathbf{i}_{(3)}$$

and also

$$0.333\mathbf{P}'_{(1)}\mathbf{i}_{(1)} + 0.667\mathbf{P}'_{(2)}\mathbf{i}_{(3)}$$

Consequently, we have the following sources:

$$\begin{pmatrix} 0.445 \\ 0.333 \\ 0.222 \end{pmatrix} \begin{matrix} 0.211 + 0.089 \\ \rightarrow 0.367 + 0.033 = \\ 0.233 + 0.067 \end{matrix} \begin{pmatrix} 0.3 \\ 0.4 \\ 0.3 \end{pmatrix}$$

and also

$$\begin{pmatrix} 0.333 \\ 0 \\ 0.667 \end{pmatrix} \begin{matrix} 0.233 + 0.067 \\ \rightarrow 0.2 \quad + 0.2 \quad = \\ 0.3 \end{matrix} \begin{pmatrix} 0.3 \\ 0.4 \\ 0.3 \end{pmatrix}$$

7.18

Example 23

To find $B_2(\bar{\mathbf{n}})$ for a given $\bar{\mathbf{n}}$, we use again the simplex method, and $\mathbf{P}_0$.

We use again formulae (7.7) to (7.10), but this time with unknown $\mathbf{n}$, so that we must add $\mathbf{n}'\mathbf{e} = 1$. This is, in tableau form, for general $\bar{\mathbf{n}}$

	n_1	n_2	n_3	$u_1(0)$	$u_2(0)$	$u_3(0)$	
$u_1(1)$	0.15	0.14	0.15	0.3	0.1	0.2	$\bar{n}_1$
$u_2(1)$	0.33	0.32	0.17	0.4	0.5	0.1	$\bar{n}_2$
$u_3(1)$	0.19	0.28	0.21	0.1	0.3	0.4	$\bar{n}_3$
s	−0.2*	−0.1	−0.3	1.0	1.0	1.0	0
t	1.0	1.0	1.0	0	0	0	1.0

s and t are artificial variables, and the unknowns are, this time, $\mathbf{n}$, $\mathbf{u}(0)$, and $\mathbf{u}(1)$.

We obtain the following sequence of tableaus:

	n_2	n_3	$u_1(0)$	$u_2(0)$	$u_3(0)$	
$u_1(1)$	0.065	−0.075	1.05	0.85	0.95	$\bar{n}_1$
$u_2(1)$	0.155	−0.325	2.05	2.15	1.75	$\bar{n}_2$
$u_3(1)$	0.185	−0.075	1.05	1.25	1.35	$\bar{n}_3$
n_1	0.5	1.5	−5.00	−5.00	−5.00	0
t	0.5	−0.5	5.00*	5.00	5.00	1.0

and then tableau T

	n_2	n_3	$u_2(0)$	$u_3(0)$	
$u_1(1)$	−0.04	0.03	−0.2	−0.1	$\bar{n}_1 - 0.21$
$u_2(1)$	−0.05	−0.12	0.1	−0.3	$\bar{n}_2 - 0.41$
$u_3(1)$	0.08	0.03	0.2	0.3	$\bar{n}_3 - 0.21$
n_1	1.00	1.00	0	0	1.00
$u_1(0)$	0.10	−0.10	1.0	1.0	0.20

For $\bar{\mathbf{n}}$ = [0.37, 0.37, 0.26] this is

	n_2	n_3	$u_2(0)$	$u_3(0)$	
$u_1(1)$	−0.04	0.03	−0.2	−0.1	0.16
$u_2(1)$	−0.05	−0.12	0.1	−0.3*	−0.04
$u_3(1)$	0.08	0.03	0.2	0.3	0.05
n_1	1.00	1.00	0	0	1.00
$u_1(0)$	0.10	−0.10	1.00	1.00	0.20

	n_2	n_3	$u_2(0)$	$u_2(1)$	
$u_1(1)$	−0.023	0.07	−0.233	−0.333	0.173
$u_3(0)$	0.167	0.40	−0.333	−3.333	0.133
$u_3(1)$	0.030	−0.09	0.300	1.000	0.010
n_1	1.000	1.00	0	0	1.000
$u_1(0)$	−0.067	−0.50	1.333	3.333	0.067

We have thus obtained one of the vertices in $(\mathbf{n}, \mathbf{u}(0), \mathbf{u}(1))$-space. Its projection into the $\mathbf{n}$-space is [1, 0, 0].

There are more vertices in the nine-dimensional space, and some of them project into the same point in the three-dimensional space, but imply different recruiting rates. The following is a full list of all vertices, obtained from tableaus of the simplex method:

n_1	1.000	1.000	1.000	0.000	0.000	0.000	0.667	0.500	0.000	0.667	0.333
n_2	0.000	0.000	0.000	0.000	0.000	0.000	0.000	0.000	0.400	0.333	0.600
n_3	0.000	0.000	0.000	1.000	1.000	1.000	0.333	0.500	0.600	0.000	0.067
$u_1(0)$	0.067	0.023	0.033	0.300	0.200	0.233	0.233	0.070	0.220	0.090	0.147
$u_2(0)$	0.000	0.033	0.000	0.000	0.100	0.000	0.000	0.178	0.000	0.000	0.000
$u_3(0)$	0.133	0.144	0.167	0.000	0.000	0.067	0.000	0.000	0.000	0.076	0.000
$u_1(1)$	0.173	0.181	0.176	0.130	0.150	0.136	0.150	0.181	0.158	0.181	0.181
$u_2(1)$	0.000	0.000	0.010	0.080	0.070	0.100	0.000	0.000	0.052	0.000	0.000
$u_3(1)$	0.010	0.000	0.000	0.020	0.000	0.000	0.040	0.000	0.000	0.000	0.000
	*	*	*	*	*	*			*	*	*

*In the projection onto $\mathbf{n}$-space the first six and the last three vectors are vertices. $B_2(\bar{\mathbf{n}})$ is their convex hull.

For instance,

$$\begin{pmatrix}0.32\\0.43\\0.25\end{pmatrix} = 0.079\begin{pmatrix}1\\0\\0\end{pmatrix} + 0.203\begin{pmatrix}0\\0\\1\end{pmatrix} + 0.718\begin{pmatrix}0.333\\0.600\\0.067\end{pmatrix}$$

7.19

We may wish to know what relationship there is between $B_1(\bar{n})$ and $B_2(\bar{n})$, for the same $\bar{n}$.

One fact is immediate: if A_1 includes A_2, strictly, i.e. if there is a point $\bar{n}$ in A_1 which is not in A_2, then $B_2(\bar{n})$ is empty, while $B_1(\bar{n})$ is not. If $\bar{n}$ is both in A_1 and in A_2, then all four of the following possibilities can be illustrated.

(i) $B_1(\bar{n})$ and $B_2(\bar{n})$ have no point in common;
(ii) $B_1(\bar{n})$ includes $B_2(\bar{n})$;
(iii) $B_2(\bar{n})$ includes $B_1(\bar{n})$;
(iv) there is a partial overlap between $B_1(\bar{n})$ and $B_2(\bar{n})$.

(i) Let $\bar{n} = [0.21, 0.58, 0.21]$.

$B_1(\bar{n})$ does not include $[1, 0, 0]$, because $A_1([1, 0, 0])$ does not include $\bar{n}$. On the other hand, $B_2(\bar{n})$ is the single point $[1, 0, 0]$. We see this from the tableau marked T in Section 7.18. The third line of it reads, for our present $\bar{n}$,

$$u_3(1) + 0.08n_2 + 0.03n_3 + 0.2u_2(0) + 0.3u_3(0) = 0$$

and the only non-negative solution is $n_2 = n_3 = 0$ (and of course also $u_2(0) = u_3(0) = u_3(1) = 0$). Then

$$\begin{pmatrix}1\\0\\0\end{pmatrix} \begin{matrix}0.3+0.2\\ \to 0.4\\ 0.1\end{matrix} = \begin{pmatrix}0.5\\0.4\\0.1\end{pmatrix} \begin{matrix}0.21\\ \to 0.41+0.17\\ 0.21\end{matrix} = \begin{pmatrix}0.21\\0.58\\0.21\end{pmatrix}$$

(ii) Let $\bar{n} = [0.30, 0.49, 0.21]$.

Again, $B_2(\bar{n})$ is the single point $[1, 0, 0]$, and the proof is the same as in case (i). We have now

$$\begin{pmatrix}1\\0\\0\end{pmatrix} \begin{matrix}0.3+0.2\\ \to 0.4\\ 0.1\end{matrix} = \begin{pmatrix}0.5\\0.4\\0.1\end{pmatrix} \begin{matrix}0.21+0.09\\ \to 0.41+0.08\\ 0.21\end{matrix} = \begin{pmatrix}0.30\\0.49\\0.21\end{pmatrix}$$

On the other hand, $B_1(\bar{n})$ does include $[1, 0, 0]$, but other points as well, for instance

$$\begin{pmatrix}0.5\\0.5\\0\end{pmatrix} \begin{matrix}0.20+0.10\\ \to 0.45+0.04\\ 0.20+0.01\end{matrix} = \begin{pmatrix}0.30\\0.49\\0.21\end{pmatrix}$$

(iii) Let $\bar{n} = [0.37, 0.37, 0.26]$. This is the example we have been dealing with in Section 7.18.

It is easy to verify that the vectors $\mathbf{v}_i$ $(i = 1, 2, 3)$ of Section 7.14, i.e. the vertices of $B_1(\bar{\mathbf{n}})$, are in $B_2(\bar{\mathbf{n}})$. It is readily seen that both $\mathbf{v}_1$ and $\mathbf{v}_2$ are on the straight line segment between [1, 0, 0] and [0, 0, 1], two vertices of $B_2(\bar{\mathbf{n}})$, while

$$\mathbf{v}_3 = 0.376\begin{pmatrix}0\\0.4\\0.6\end{pmatrix} + 0.343\begin{pmatrix}0.667\\0.333\\0\end{pmatrix} + 0.281\begin{pmatrix}0.333\\0.600\\0.067\end{pmatrix}$$

This means that from any point, from which $\bar{\mathbf{n}}$ can be attained in one step, it can also be attained in two steps. For instance

$$\begin{pmatrix}0.371\\0.368\\0.261\end{pmatrix} \rightarrow \begin{matrix}0.2003 + 0.1697\\0.3585 + 0.0115\\0.2519 + 0.0081\end{matrix} = \begin{pmatrix}0.37\\0.37\\0.26\end{pmatrix}$$

and also

$$\begin{pmatrix}0.371\\0.368\\0.261\end{pmatrix} \rightarrow \begin{matrix}0.2003 + 0.1893\\0.3585\\0.2519\end{matrix} = \begin{pmatrix}0.3896\\0.3585\\0.2519\end{pmatrix} \rightarrow \begin{matrix}0.203 + 0.167\\0.360 + 0.010\\0.247 + 0.013\end{matrix} = \begin{pmatrix}0.37\\0.37\\0.26\end{pmatrix}$$

(iv) Let $\bar{\mathbf{n}} = [0.33, 0.35, 0.32]$.

It can be attained in one step from [0.70, 0.10, 0.20] thus:

$$\begin{pmatrix}0.70\\0.10\\0.20\end{pmatrix} \rightarrow \begin{matrix}0.26 + 0.07\\0.35 + 0\\0.18 + 0.14\end{matrix} = \begin{pmatrix}0.33\\0.35\\0.32\end{pmatrix}$$

but not in two steps, as is seen again from the third row of tableau T. Also, it can be attained from [0, 1, 0] in two steps, thus:

$$\begin{pmatrix}0\\1\\0\end{pmatrix} \rightarrow \begin{matrix}0.1\\0.5\\0.3 + 0.1\end{matrix} = \begin{pmatrix}0.1\\0.5\\0.4\end{pmatrix} \rightarrow \begin{matrix}0.16 + 0.17\\0.33 + 0.02\\0.32\end{matrix} = \begin{pmatrix}0.33\\0.35\\0.32\end{pmatrix}$$

but not in one step. Finally, from [0.30, 0, 0.70], it can be attained in one step:

$$\begin{pmatrix}0.30\\0\\0.70\end{pmatrix} \rightarrow \begin{matrix}0.23 + 0.10\\0.19 + 0.16\\0.31 + 0.01\end{matrix} = \begin{pmatrix}0.33\\0.35\\0.32\end{pmatrix}$$

but also in two steps

$$\begin{pmatrix}0.30\\0\\0.70\end{pmatrix} \rightarrow \begin{matrix}0.23 + 0.27\\0.19\\0.31\end{matrix} = \begin{pmatrix}0.50\\0.19\\0.31\end{pmatrix} \rightarrow \begin{matrix}0.231 + 0.099\\0.326 + 0.024\\0.231 + 0.089\end{matrix} = \begin{pmatrix}0.33\\0.35\\0.32\end{pmatrix}$$

7.20

In Section 5.24 we considered the requirement of keeping a weighted total of a population, its 'efficiency', constant, rather than its total membership.

We may be interested in knowing which structures can be transformed into others, of the same efficiency, with non-negative recruiting.

If the weights are all the same, then this question has a trivial answer: when the total wastage is non-negative, then any structure can be transformed into others with equal efficiency. But when the weights f_i are different, then this is not always true.

For illustration, let the transition matrix be again $\mathbf{P}_0$, and let $\mathbf{f} = [1, 2, 4]$. We then see at once that [1, 0, 0] or [0, 1, 0] cannot be transformed in the required way, because [1. 0. 0], with efficiency 1, transforms even before recruiting into [0.3, 0.4, 0.1] which already has efficiency 1.5, while [0, 1, 0] has efficiency 2 and transforms into [0.1, 0.5, 0.3] with efficiency 2.3.

On the other hand, [0, 0, 1], with efficiency 4, transforms into [0.2, 0.1, 0.4] with efficiency 2 and the deficiency can be made up in an infinity of ways.

7.21

To obtain an overall view, i.e. to find the vertices, in $(\mathbf{n}, \mathbf{u}, \bar{\mathbf{n}})$-space, of the set of those sets whose efficiency can be maintained after one step, we use again the simplex method. We have to solve

$$\bar{\mathbf{n}}_i = p_{1i}n_1 + p_{2i}n_2 + \ldots + p_{ki}n_k + u_i \quad (i = 1, \ldots, k) \tag{7.22}$$

$$n_1 f_1 + \ldots + n_k f_k = \bar{n}_1 f_1 + \ldots + \bar{n}_k f_k \quad n_i \geqslant 0, u_i \geqslant 0 \quad (\text{all } i) \tag{7.23}$$

and we normalize by

$$n_1 + \ldots + n_k = 1 \tag{7.24}$$

This leads to the initial tableau

	n_1	n_2	n_3	$\bar{n}_1$	$\bar{n}_2$	$\bar{n}_3$	
u_1	0.3	0.1	0.2	−1.0			0
u_2	0.4	0.5	0.1		−1.0		0
u_3	0.1	0.3	0.4			−1.0	0
s_1	1.0	2.0	4.0	−1.0	−2.0	−4.0	0
s_2	1.0	1.0	1.0	0	0	0	1.0

We obtain eventually the following extreme cases.
[0, 0, 1] appears three times, as follows:

$$\begin{pmatrix} 0 \\ 0 \\ 1 \end{pmatrix} \rightarrow \begin{matrix} 0.2 \\ 0.1 \\ 0.4 \end{matrix} \quad \text{and then} \quad \begin{pmatrix} 2.2 \\ 0.1 \\ 0.4 \end{pmatrix} \quad \text{when } u_1 = 2$$

$$\begin{pmatrix} 0.2 \\ 1.1 \\ 0.4 \end{pmatrix} \quad \text{when } u_2 = 1$$

$$\begin{pmatrix} 0.2 \\ 0.1 \\ 0.9 \end{pmatrix} \quad \text{when } u_3 = 0.5$$

In these three cases the total membership increases. Moreover, we have two cases which do not require any new entrants – in which case the total is necessarily reduced:

$$\begin{pmatrix} 0.8 \\ 0 \\ 0.2 \end{pmatrix} \to \begin{pmatrix} 0.28 \\ 0.34 \\ 0.16 \end{pmatrix} \quad \text{efficiency } 1.6$$

and

$$\begin{pmatrix} 0 \\ 0.87 \\ 0.13 \end{pmatrix} \to \begin{pmatrix} 0.113 \\ 0.448 \\ 0.313 \end{pmatrix} \quad \text{efficiency } 2.26$$

7.22

We see that no structure with efficiency less than 1.6, or more than 4, can maintain its efficiency after one step. The last mentioned fact follows, of course, from 4 being the largest of f_i. But the smallest of the f_i is 1, and it is due to $\mathbf{P}_0$ that no structure with this efficiency (e.g. [1, 0, 0]) can be maintained.

Let us take now a structure with intermediate efficiency, say

$$[0.5, 0.3, 0.2] = 0.03\begin{pmatrix} 0 \\ 0 \\ 1 \end{pmatrix} + 0.625\begin{pmatrix} 0.8 \\ 0 \\ 0.2 \end{pmatrix} + 0.345\begin{pmatrix} 0 \\ 0.87 \\ 0.13 \end{pmatrix}$$

Its efficiency, $1.900 = 0.3 \times 4 + 0.625 \times 1.6 + 0.345 \times 0.226$. It is possible to maintain this efficiency after one step, with non-negative recruiting rate. What this rate is to be, depends on whether the entrants join state 1, 2, or 3. The rate of entry is then, respectively, $0.03 \times 2 = 0.06$, or $0.03 \times 1 = 0.03$, or $0.03 \times 0.5 = 0.015$. The other constituents do not contribute to the recruiting requirement.

7.23

The same method could be used if we wanted to determine those structures whose efficiency can be maintained through more than one step. We do not pursue this question any further, apart from mentioning that of those structures obtained above, the efficiency of all except [2.2, 0.1, 0.4] can be maintained for at least one more step. Indeed, the efficiency of [0.75, 0.97, 0.41] into which this structure develops before recruiting is already 4.33. On the other hand, [0.2, 1.1, 0.4] transforms into [0.25, 0.67, 0.51] whose efficiency is only 3.63, before recruitment..

7.24

Example 24

We shall now derive the set of those structures which can be derived from a given structure, keeping the efficiency constant after one step, and also after the second step.

The formulae we have to use now are (7.4), and instead of (7.5) we use this formula but replacing $\mathbf{e} = [1, \ldots, 1]$ by $\mathbf{f} = [f_1, \ldots, f_k]$, i.e.

$$\mathbf{u}(0)'\mathbf{f} = \mathbf{n}'(\mathbf{I} - \mathbf{P})\mathbf{f}, \quad \mathbf{u}(1)'\mathbf{f} = \mathbf{n}'\mathbf{P}(\mathbf{I} - \mathbf{P})\mathbf{f} + \mathbf{u}(0)'(\mathbf{I} - \mathbf{P})\mathbf{f} \tag{7.5f}$$

With $\mathbf{f} = [1, 2, 4]$ we have

$$\mathbf{P}_0(\mathbf{I} - \mathbf{P}_0)\mathbf{f} = \begin{pmatrix} 0.3 & 0.4 & 0.1 \\ 0.1 & 0.5 & 0.3 \\ 0.2 & 0.1 & 0.4 \end{pmatrix} \begin{pmatrix} -0.5 \\ -0.3 \\ 2.0 \end{pmatrix} = \begin{pmatrix} -0.07 \\ 0.40 \\ 0.67 \end{pmatrix}$$

Formulae (7.7), (7.8), and (7.9) remain valid, and for (7.10) and (7.11) we have now

$$u_1(0) + 2u_2(0) + 4u_3(0) = -0.5n_1 - 0.3n_2 + 2.0n_3 \tag{7.10f}$$

$$\begin{aligned} &0.5u_1(0) + 0.3u_2(0) - 2.0u_3(0) + u_1(1) + 2u_2(1) + 4u_3(1) \\ &\quad = -0.07n_1 + 0.40n_2 + 0.67n_3 \end{aligned} \tag{7.11f}$$

where $[n_1, n_2, n_3]$ is the initial structure.

If we start with [500, 300, 200], efficiency 1900, then we have, to begin with, the tableau

	$u_1(0)$	$u_2(0)$	$u_3(0)$	$u_1(1)$	$u_2(1)$	$u_3(1)$	
$\bar{n}_1$	−0.3	−0.1	−0.2	−1.0	0	0	147
$\bar{n}_2$	−0.4	−0.5	−0.1	0	−1.0	0	295
$\bar{n}_3$	−0.1	−0.3	−0.4	0	0	−1.0	221
s_1	1.0	2.0	4.0	0	0	0	60
s_2	0.5	0.3	−2.0	1.0	2.0	4.0	219

First we drop s_1 and s_2 and then we obtain the following nine vertices of the set we are looking for:

$\bar{n}_1$	354	360	399	165	150	150	166	150	150
$\bar{n}_2$	319	310	296.5	413.5	415	421	319	310	296.5
$\bar{n}_3$	227	230	227	227	230	227	274	282.5	289
$u_1(0)$	60			60			60		
$u_2(0)$		30			30			30	
$u_3(0)$			15			15			15
$u_1(1)$	189	210	249						
$u_2(1)$				94.5	105	124.5			
$u_3(1)$							47	52.5	62

The first column repeats the result after two years given in Section 5.26, where we considered only entries into state 1.

The list shows the results after two steps. It contains information about the first step, containing $u_i(0)$. These values, 60, or 30, or 15, confirm the results of Section 7.25, referring to [500, 300, 200].

8

Re-attainable Structures

8.1

We have looked at regions $A_t(\mathbf{n})$, i.e. sets of structures attainable from $\mathbf{n}$ after t steps, and at regions $B_t(\mathbf{n})$, i.e. sets from which $\mathbf{n}$ can be reached in t steps. In all these cases it is assumed that at intermediate steps the total of the population remains constant.

If $\mathbf{n}$ is in $A_t(\mathbf{n})$, then it is also in $B_t(\mathbf{n})$. In such a case we call $\mathbf{n}$ re-attainable after t steps. (The set of such structures is denoted by S_t in Davies (1973), and by M_t in Davies (1975).)

We consider first structures re-attainable after one step. They are also re-attainable after any number of steps. In Part I we have called them stationary, and in the present context we call them 'strictly maintainable'.

In Part I we have seen how we can find such structures. Here we shall use for this purpose a method based on the simplex method of linear programming, and we shall see how it can be generalized to find structures which are re-attainable after $t = 2, 3, \ldots$ steps.

Our problem is that of finding vectors $\mathbf{n}$ such that

$$u_i = n_i - (p_{1i}n_1 + \ldots + p_{ki}n_k) \geqslant 0 \quad (i = 1, \ldots, k) \tag{8.1}$$

The u_i are the required numbers of new entrants into state i, so as to retain the totals within each state. The n_i must be non-negative, and we shall find the vertices of the set of strictly maintainable structures by the simplex method.

8.2

Example 25

As an example, we choose the total membership to be 1, and we use the transition matrix $\mathbf{P}_0$. The initial tableau is then

	n_1	n_2	n_3	
u_1	−0.7	0.1	0.2	0
u_2	0.4	−0.5	0.1	0
u_3	0.1	0.3	−0.6	0
s	1.0	1.0	1.0	1.0

Eventually, we obtain the following vertices in $(\mathbf{n}, \mathbf{u})$-space:

	$\mathbf{w}_1$	$\mathbf{w}_2$	$\mathbf{w}_3$
n_1	0.392	0.162	0.193
n_2	0.362	0.541	0.263
n_3	0.246	0.297	0.544
u_1	0.189	0	0
u_2	0	0.176	0
u_3	0	0	0.228

For each vertex only one single u_i differs from zero. We remark that

$$\begin{pmatrix} 0.37 \\ 0.37 \\ 0.26 \end{pmatrix} = 0.899\mathbf{w}_1 + 0.065\mathbf{w}_2 + 0.036\mathbf{w}_3$$

and is therefore strictly maintainable:

$$\begin{pmatrix} 0.37 \\ 0.37 \\ 0.26 \end{pmatrix} \to \begin{matrix} 0.200 + 0.170 \\ 0.359 + 0.011 \\ 0.252 + 0.008 \end{matrix} = \begin{pmatrix} 0.37 \\ 0.37 \\ 0.26 \end{pmatrix}$$

On the other hand

$$\begin{pmatrix} 0.32 \\ 0.43 \\ 0.25 \end{pmatrix} = 0.693\mathbf{w}_1 + 0.354\mathbf{w}_2 - 0.047\mathbf{w}_3$$

and is, therefore, not a strictly maintainable structure.

8.3

We interpolate a brief remark about two-state structures. In this case the set of strictly maintainable structures can be found by a simple algorithm, which we illustrate by an example.

Let the transition matrix be

$$\begin{pmatrix} 0.3 & 0.1 \\ 0.4 & 0.2 \end{pmatrix}$$

Then $[n_1, n_2], n_1 + n_2 = 1, n_1, n_2 \geqslant 0$ will be transformed into

$$[0.3n_1 + 0.4n_2, 0.1n_1 + 0.2n_2] = [0.4 - 0.1n_1, 0.2 - 0.1n_1]$$

For $[n_1, n_2]$ to be strictly maintainable, we must have

$$0.4 - 0.1n_1 \leqslant n_1 \qquad \text{or} \qquad 0.4 \leqslant 1.1n_1$$

and

$$0.2 - 0.1n_1 \leqslant 1 - n_1 \qquad \text{or} \qquad 0.8 \geqslant 0.9n_1$$

Hence the vertices we are looking for are $[4/11, 7/11]$ and $[8/9, 1/9]$.

8.4

We look now for structures which can be re-attained after t steps, $t \geqslant 2$.

If, at the sth step, the transition matrix, including the new entrants after the transition, is

$$\mathbf{R}^{(s)} = \begin{pmatrix} r_{11}^{(s)} & \cdots & r_{k1}^{(s)} \\ \vdots & & \vdots \\ r_{1k}^{(s)} & \cdots & r_{kk}^{(s)} \end{pmatrix}$$

where

$$r_{ij}^{(s)} = p_{ij} + \rho_j^{(s)} w_i \qquad \sum_{j=1}^{k} r_{ij}^{(s)} = 1 \qquad \text{for all } i$$

then, after t steps, $\mathbf{n}(t) = \mathbf{R}^{(t)} \ldots \mathbf{R}^{(1)}\mathbf{n}(0)$.

The $\rho_j^{(s)}$ are the proportions of new entrants which join state j at the sth step. The notation is analogous to that in Section 2.19, but we allow here different proportions at the different steps. We did not do this in Part I.

The structure $\mathbf{n}$ is re-attainable after t steps, if

$$(\mathbf{R}^{(t)} \ldots \mathbf{R}^{(1)} - \mathbf{I})\mathbf{n} = 0 \tag{8.2}$$

To know that this system has a non-trivial solution $\mathbf{n}$, we must know that the matrix of (8.2) is singular, i.e. that the matrix product $\mathbf{R}^{(t)} \ldots \mathbf{R}^{(1)}$ has a latent root equal to unity.

We know it of $\mathbf{R}^{(1)}$, because its columns all add up to 1. By induction, we convince ourselves that this is also true of $\mathbf{R}^{(2)}\mathbf{R}^{(1)}$, of $\mathbf{R}^{(3)}\mathbf{R}^{(2)}\mathbf{R}^{(1)}$ and so on.

In particular, there exist k^t structures $\mathbf{n}_u$, re-attainable after t years, such that each structure recruits, at each step, only into one single state, not necessarily into the same state at each step. They are the solutions of equation (8.2) when $\mathbf{R}^{(s)} = \mathbf{P}'_{(v)}$, v being the number of some row. (The notation is that of the lemma of Chapter 6).

For instance, using $\mathbf{P}_0$ and choosing $k = 3$ and $t = 2$, we have the nine structures (the subscripts indicate the states into which new members enter at the first, and at the second step)

$\mathbf{w}_{11}$	$\mathbf{w}_{12}$	$\mathbf{w}_{13}$	$\mathbf{w}_{21}$	$\mathbf{w}_{22}$	$\mathbf{w}_{23}$	$\mathbf{w}_{31}$	$\mathbf{w}_{32}$	$\mathbf{w}_{33}$
0.392	0.196	0.210	0.337	0.162	0.168	0.399	0.181	0.193
0.362	0.543	0.339	0.376	0.541	0.356	0.298	0.505	0.263
0.246	0.261	0.451	0.287	0.297	0.476	0.303	0.314	0.544
*	*			*	*	*		*

Those marked with an asterisk are vertices in their convex hull. Figure 6 shows the points in barycentric coordinates. Those with two equal subscripts are the vertices of the region of strictly maintainable structures.

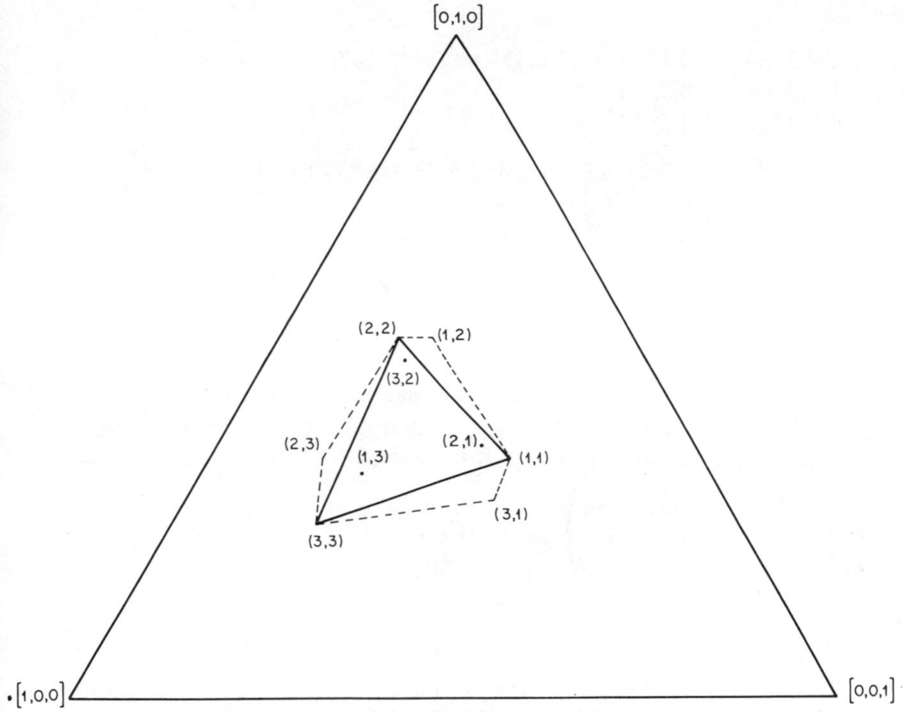

Figure 6

8.5

We prove now that a structure is re-attainable after t steps if and only if it lies in the convex hull of the structures $\mathbf{n}_u$ defined above. We write m for k^t.

(i) A structure $a_1\mathbf{n}_1 + \ldots + a_m\mathbf{n}_m$ will be re-attained after t steps by recruiting, at each step, these numbers which enter at that step into $\mathbf{n}_1, \ldots, \mathbf{n}_m$ respectively, multiplied by the weights $a_1, \ldots, a_m$.

For instance, when $k = 3$ and $t = 3$, and we use again $\mathbf{P}_0$, consider $\mathbf{n}_{111} = [0.392, 0.362, 0.246]$, which is strictly maintainable, and $\mathbf{n}_{113} = [0.208, 0.358, 0.434]$, whose subscripts are justified by the following transitions:

$$\begin{pmatrix}0.208\\0.358\\0.434\end{pmatrix} \to \begin{matrix}0.185+0.207\\0.306\\0.302\end{matrix} = \begin{pmatrix}0.392\\0.306\\0.302\end{pmatrix} \to \begin{matrix}0.209+0.199\\0.340\\0.252\end{matrix}$$

$$= \begin{pmatrix}0.408\\0.340\\0.252\end{pmatrix} \to \begin{matrix}0.208\\0.358\\0.244+0.190\end{matrix} = \begin{pmatrix}0.208\\0.358\\0.434\end{pmatrix}$$

Consider now

$$0.6\mathbf{n}_{111} + 0.4\mathbf{n}_{113} = [0.3184, 0.3604, 0.3212]$$

We have

$$\begin{pmatrix}0.3184\\0.3604\\0.3212\end{pmatrix} \begin{array}{l} \quad 0.1958 + 0.6(0.189) + 0.4(0.207)\\ \to 0.3396\\ \quad 0.2684\end{array}$$

$$= \begin{pmatrix}0.3920\\0.3396\\0.2684\end{pmatrix} \begin{array}{l} \quad 0.2052 + 0.6(0.189) + 0.4(0.199)\\ \to 0.3532\\ \quad 0.2484\end{array}$$

$$= \begin{pmatrix}0.3984\\0.3532\\0.2484\end{pmatrix} \begin{array}{l} \quad 0.2045 + 0.6(0.189)\\ \to 0.3604\\ \quad 0.2453 + 0.4(0.190)\end{array} = \begin{pmatrix}0.3184\\0.3804\\0.3212\end{pmatrix}$$

A general proof is immediate. It depends on the fact that after each number of steps, the structure reached by the weighted average is the average of those structures obtained by $\mathbf{n}_1, \ldots, \mathbf{n}_m$. For instance,

$$\begin{pmatrix}0.3920\\0.3396\\0.2684\end{pmatrix} = 0.6\begin{pmatrix}0.392\\0.362\\0.246\end{pmatrix} + 0.4\begin{pmatrix}0.392\\0.306\\0.302\end{pmatrix}$$

and

$$\begin{pmatrix}0.3984\\0.3532\\0.2484\end{pmatrix} = 0.6\begin{pmatrix}0.392\\0.362\\0.246\end{pmatrix} + 0.4\begin{pmatrix}0.408\\0.340\\0.252\end{pmatrix}$$

(ii) All structures re-attainable after t steps are in the convex hull of the m structures $\mathbf{n}_{\mu_1}, \ldots, \mathbf{n}_{\mu m}$ defined above.

We prove this for $t = 2$, $m = k^2$, but it will be seen that the proof can be extended to cover any t.

A structure $\mathbf{n}_{ij}$ has components proportional to the co-factors of, say, the first row of the matrix $(\mathbf{P}'_{(i)}\mathbf{P}'_{(j)} - \mathbf{I})$. Denote the co-factors by $A_1(i, j), \ldots, A_k(i, j)$.

On the other hand, a structure $n_{\rho\sigma}$ which is the solution of

$$(\mathbf{R}(\rho)\mathbf{R}(\sigma) - \mathbf{I})\mathbf{n} = 0$$

where

$$\mathbf{R}(\rho) = \sum_i \rho_{(i)}\mathbf{P}'_{(i)} \qquad \mathbf{R}(\sigma) = \sum_j \sigma_{(j)}\mathbf{P}'_{(j)}$$

$$\sum_i \rho_i = \sum_j \rho_j = 1 \qquad \text{all } \rho_i \text{ and } \sigma_j \text{ non-negative}$$

has components proportional to the co-factors of, say, the first row of the matrix

$$(\mathbf{R}(\rho)\mathbf{R}(\sigma) - \mathbf{I}) = \left(\sum_i\sum_j \tau_{ij}\mathbf{P}'_{(i)}\mathbf{P}'_{(j)} - \mathbf{I}\right)$$

$$= \left(\sum_i\sum_j \tau_{ij}[\mathbf{P}'_{(j)} - \mathbf{I}]\right)$$

where $\tau_{ij} = \rho_i\sigma_j$, and hence $\Sigma_i\Sigma_j\tau_{ij} = 1$. Denote these co-factors by $A_1(\rho, \sigma), \ldots,$

$A_k(\rho, \sigma)$. The $A_l(\rho, \sigma)$ are proportional to $\Sigma_i \Sigma_j \tau_{ij} A_l(i, j)$ and if we normalize by making $\mathbf{n}'\mathbf{e} = 1$, then the two expressions are equal, thus:

$$A_l(\rho, \sigma) = \sum_{i=1}^{k} \sum_{j=1}^{k} \tau_{ij} A_l(i, j) \tag{8.3}$$

and

$$\mathbf{n}_{\rho\sigma} = \sum_i \sum_j \tau_{ij} \mathbf{n}_{ij}, \tag{8.4}$$

i.e. any $\mathbf{n}_{\rho\sigma}$ is in the convex hull of the n_{ij}.

8.6

If we derive the structures which are re-attainable after t steps by solving equation (8.2), then we do not obtain immediately the number of new entrants required at the successive steps. We use therefore again the simplex method to determine the vertices of the region in $(\mathbf{n}, \mathbf{u}(0), \ldots, \mathbf{u}(t-1))$-space.

A preliminary observation is in order here, which helps to reduce the volume of the computations involved.

If we wish to find the vertices of the region of structures re-attainable after t steps, then it is not necessary to compute every one of them from the tableaus. Having obtained one of them, then the path of re-attainment passes through $t - 1$ of the other vertices. For instance (anticipating a result for $t = 3$ which we establish later, see Section 8.10), [0.204, 0.547, 0.249] is re-attainable after three steps as follows:

$$\begin{pmatrix} 0.204 \\ 0.547 \\ 0.249 \end{pmatrix} \begin{matrix} 0.166 + 0.170 \\ \rightarrow 0.380 \\ 0.284 \end{matrix} = \begin{pmatrix} 0.336 \\ 0.380 \\ 0.284 \end{pmatrix} \begin{matrix} 0.196 + 0.190 \\ \rightarrow 0.353 \\ 0.261 \end{matrix}$$

$$= \begin{pmatrix} 0.386 \\ 0.353 \\ 0.261 \end{pmatrix} \begin{matrix} 0.204 \\ \rightarrow 0.357 + 0.190 \\ 0.249 \end{matrix} = \begin{pmatrix} 0.204 \\ 0.547 \\ 0.249 \end{pmatrix}$$

We see that the first structure can be written $\mathbf{n}_{112}$, the next $\mathbf{n}_{121}$, and the third $\mathbf{n}_{211}$, since the results emerge in cyclic periodicity.

8.7

Example 26

To determine the structures re-attainable after two steps, we start with the tableau representing equations (6.4) and (6.6)

	n_1	n_2	n_3	$u_1(0)$	$u_2(0)$	$u_3(0)$	
$u_1(1)$	0.15	0.14	0.15	0.3	0.1	0.2	n_1
$u_2(1)$	0.33	0.32	0.17	0.4	0.5	0.1	n_2
$u_3(1)$	0.19	0.28	0.21	0.1	0.3	0.4	n_3
s	−0.20	−0.10	−0.30	1.0	1.0	1.0	0
t	1.00	1.00	1.00	0	0	0	1

This is the tableau of Section 7.18, but now the n_i appear not only as labels of columns, but also on the right-hand side. Collecting them, we have

	n_1	n_2	n_3	$u_1(0)$	$u_2(0)$	$u_3(0)$	
$u_1(1)$	−0.85	0.14	0.15	0.3	0.1	0.2	0
$u_2(1)$	0.33	−0.68	0.17	0.4	0.5	0.1	0
$u_3(1)$	0.19	0.28	−0.79	0.1	0.3	0.4	0
s	−0.20	−0.10	−0.30	1.0	1.0	1.0	0
t	1.00	1.00	1.00	0	0	0	1

(T.2)

Eventually we obtain the nine $\mathbf{w}_{ij}$ quoted in Section 8.4, and also the values for

$u_i(0)$	0.189	0.172	0.212	0.191	0.176	0.212	0.200	0.181	0.228
$u_i(1)$	0.189	0.191	0.200	0.172	0.176	0.181	0.212	0.212	0.228
For entries into states	1, 1	1, 2	1, 3	2, 1	2, 2	2, 3	3, 1	3, 2	3, 3

The structures for (1, 1), (2, 2), and (3, 3) are, of course, strictly maintainable. In these cases $\mathbf{u}(0) = \mathbf{u}(1)$. In the other cases we observe that for pairs (i, j) and (j, i) the values of $u_i(0)$ and $u_j(1)$ are reversed. This conforms with the observation made in the last section.

If we are prepared to wait until the end of two steps, before we re-attain a given structure, and do not insist on filling up after one step to the initial total, then we have to find rows of $(\mathbf{I} - \mathbf{P}^2)^{-1}$. This will give the vertices of the region of these structures which can be re-attained after two steps

For instance,

$$(\mathbf{I} - \mathbf{P}_0^2)^{-1} = \begin{pmatrix} 1.431 & 0.855 & 0.648 \\ 0.445 & 1.879 & 0.772 \\ 0.366 & 0.565 & 1.553 \end{pmatrix}$$

and we find, with entries into the first, the second, the third state respectively

$$\begin{pmatrix} 1431 \\ 855 \\ 648 \end{pmatrix} \to \begin{pmatrix} 644 \\ 1065 \\ 659 \end{pmatrix} \to \begin{pmatrix} 431 + 1000 \\ 855 \\ 648 \end{pmatrix}$$

$$\begin{pmatrix} 445 \\ 1879 \\ 772 \end{pmatrix} \to \begin{pmatrix} 476 \\ 1194 \\ 917 \end{pmatrix} \to \begin{pmatrix} 445 \\ 879 + 1000 \\ 772 \end{pmatrix}$$

$$\begin{pmatrix} 366 \\ 565 \\ 1553 \end{pmatrix} \to \begin{pmatrix} 477 \\ 584 \\ 827 \end{pmatrix} \to \begin{pmatrix} 366 \\ 565 \\ 553 + 1000 \end{pmatrix}$$

8.8

Every strictly maintainable structure is, of course, re-attainable after two steps, but it may be re-attainable by different routes as well.

For instance, the lists above show that $\mathbf{w}_{32}$ is re-attainable as follows:

$$\begin{pmatrix}0.181\\0.505\\0.314\end{pmatrix} \begin{matrix}0.168\\ \rightarrow 0.356\\ 0.295+0.181\end{matrix} = \begin{pmatrix}0.168\\0.356\\0.476\end{pmatrix} \begin{matrix}0.181\\ \rightarrow 0.293+0.212=\\ 0.314\end{matrix} \begin{pmatrix}0.181\\0.505\\0.314\end{pmatrix}$$

However,

$$\mathbf{w}_{32} = 0.0713\mathbf{w}_{11} + 0.8451\mathbf{w}_{22} + 0.0836\mathbf{w}_{33}$$

and is therefore strictly maintainable, so that also

$$\begin{pmatrix}0.181\\0.505\\0.314\end{pmatrix} \begin{matrix}0.168+0.013\\ \rightarrow 0.356+0.149=\\ 0.295+0.019\end{matrix} \begin{pmatrix}0.181\\0.505\\0.314\end{pmatrix} \begin{matrix}0.168+0.013\\ \rightarrow 0.356+0.149=\\ 0.295+0.019\end{matrix} \begin{pmatrix}0.181\\0.505\\0.314\end{pmatrix}$$

Furthermore,

$$\mathbf{w}_{32} = 0.302\mathbf{w}_{12} + 0.181\mathbf{w}_{13} + 0.517\mathbf{w}_{22}$$

and hence

$$\begin{pmatrix}0.181\\0.505\\0.314\end{pmatrix} \begin{matrix}0.168+0.302(0.172)+0.181(0.212)\\ \rightarrow 0.356+0.517(0.176)\\ 0.295\end{matrix} \begin{matrix}=0.168+0.090\\ =0.356+0.091\\ =0.295\end{matrix}$$

$$\begin{matrix}=\\=\\=\end{matrix} \begin{pmatrix}0.258\\0.447\\0.295\end{pmatrix} \begin{matrix}0.181\\ \rightarrow 0.356+0.302(0.191)+0.517(0.176)\\ 0.278+0.181(0.200)\end{matrix} \begin{matrix}=0.181\\ =0.356+0.149\\ =0.278+0.036\end{matrix}$$

$$\begin{matrix}=\\=\\=\end{matrix} \begin{pmatrix}0.181\\0.505\\0.314\end{pmatrix}$$

8.9

The results of Section 8.8 might lead us to ask for an identification of all possibilities of obtaining [0.181, 0.505, 0.314] again after two steps.

To answer this question, we use the procedure of Section 7.12 and start from the tableau

	$u_1(0)$	$u_2(0)$	$u_3(0)$	
$u_1(1)$	0.3	0.1	0.2	0.181 − 0.145 = 0.036
$u_2(1)$	0.4	0.5	0.1	0.505 − 0.275 = 0.230
$u_3(1)$	0.1	0.3	0.4	0.314 − 0.242 = 0.072
s	1.0	1.0	1.0	0.181

The simplex method leads to the following three vertices in $(\mathbf{u}(0), \mathbf{u}(1))$-space:

	(a)	(b)	(c)
$u_1(0)$	0.090		
$u_2(0)$	0.091	0.181	
$u_3(0)$			0.181
$u_1(1)$		0.018	
$u_2(1)$	0.149	0.140	0.212
$u_3(1)$	0.036	0.018	

(c) is the same as $\mathbf{w}_{32}$ in Section 8.7. This was to be expected, because the structure we consider is a vertex of the set of these re-attainable after two steps. (a) is the last example in Section 8.8, while the last but one example of that section equals

$$0.145(a) + 0.750(b) + 0.105(c)$$

In this case the recruitment was the same in both years, due to the fact that the structure was strictly maintainable.

8.10

We list now the set of structures re-attainable after three steps, in $(\mathbf{n}, \mathbf{u}(0), \mathbf{u}(1), \mathbf{u}(2))$-space. We can use again the simplex method and obtain the three vertices which are strictly maintainable, and the following twenty-four which we exhibit in triplets, as explained in Section 8.6:

$$\begin{pmatrix}0.204\\0.547\\0.249\end{pmatrix} \to \begin{matrix}0.166+0.170\\0.380\\0.284\end{matrix} = \begin{pmatrix}0.336\\0.380\\0.284\end{pmatrix} \to \begin{matrix}0.196+0.190\\0.353\\0.261\end{matrix}$$

$$= \begin{pmatrix}0.386\\0.353\\0.261\end{pmatrix} \to \begin{matrix}0.204\\0.257+0.190\\0.249\end{matrix} = \begin{pmatrix}0.204\\0.547\\0.249\end{pmatrix}$$

$$\begin{pmatrix}0.207\\0.359\\0.434\end{pmatrix} \to \begin{matrix}0.184+0.208\\0.306\\0.302\end{matrix} = \begin{pmatrix}0.392\\0.306\\0.302\end{pmatrix} \to \begin{matrix}0.209+0.199\\0.340\\0.252\end{matrix}$$

$$= \begin{pmatrix}0.408\\0.340\\0.252\end{pmatrix} \to \begin{matrix}0.207\\0.359\\0.244+0.190\end{matrix} = \begin{pmatrix}0.207\\0.359\\0.434\end{pmatrix}$$

$$\begin{pmatrix}0.166\\0.547\\0.287\end{pmatrix} \to \begin{matrix}0.162+0.174\\0.369\\0.295\end{matrix} = \begin{pmatrix}0.336\\0.369\\0.295\end{pmatrix} \to \begin{matrix}0.197\\0.348+0.193\\0.262\end{matrix}$$

$$= \begin{pmatrix}0.197\\0.541\\0.262\end{pmatrix} \to \begin{matrix}0.166\\0.375+0.172\\0.287\end{matrix} = \begin{pmatrix}0.166\\0.547\\0.287\end{pmatrix}$$

$$\begin{pmatrix}0.188\\0.297\\0.515\end{pmatrix} \to \begin{matrix}0.189+0.222\\0.275\\0.314\end{matrix} = \begin{pmatrix}0.411\\0.275\\0.314\end{pmatrix} \to \begin{matrix}0.214\\0.333\\0.249+0.204\end{matrix}$$

$$= \begin{pmatrix}0.214\\0.333\\0.453\end{pmatrix} \begin{array}{l}\,0.188\\ \rightarrow 0.297\\ \,0.303+0.212\end{array} = \begin{pmatrix}0.188\\0.297\\0.515\end{pmatrix}$$

$$\begin{pmatrix}0.163\\0.365\\0.472\end{pmatrix} \begin{array}{l}\,0.180\\ \rightarrow 0.295+0.211\\ \,0.314\end{array} = \begin{pmatrix}0.180\\0.506\\0.314\end{pmatrix} \begin{array}{l}\,0.168\\ \rightarrow 0.356+0.180\\ \,0.296\end{array}$$

$$= \begin{pmatrix}0.168\\0.536\\0.296\end{pmatrix} \begin{array}{l}\,0.163\\ \rightarrow 0.365\\ \,0.296+0.176\end{array} = \begin{pmatrix}0.163\\0.365\\0.472\end{pmatrix}$$

$$\begin{pmatrix}0.181\\0.293\\0.526\end{pmatrix} \begin{array}{l}\,0.189\\ \rightarrow 0.271+0.224\\ \,0.316\end{array} = \begin{pmatrix}0.189\\0.495\\0.316\end{pmatrix} \begin{array}{l}\,0.169\\ \rightarrow 0.355\\ \,0.294+0.182\end{array}$$

$$= \begin{pmatrix}0.169\\0.355\\0.476\end{pmatrix} \begin{array}{l}\,0.181\\ \rightarrow 0.293\\ \,0.314+0.212\end{array} = \begin{pmatrix}0.181\\0.293\\0.526\end{pmatrix}$$

$$\begin{pmatrix}0.167\\0.378\\0.455\end{pmatrix} \begin{array}{l}\,0.179+0.208\\ \rightarrow 0.310\\ \,0.312\end{array} = \begin{pmatrix}0.387\\0.301\\0.312\end{pmatrix} \begin{array}{l}\,0.209\\ \rightarrow 0.336+0.201\\ \,0.254\end{array}$$

$$= \begin{pmatrix}0.209\\0.537\\0.254\end{pmatrix} \begin{array}{l}\,0.167\\ \rightarrow 0.378\\ \,0.284+0.171\end{array} = \begin{pmatrix}0.167\\0.378\\0.455\end{pmatrix}$$

$$\begin{pmatrix}0.185\\0.510\\0.305\end{pmatrix} \begin{array}{l}\,0.168+0.179\\ \rightarrow 0.360\\ \,0.293\end{array} = \begin{pmatrix}0.347\\0.360\\0.293\end{pmatrix} \begin{array}{l}\,0.199\\ \rightarrow 0.348\\ \,0.260+0.193\end{array}$$

$$= \begin{pmatrix}0.199\\0.348\\0.453\end{pmatrix} \begin{array}{l}\,0.185\\ \rightarrow 0.299+0.211\\ \,0.305\end{array} = \begin{pmatrix}0.185\\0.510\\0.305\end{pmatrix}$$

8.10

If a structure is strictly maintainable, then it is re-attainable after any number of steps. If it is re-attainable after t (>1) steps, but not after one step, then it might be re-attainable after $t+1$ steps as well (though obviously through different first t steps), or it might not be. We give here an example for each of these possibilities.

Consider the structure [0.1885, 0.5240, 0.2875]. It equals

$$0.5\mathbf{w}_{12} + 0.5\mathbf{w}_{32} \quad \text{and also} \quad 0.117\mathbf{w}_{11} + 0.090\mathbf{w}_{22} - 0.014\mathbf{w}_{33}$$

It is therefore not strictly maintainable, but re-attainable after two steps. We can show that it is re-attainable after three steps as well:

$$\begin{pmatrix}0.1885\\0.5240\\0.2875\end{pmatrix} \begin{array}{l}\,0.1665+0.1763\\ \rightarrow 0.3662\\ \,0.2910\end{array} = \begin{pmatrix}0.3428\\0.3662\\0.2910\end{pmatrix} \begin{array}{l}\,0.1977+0.1146\\ \rightarrow 0.3493+0.0078\\ \,0.2606\end{array}$$

$$= \begin{pmatrix} 0.3125 \\ 0.4271 \\ 0.2606 \end{pmatrix} \rightarrow \begin{matrix} 0.1885 \\ 0.3645 + 0.1595 = \\ 0.2636 + 0.0239 \end{matrix} \begin{pmatrix} 0.1885 \\ 0.5240 \\ 0.2875 \end{pmatrix}$$

On the other hand, $\mathbf{w}_{23}$, which is not strictly maintainable, but re-attainable after two steps, is not re-attainable after three steps. This can be established as follows. We set up the tableau for formulae (6.4) to (6.6), viz.

$$(\mathbf{P}')^3\mathbf{n} + (\mathbf{P}')^2\mathbf{u}(0) + \mathbf{P}'\mathbf{u}(1) + \mathbf{u}(2) = \mathbf{n} \tag{8.5}$$

$$\mathbf{u}(0)'\mathbf{e} = \mathbf{n}'(\mathbf{I} - \mathbf{P})\mathbf{e} \quad \mathbf{u}(1)'\mathbf{e} = \mathbf{n}'\mathbf{P}(\mathbf{I} - \mathbf{P})\mathbf{e} + \mathbf{u}(0)'(\mathbf{I} - \mathbf{P})\mathbf{e} \tag{8.6}$$

For the transition matrix $\mathbf{P}_0$, this is

	n_1	n_2	n_3	$u_1(0)$	$u_2(0)$	$u_3(0)$	$u_1(1)$	$u_2(1)$	$u_3(1)$	
$u_1(2)$	−0.884	0.130	0.104	0.15	0.14	0.15	0.3	0.1	0.2	0
$u_2(2)$	0.244	−0.756	0.166	0.33	0.32	0.17	0.4	0.5	0.1	0
$u_3(2)$	0.190	0.222	−0.850	0.19	0.28	0.21	0.1	0.3	0.4	0
s_1	−0.200	−0.100	−0.300	1.00	1.00	1.00	0	0	0	0
s_2	−0.130	−0.160	−0.170	−0.20	−0.10	−0.30	1.0	1.0	1.0	0

After dropping the artificial variables s_1 and s_2, and inserting the components of $\mathbf{w}_{23}$, we reach

	$u_2(0)$	$u_3(0)$	$u_2(1)$	$u_3(1)$	
$u_1(2)$	−0.04	0.03	−0.2	0.1	−0.040
$u_2(2)$	−0.05	−0.12	0.1	−0.3	−0.002
$u_3(2)$	0.08	0.03	0.2	0.3	0.233
$u_1(0)$	1.00	1.00	0	0	0.213
$u_1(1)$	0.10	−0.10	1.0	1.0	0.202

After three more transformations we obtain the tableau

	$u_1(0)$	$u_1(2)$	$u_2(2)$	$u_3(1)$	
$u_2(0)$	3.0	14.286	28.561	−7.140	0.013
$u_3(0)$	−2.0	−14.286	−28.561	7.140	0.200
$u_1(1)$	0.4	7.142	4.284	0.429	−0.006
$u_2(1)$	−0.9	−10.000	−10.000	2.000	0.227
$u_3(2)$	0	1.286	0.571	0.257	0.181

The third row of this tableau cannot be satisfied by non-negative values. Hence no solution exists, and $\mathbf{w}_{23}$ is not re-attainable after three steps.

Another counter example to the assumption that if a structure is re-attainable after t steps, it is also re-attainable after $t + 1$ steps, is contained in Davies (1975).

Many of the results above are published in Vajda (1975).

8.11

Because the set $2s + 3t$ ($s, t = 0, 1, \ldots$) contains all integers above 1, structures which are re-attainable after two, and also after three steps, are re-attainable after any number of steps larger than one. Sums of these are, of course, also strictly maintainable.

8.12

J. Haigh (1976) has shown for upper triangular transition matrices of order two that every vector re-attainable after t steps is re-attainable after $t + 1$ steps. His proof is as follows.

Let the transition matrix be

$$\begin{pmatrix} a & b \\ 0 & c \end{pmatrix}$$

We distinguish the two cases: (i) $c \geqslant b$; and (ii) $c < b$.

(i) Denote $c - b$ by d. We shall prove, by induction, the lemma that the vector $\mathbf{y} = [y_1, 1 - y_1]$ is attainable from $\mathbf{x} = [x_1, 1 - x_1]$ in t steps if and only if

$$a^t x_1 \leqslant y_1 \leqslant (1 - c)(1 + d + \ldots + d^{t-1}) + d^t x_1 \tag{8.7}$$

This is true for $t = 1$, since

$$\begin{pmatrix} a & b \\ 0 & c \end{pmatrix}' \begin{pmatrix} x_1 \\ 1 - x_1 \end{pmatrix} = \begin{pmatrix} ax_1 \\ c - dx_1 \end{pmatrix}$$

and $\mathbf{y}$ is attainable in one step if

$$ax_1 \leqslant y_1 \quad \text{and} \quad c - dx_1 \leqslant 1 - y_1 \quad \text{or} \quad y_1 \leqslant (1 - c) + dx_1$$

$\mathbf{y}$ is re-attainable in $t + 1$ steps from $\mathbf{x}$, if it is attainable in one step from some $\mathbf{z} = [z_1, 1 - z_1]$ which is itself attainable after t steps from $\mathbf{x}$.

Assuming the lemma to be true for t, this means that

$$a^t x_1 \leqslant z_1 \leqslant (1 - c)(1 + d + \ldots + d^{t-1}) + d^t x_1 \tag{8.8}$$

and y_1 must satisfy

$$az_1 \leqslant y_1 \leqslant (1 - c) + dz_1$$

In view of inequality (8.8) this is equivalent to

$$\begin{aligned} a^{t+1} x_1 \leqslant y_1 &\leqslant (1 - c) + d(1 - c)(1 + d + \ldots + d^{t-1}) + d^{t+1} x_1 \\ &= (1 - c)(1 + d + \ldots + d^t) + d^{t+1} x_1 \end{aligned} \tag{8.9}$$

Hence the lemma is established.

By the lemma, x will be re-attainable after t steps if and only if inequality (8.8) holds for $\mathbf{z} = \mathbf{x}$. Now the first inequality is always satisfied, because $0 \leqslant a \leqslant 1$, being an element of a transition matrix.

The right-hand inequality is satisfied when $c = d = 1$. Otherwise it means

$$x_1 \leqslant (1-c)[(c-b)^t - 1]/(c-b-1) + (c-b)^t x_1$$

which can be written

$$x_1[1-(c-b)^t] \leqslant (1-c)[1-(c-b)^t]/(1-c+b) \tag{8.10}$$

Now $1 \geqslant c - b \geqslant 0$, hence from inequality (8.10)

$$x_1 \leqslant 1 - c + (c-b)x_1 \tag{8.11}$$

This is the condition for **x** to be strictly maintainable. Hence **x** is maintainable after t steps if and only if it is strictly maintainable. Trivially, it is then also maintainable after $t + 1$ steps.

(ii) In this case we shall prove, again by induction, the lemma that $\mathbf{y} = [y_1, 1 - y_1]$ is attainable in t steps from $[x_1, 1 - x_1]$ if and only if

$$a^t x_1 \leqslant y_1 \leqslant (1-c) + a^{t-1}(c-b)x_1 \tag{8.12}$$

This is true for $t = 1$, as in (i).

y is attainable after $t + 1$ steps from **x** if it is attainable in one step from some $\mathbf{z} = [z_1, 1 - z_1]$ which is itself attainable after t steps from **x**.

Assuming the lemma to be true for t, this means that

$$a^t x_1 \leqslant z_1 \leqslant (1-c) + a^{t-1}(c-b)z_1 \tag{8.13}$$

and y_1 must satisfy

$$az_1 \leqslant y_1 \leqslant (1-c) + (c-b)z_1$$

Now $c - b \leqslant 0$ and $z_1(c-b) \leqslant a^t(c-b)x_1$ and therefore this is equivalent to

$$a^{t+1}x_1 \leqslant y_1 \leqslant (1-c) + (c-b)z_1 \leqslant (1-c) + a^t(c-b)x_1 \tag{8.14}$$

Hence the lemma is established.

By the lemma, **x** will be re-attainable after t steps if and only if inequality (8.13) holds for $\mathbf{z} = \mathbf{x}$. The first inequality is redundant, **x** will be re-attainable after $t + 1$ steps if

$$x_1 \leqslant (1-c) + a^t(c-b)x_1 \tag{8.15}$$

But inequality (8.15) will hold if inequality (8.13) holds for $\mathbf{x} = \mathbf{z}$, because

$$a^t(c-b)x_1 - a^{t-1}(c-b)x_1 = a^{t-1}x_1(c-b)(a-1) \geqslant 0$$

in view of $a \leqslant 1, c < b$.

Hence, if **x** is re-attainable after t steps, then it is also re-attainable after $t + 1$ steps.

8.13

Example 27

We illustrate the result by two transition matrices

(a) $\begin{pmatrix} 0.3 & 0.2 \\ 0 & 0.6 \end{pmatrix}$

Vertices of the region re-attainable after t steps:

$t = 1$

$\mathbf{w}_1 = \begin{pmatrix} 0.67 \\ 0.33 \end{pmatrix}$ $\quad \mathbf{w}_2 = \begin{pmatrix} 0 \\ 1 \end{pmatrix}$

$t = 2$

$\mathbf{w}_{11} = \begin{pmatrix} 0.67 \\ 0.33 \end{pmatrix}$ $\quad \mathbf{w}_{21} = \begin{pmatrix} 0.46 \\ 0.54 \end{pmatrix}$ $\quad \mathbf{w}_{12} = \begin{pmatrix} 0.14 \\ 0.86 \end{pmatrix}$ $\quad \mathbf{w}_{22} = \begin{pmatrix} 0 \\ 1 \end{pmatrix}$

$t = 3$

$\mathbf{w}_{111} = \begin{pmatrix} 0.67 \\ 0.33 \end{pmatrix}$ $\quad \mathbf{w}_{211} = \begin{pmatrix} 0.59 \\ 0.41 \end{pmatrix}$ $\quad \mathbf{w}_{121} = \begin{pmatrix} 0.47 \\ 0.53 \end{pmatrix}$ $\quad \mathbf{w}_{112} = \begin{pmatrix} 0.18 \\ 0.82 \end{pmatrix}$ $\quad \mathbf{w}_{222} = \begin{pmatrix} 0 \\ 1 \end{pmatrix}$

(In this case all three regions are the same.)

(b) $\begin{pmatrix} 0.3 & 0.6 \\ 0 & 0.2 \end{pmatrix}$

$t = 1$

$\mathbf{w}_1 = \begin{pmatrix} 4/7 \\ 3/7 \end{pmatrix}$ $\quad \mathbf{w}_2 = \begin{pmatrix} 0 \\ 1 \end{pmatrix}$

$t = 2$

$\mathbf{w}_{21} = \begin{pmatrix} 0.71 \\ 0.29 \end{pmatrix}$ $\quad \mathbf{w}_{11} = \begin{pmatrix} 4/7 \\ 3/7 \end{pmatrix}$ $\quad \mathbf{w}_{12} = \begin{pmatrix} 0.21 \\ 0.79 \end{pmatrix}$ $\quad \mathbf{w}_{22} = \begin{pmatrix} 0 \\ 1 \end{pmatrix}$

$t = 3$

$\mathbf{w} = \begin{pmatrix} 0.74 \\ 0.26 \end{pmatrix}$ $\quad \mathbf{w}_{111} = \begin{pmatrix} 4/7 \\ 3/7 \end{pmatrix}$ $\quad \mathbf{w}_{211} = \begin{pmatrix} 0.5 \\ 0.5 \end{pmatrix}$ $\quad \mathbf{w}_{112} = \begin{pmatrix} 0.15 \\ 0.85 \end{pmatrix}$ $\quad \mathbf{w}_{222} = \begin{pmatrix} 0 \\ 1 \end{pmatrix}$

We see that the region for higher t contains strictly that for smaller t.

8.14

We turn now again to the concept of efficiency, and ask which structures, with given efficiency, can be strictly maintained. We shall find that the vertices of the set of such structures will be those of strictly maintainable structures, with such total which produces that required efficiency. In our example we require total efficiency 1900.

Example 28

Using the simplex method, we start from the tableau

	n_1	n_2	n_3	
u_1	−0.7	0.1	0.2	0
u_2	0.4	−0.5	0.1	0
u_3	0.1	0.3	−0.6	0
s	1.0	2.0	4.0	1900

where as in earlier examples, $\mathbf{f} = [1, 2, 4]$ and the transition matrix is $\mathbf{P}_0$. The final tableaus give the vertices of the set

n_1	354	128	127
n_2	327	422	173
n_3	223	232	357
u_1	170		
u_2		137	
u_3			149

The n_i components of these vertices in $(\mathbf{n}, \mathbf{u})$-space are strictly maintainable structures quoted, for instance, in Section 3.6, multiplied, respectively, by 904, 782, 657.

9

Partially Re-attainable Structures

9.1

In Chapter 3 we have considered the stationary population and in Chapter 4 the semi-stationary one. In the former case, recruitment was such that the total of each state was retained after one, and hence any number of steps. In the latter case, the totals of one or more subsets of states were retained after any number of steps, though the pattern of recruitment had to be adapted at each step. Apart from the stationary structures, semi-stationary ones do not exist for all transition matrices, whose rates are independent of the order of steps.

In Chapter 8 we have dealt with re-attainable structures, those which can be recovered after a given number of steps, with appropriate recruitment in between, to keep the total of the population constant. The structures which are re-attainable after one step were called strictly maintainable. They are identical with the stationary structures of Chapter 3.

In the present chapter we are interested in a generalization of the concept of semi-stationarity. We call a structure partially re-attainable after t steps for a given subset of states, if the total of these states can be made the same after t steps, as it was initially, keeping the in between grand-totals constant.

9.2

It might be informative to show here how the concept of partial re-attainment differs in essentials from that of semi-stationarity. To begin with, the latter assumes an unchanging pattern of recruitment throughout, while the former does not make such an assumption, but allows changing patterns of recruitment from step to step.

Also, partial re-attainability after one step does not ensure partial re-attainability after further numbers of steps. For instance, using again the transition matrix $\mathbf{P}_0$ which does not allow semi-stationary structures (apart from those which are stationary) we can preserve the first two strata of

$$\begin{pmatrix} 0 \\ 0.429 \\ 0.571 \end{pmatrix} \rightarrow \begin{matrix} 0.157 \\ 0.272 \\ 0.357 + 0.214 \end{matrix} = \begin{pmatrix} 0.157 \\ 0.272 \\ 0.571 \end{pmatrix}$$

for one year, but no longer, because

$$\begin{pmatrix}0.157\\0.272\\0.571\end{pmatrix} \quad \text{transforms, before recruitment, into} \quad \begin{pmatrix}0.188\\0.256\\0.326\end{pmatrix}$$

and 0.188 + 0.256 is already larger than 0.429.

On the other hand,

$$\begin{pmatrix}0.5\\0\\0.5\end{pmatrix} \to \begin{matrix}0.25\\0.25\\0.25+0.25\end{matrix} = \begin{pmatrix}0.25\\0.25\\0.50\end{pmatrix}$$

is partially re-attained after one step, and also after two steps:

$$\begin{pmatrix}0.25\\0.25\\0.50\end{pmatrix} \to \begin{matrix}\left.\begin{matrix}0.200\\0.275\end{matrix}\right\} + 0.025 = 0.50\\0.300 \quad +0.200\end{matrix}$$

though this time it is necessary to recruit into more states than one.

9.3

We define the region R_1 of partially maintainable structures, i.e. those partially re-attainable after one step, the region R_2 of structures partially re-attainable after two steps, and the region R_{12} of structures which are partially re-attainable after one, and then again after a further step, and we shall find them for the total of the first two states, and hence also for the third state on its own, for the transition matrix $\mathbf{P}_0$. For this purpose, we shall use the simplex technique.

Clearly, R_1 as well as R_2 contain R_{12}, and R_{12} contains all those re-attainable after two steps, and hence all strictly maintainable structures. R_{12}, and hence R_1 as well as R_2, will also contain all semi-stationary structures which might, however, only be stationary ones. This will certainly be so when we use the transition matrix $\mathbf{P}_0$.

We shall also add a few remarks concerning the region of structures with given total of the first two states combined.

9.4

Example 29

To determine the region R_1 of partially maintainable structures we start from the initial tableau in Section 8.2, but add the first two rows. We call the rate of recruitment into states 1 and 2 combined u_{12}, and have the tableau

	n_1	n_2	n_3	
u_{12}	−0.3	−0.4	0.3	0
u_3	0.1	0.3	−0.6	0
s	1.0	1.0	1.0	1.0

Eventually we obtain the following vertices in $(\mathbf{n}, \mathbf{u})$-space:

	$\mathbf{v}_1$	$\mathbf{v}_2$	$\mathbf{v}_3$	$\mathbf{v}_4$
n_1	0.5	0	0.857	0
n_2	0	0.429	0	0.667
n_3	0.5	0.571	0.143	0.333
u_{12}	0	0	0.214	0.167
u_3	0.25	0.214	0	0

The convex hull of these points contains, of course, all strictly maintainable structures. In fact, the segment $\mathbf{v}_3\mathbf{v}_4$ contains a side of that region:

$$[0.392, 0.362, 0.246] = 0.457\mathbf{v}_3 + 0.543\mathbf{v}_4$$

and

$$[0.162, 0.541, 0.297] = 0.189\mathbf{v}_3 + 0.811\mathbf{v}_4$$

and the third vertex of the strictly maintainable region lies on the segment $\mathbf{v}_1\mathbf{v}_2$, thus:

$$[0.193, 0.263, 0.544] = 0.386\mathbf{v}_1 + 0.614\mathbf{v}_2$$

We have used $\mathbf{v}_2$ as an example in Section 9.2, and the structure [0.25, 0.25, 0.50], also mentioned in that section, equals

$$0.3\mathbf{v}_1 + 0.583\mathbf{v}_2 + 0.117\mathbf{v}_3$$

9.5

To determine the region R_2 of structures partially re-attainable after two steps, we can start from tableau (T.2) in Section 8.7 and add up the first two rows, to obtain

	n_1	n_2	n_3	$u_1(0)$	$u_2(0)$	$u_3(0)$	
$u_{12}(1)$	−0.52	−0.54	0.32	0.7	0.6	0.3	0
$u_3(1)$	0.19	0.28	−0.79	0.1	0.3	0.4	0
s	−0.20	−0.10	−0.30	1.0	1.0	1.0	0
t	1.00	1.00	1.00	0	0	0	1.0

This leads, eventually, to the following vertices in $(\mathbf{n}, \mathbf{u}(0), \mathbf{u}(1))$-space:

n_1	0.783	0.737	0.713	0.582	0.556	0.471
n_2	0	0	0	0	0	0
n_3	0.217	0.263	0.287	0.418	0.444	0.529
$u_1(0)$	0.221	0	0	0.241	0	0
$u_2(0)$	0	0.226	0	0	0.244	0
$u_3(0)$	0	0	0.229	0	0	0.253
$u_{12}(1)$	0.183	0.163	0.210	0	0	0
$u_3(1)$	0	0	0	0.195	0.172	0.227
	*					*

n_1	0	0	0	0	0	0
n_2	0.723	0.693	0.676	0.530	0.510	0.446
n_3	0.277	0.307	0.324	0.470	0.490	0.554
$u_1(0)$	0.155	0	0	0.194	0	0
$u_2(0)$	0	0.162	0	0	0.198	0
$u_3(0)$	0	0	0.165	0	0	0.211
$u_{12}(1)$	0.193	0.178	0.162	0	0	0
$u_3(1)$	0	0	0	0.203	0.185	0.228
	*					*

Only one of $u_i(0)$ is positive in all these cases.

The vertices of the projection onto **n**-space are marked by asterisks.

The regions R_1 and R_2 overlap in parts. The strictly maintainable structure [0.193, 0.263, 0.544] is the intersection of the projection of $\mathbf{v}_1\mathbf{v}_2$ on R_1, and of the boundary of the projection of R_2 defined by the sixth and the twelfth columns above (both vertices).

9.6

We deal now with R_{12}. It differs from the region R_2 in that its structures preserve the total of a chosen subset of states after the first as well as after the second step. It contains precisely those structures of R_1 which can once more be partially maintained.

We start again from tableau (T.2), the initial tableau in Section 9.5, but remember that there the s row only ensures that the total of the whole structure is filled up to unity after the first step. This is not enough now. We require that the first and the second states be preserved after the first step already, not only after the second step.

In the present example, where there are only three states, this means that, also, the third state be filled up again to n_3.

The first requirement mentioned means

$$u_1(0) + u_2(0) + 0.7n_1 + 0.6n_2 + 0.3n_3 = n_1 + n_2$$

i.e.

$$-0.3n_1 - 0.4n_2 + 0.3n_3 + u_1(0) + u_2(0) = 0 \tag{9.1}$$

and the second means that

$$u_3(0) + 0.1n_1 + 0.3n_2 + 0.4n_3 = n_3$$

i.e.

$$0.1n_1 + 0.3n_2 - 0.6n_3 + u_3(0) = 0 \tag{9.2}$$

We substitute

$$u_3(0) = -0.1n_1 - 0.3n_2 + 0.6n_3 \tag{9.3}$$

in the tableau, add constraint (9.1) with an artificial variable, and constraint (9.2) using $u_3(0)$ as a basic variable. Thus we obtain

	n_1	n_2	n_3	$u_1(0)$	$u_2(0)$	
$u_{12}(1)$	−0.55	−0.63	0.50	0.7	0.6	0
$u_3(1)$	0.15	0.16	−0.55	0.1	0.3	0
$u_3(0)$	0.10	0.30	−0.60	0	0	0
s	−0.30	−0.40	0.30	1.0	1.0	0
t	1.00	1.00	1.00	0	0	1.0

After dropping s and t we get

	n_2	n_3	$u_2(0)$	
$u_{12}(1)$	−0.01	0.63	−0.1	0.34
$u_3(1)$	0.02	−0.76*	0.2	−0.18
$u_1(0)$	−0.10	0.60	1.0	0.30
$u_3(0)$	0.20	−0.70	0	−0.10
n_1	1.00	1.00	0	1.00

Now we have to use the dual simplex method (see Appendix II) using the indicated pivot, and eventually ten vertices emerge.

First, we quote three vertices:

	$\mathbf{w}_1$	$\mathbf{w}_2$	$\mathbf{w}_3$
n_1	0.392	0.162	0.193
n_2	0.362	0.541	0.263
n_3	0.246	0.297	0.544
$u_1(0)$	0.189	0	0
$u_2(0)$	0	0.176	0
$u_3(0)$	0	0	0.228
$u_{12}(1)$	0.189	0.176	0
$u_3(1)$	0	0	0.228

These correspond, of course, to the vertices of the strictly maintainable structures (Section 8.2). In $\mathbf{w}_1$, $u_{12}(1)$ can be interpreted as $u_1(1) = 0.189$, $u_2(1) = 0$, and in $\mathbf{w}_2$ as $u_1(1) = 0$, $u_2(1) = 0.176$, to get precisely the strictly maintainable structures.

Furthermore, we have the vertices

	$n_1 = 0$			
n_2	0.667	0.667	0.452	0.450
n_3	0.333	0.333	0.548	0.550
$u_1(0)$	0.167	0	0.017	0
$u_2(0)$	0	0.167	0	0.015
$u_3(0)$	0	0	0.193	0.195
$u_{12}(1)$	0.137	0.150	0	0
$u_3(1)$	0.060	0.027	0.227	0.226

and with

	$n_2 = 0$		
n_1	0.763	0.500	0.727
n_3	0.237	0.500	0.273
$u_1(0)$	0.157	0	0
$u_2(0)$	0	0	0.136
$u_3(0)$	0.066	0.250	0.091
$u_{12}(1)$	0.191	0.025	0.182
$u_3(1)$	0	0.200	0

We observe that any three of the parameters $u_1(0), \ldots, u_3(1)$ which are positive in the set with $n_1 = 0$ will not be all positive in the set with $n_2 = 0$, and vice versa.

9.7

Our example is somewhat special in that state 3 is to be preserved on its own. It follows that n_3 cannot possibly be zero. We leave the question of which of the observed other facts and relationships would appear in other examples as well unresolved for the time being. Also, we do not explore cases of more than two steps.

9.8

A question related to those considered above is the preservation of states with given totals.

Example 30

For instance, let us ask for all those structures of three states where the first two states total 0.700 together and which can be preserved after the first, and also after the second step, using the transitions matrix $\mathbf{P}_0$.

Since state 3 is to be preserved on its own, it is simplest to insist on $n_3 = 0.300$ in our initial tableau, or in any of those of a later stage, and to proceed from there.

Starting from the second tableau in Section 9.6, i.e. that obtained after having dropped the artificial variables, we have, when $n_3 = 0.300$

	n_2	$u_2(0)$	
$u_{12}(1)$	−0.01	−0.1	0.151
$u_3(1)$	0.02	0.2	0.048
$u_1(0)$	−0.10	1.0	0.120
$u_3(0)$	0.20	0	0.110
n_1	1.00	0	0.700

This is one vertex, indicating

$$\begin{pmatrix}0.700\\0\\0.300\end{pmatrix} \begin{matrix}0.270+0.120\\ \to 0.310\\ 0.190+0.110\end{matrix} = \begin{pmatrix}0.390\\0.310\\0.300\end{pmatrix} \begin{matrix}\left.\begin{matrix}0.208\\ \to 0.341\end{matrix}\right\} + 0.151\\ 0.252 \quad +0.048\end{matrix} \begin{matrix}\left.\right\} = \\ \end{matrix} \begin{pmatrix}0.700\\ \\0.300\end{pmatrix}$$

There are altogether four vertices, as follows:

n_1	0.700	0.700	0.150	0.150
n_2	0	0	0.550	0.550
n_3	0.300	0.300	0.300	0.300
$u_1(0)$	0.120	0	0.175	0
$u_2(0)$	0	0.120	0	0.175
$u_3(0)$	0.110	0.110	0	0
$u_{12}(1)$	0.151	0.163	0.157	0.174
$u_3(1)$	0.048	0.024	0.037	0.002

10

Stable Populations

10.1

We shall now deal with expanding or contracting structures, using methods analogous to those which we have used previously in Part II of this book.

For instance, let us determine the region of structures which can be stable for given α. We choose $\alpha = 0.2$, and use again the transition matrix $\mathbf{P}_0$. Also, we are looking for structures with total 1.

Example 31

We have to solve the system

$$(1+\alpha)n_j = p_{1j}n_1 + \ldots + p_{kj}n_k + u_j \quad (j = 1, \ldots, k) \tag{10.1}$$

$$n_1 + \ldots + n_k = 1$$

for non-negative $\mathbf{n}$ and $\mathbf{u}$.

The first simplex tableau is then

	n_1	n_2	n_3	
u_1	−0.9	0.1	0.2	0
u_2	0.4	−0.7	0.1	0
u_3	0.1	0.3	−0.8	0
s	1.0	1.0	1.0	1.0

This is analogous to the tableau in Section 8.2, to find strictly maintainable structures.

Eventually, we obtain the following vertices in $(\mathbf{n}, \mathbf{u})$-space:

n_1	0.505	0.124	0.165
n_2	0.314	0.626	0.186
n_3	0.181	0.250	0.649
u_1	0.388	0	0
u_2	0	0.364	0
u_3	0	0	0.447

Again, for each of these vertices only one single u_i differs from zero.

The vertices are the structures $\mathbf{S}_i^{(0.2)}$ derived in Section 5.11 by another method, multiplied respectively by

1/2585 1/2755 1/2241

10.2

The search for a structure with total 1 from which an expanded (or contracted) structure can be obtained may be viewed as a problem of parametric linear programming (see Appendix II).

Example 32

For instance, to find sources from which $(1+\alpha)[0.37, 0.37, 0.26]$ can be obtained using $\mathbf{P}_0$, we start from the tableau

	n_1	n_2	n_3	
u_1	0.3	0.1	0.2	$(1+\alpha)(0.37)$
u_2	0.4	0.5	0.1	$(1+\alpha)(0.37)$
u_3	0.1	0.3	0.4	$(1+\alpha)(0.26)$
s	1.0	1.0	1.0	1.0

We have shown in Appendix II how to find the vertices in $(\mathbf{n}, \mathbf{u})$-space, depending on various ranges of α, they are as follows:

n_1	1.0	$0.9+1.23\alpha$	$1.3-3.7\alpha$	0
n_2	0	0	$-0.3+3.7\alpha$	1.0
n_3	0	$0.1-1.23\alpha$	0	0
u_1	$0.07+0.37\alpha$	$0.08+0.247\alpha$	$0.01+1.11\alpha$	$0.27+0.37\alpha$
u_2	$-0.03+0.37\alpha$	0	0	$-0.13+0.37\alpha$
u_3	$0.16+0.26\alpha$	$0.13+0.63\alpha$	$0.22-0.48\alpha$	$-0.04+0.26\alpha$
Valid for α in	[0.081, . . .)	[−0.206, 0.081]	[0.081, 0.351]	[0.351, . . .)

1	$0.467-0.867\alpha$	0	$0.322-1.567\alpha$	0	0
2	0	0	$0.433+2.1\alpha$	$0.675-0.92\alpha$	$1.4-2.6\alpha$
3	$0.533+0.867\alpha$	1	$0.245-0.533\alpha$	$0.325-0.92\alpha$	$-0.4+2.6\alpha$
	$0.123+0.457\alpha$	$0.17+0.37\alpha$	$0.181+0.737\alpha$	$0.2375+0.457\alpha$	$0.31+0.11\alpha$
2	$0.13+0.63\alpha$	$0.27+0.37\alpha$	0	0	$-2.9+1.41\alpha$
	0	$-0.14+0.26\alpha$	0	$-0.0725+0.35\alpha$	0
alid for in	[−0.206, 0.539]	[0.539, . . .]	[−0.206, 0.204]	[0.204, 0.351]	[0.204, 0.539]

If $\alpha < -0.206$, then there is no structure with total 1 from which $(1+\alpha)[0.37, 0.37, 0.26]$ can be obtained in one step, or any structure with total $1/(1+\alpha)$ from which [0.37, 0.37, 0.26] could be obtained in one step.

10.3

We might be interested in re-attaining the present structure after t steps, multiplied by $(1+\alpha)^t$, while at intermediate stages we merely insist on the original total to be changed into $(1+\alpha)^s$ times after the sth step.

To find the initial structures for which this is possible, we have to solve

$$\mathbf{n}(t) = (\mathbf{P}')^t\mathbf{n} + (\mathbf{P}')^{t-1}\mathbf{u}(0) + \ldots + \mathbf{u}(t-1) \tag{10.2}$$

and

$$\mathbf{u}(s)'\mathbf{e} = \mathbf{n}(s)'(\mathbf{I}-\mathbf{P})\mathbf{e} + \alpha\mathbf{n}(s)'\mathbf{e} \quad \text{for } s = 0, \ldots, t-2 \tag{10.3}$$

(Such an equation for $s = t-1$ would be redundant.)

We shall also normalize by $\mathbf{n}'\mathbf{e} = 1$.

Our task can be simplified by the following argument. If the new entrants join the same state at each step, then we repeat at each step the same procedure, enlarging after each step by $(1+\alpha)$. Thus all vertices of the region we are looking for, with the same state entered at each step, can be found by taking $t = 1$. Only for the other vertices are we forced to use more extensive tableaus.

For $\alpha = 0.2$, and $\mathbf{P}_0$, we find the vertices given in Section 10.1. We observe that, in fact, in this case not only the total membership, but each state expands at the same rate, viz. $(1+\alpha)$.

10.4

For the other vertices, we have to use the tableau appropriate to the chosen value of t. For instance, for $t = 2$, we have the following example.

Example 33

	n_1	n_2	n_3	$u_1(0)$	$u_2(0)$	$u_3(0)$	
$u_1(1)$	0.15	0.14	0.15	0.3	0.1	0.2	$1.44n_1$
$u_2(1)$	0.33	0.32	0.17	0.4	0.5	0.1	$1.44n_2$
$u_3(1)$	0.19	0.28	0.21	0.1	0.3	0.4	$1.44n_3$
s	−0.20	−0.10	−0.30	1.0	1.0	1.0	$0.2n_1 + 0.2n_2 + 0.2n_3$
t	1.00	1.00	1.00	0	0	0	1.00

i.e., combining the various positions of n_i

	n_1	n_2	n_3	$u_1(0)$	$u_2(0)$	$u_3(0)$	
$u_1(1)$	−1.29	0.14	0.15	0.3	0.1	0.2	0
$u_2(1)$	0.33	1.12	0.17	0.4	0.5	0.1	0
$u_3(1)$	0.19	0.28	−1.23	0.1	0.3	0.4	0
s	−0.40	−0.30	−0.50	1.0	1.0	1.0	0
t	1.00	1.00	1.00	0	0	0	1.0

where s and t are artificial variables.

In this manner we obtain, for instance, the vertex

$$\mathbf{n} = [0.175, 0.626, 0.199] \qquad u_1(0) = 0.358 \qquad u_2(1) = 0.469$$

thus:

$$\underset{1.000}{\begin{pmatrix} 0.175 \\ 0.626 \\ 0.199 \end{pmatrix}} \rightarrow \begin{matrix} 0.155 + 0.358 \\ 0.402 \\ 0.285 \end{matrix} = \underset{1.200}{\begin{pmatrix} 0.513 \\ 0.402 \\ 0.285 \end{pmatrix}} \rightarrow \begin{matrix} 0.251 \\ 0.435 + 0.469 = \\ 0.285 \end{matrix} \underset{1.440}{\begin{pmatrix} 0.251 \\ 0.904 \\ 0.285 \end{pmatrix}}$$

From this, we can deduce the structure with entries first into state 2, and at the next step into state 1. If we normalize, for convenience at a total of 1200, we have

$$\underset{1.200}{\begin{pmatrix} 0.513 \\ 0.402 \\ 0.285 \end{pmatrix}} \rightarrow \begin{matrix} 0.251 \\ 0.435 + 0.469 = \\ 0.285 \end{matrix} \underset{1.440}{\begin{pmatrix} 0.251 \\ 0.904 \\ 0.285 \end{pmatrix}} \rightarrow \begin{matrix} 0.223 + 0.517 \\ 0.579 \\ 0.409 \end{matrix} = \underset{1.728}{\begin{pmatrix} 0.740 \\ 0.589 \\ 0.409 \end{pmatrix}}$$

The last input, 0.517, is of course $0.358\ (1 + \alpha)^2$.

The same considerations apply to any pair of states with alternative inputs.

11

Optimization

11.1

We have seen that in many cases a desired result – a structure to be obtained from a given one – can be attained in a number of ways. For instance, in Section 7.12 we have exhibited a number of two-step paths from [0.32, 0.43, 0.25] to [0.37, 0.37, 0.25], while in Section 8.8 we found various ways of re-attaining [0.181, 0.505, 0.314], after two steps.

This suggests the question of whether some way of achieving the final result may be preferable to others.

We shall now take into account the cost of supporting a state, and the cost of recruiting. These costs will, in general, depend on the state (e.g. salary scales), and they may differ from step to step.

In the following sections we deal, first, with a case of 'weak maintainability', i.e. we wish merely to maintain the total membership irrespective of their distribution through the states, through four steps.

Then, we shall deal with a case of re-attainability after four steps.

In each case the initial structure will be [0.181, 0.505, 0.314], and we shall use the transition matrix $\mathbf{P}_0$.

11.2

Example 34

The costs we shall use are, in some arbitrary monetary unit, as follows:

$n_i(1)$ all i	$n_i(2)$ all i	$n_i(3)$ all i	$n_i(4)$ all i		
20	25	30	35		
$u_1(0)$	$u_2(0)$	$u_3(0)$	$u_1(1)$	$u_2(1)$	$u_3(1)$
3	2	2	4	3	5
$u_1(2)$	$u_2(2)$	$u_3(2)$	$u_1(3)$	$u_2(3)$	$u_3(3)$
1	3	6	2	1	4

Since $\mathbf{n}(0)$ is given, the cost of supporting it, or of obtaining it initially, can be ignored for the purpose of optimization.

Using

$$\mathbf{n}(t) = (\mathbf{P}')^t\mathbf{n}(0) + (\mathbf{P}')^{t-1}\mathbf{u}(0) + \ldots + \mathbf{P}'\mathbf{u}(t-2) + \mathbf{u}(t-1)$$

(i.e. equation (6.4)) we can express the costs of $\mathbf{n}(t)$ as costs of $\mathbf{u}(0), \ldots, \mathbf{u}(t-1)$ and use only these for our computations.

We obtain, ignoring $(\mathbf{P}')^t\mathbf{n}(0)$, the following costs:

$u_1(0)$	$u_2(0)$	$u_3(0)$	$u_1(1)$	$u_2(1)$	$u_3(1)$
3	2	2	4	3	5
20	20	20	0	0	0
20	22.5	17.5	25	25	25
20.1	22.2	15.9	24	27	21
19.25	20.86	14.70	23.45	25.90	18.55
82.35	87.56	70.10	76.45	80.90	69.55

$u_1(2)$	$u_2(2)$	$u_3(2)$	$u_1(3)$	$u_2(3)$	$u_3(3)$
1	3	6	2	1	4
0	0	0	0	0	0
0	0	0	0	0	0
30	30	30	0	0	0
28	31.5	24.5	35	35	35
59.0	64.5	60.5	37	36	39

In these twelve columns, the first entry is the cost of $u_i(t)$, the second is the result of $20[\mathbf{P}'\mathbf{n}(0) + \mathbf{u}(0)]$, the third of

$$25[(\mathbf{P}')^2\mathbf{n}(0) + \mathbf{P}'\mathbf{u}(0) + \mathbf{u}(1)]$$

the fourth of

$$30[(\mathbf{P}')^3\mathbf{n}(0) + (\mathbf{P}')^2\mathbf{u}(0) + \mathbf{P}'\mathbf{u}(1) + \mathbf{u}(2)]$$

and the fifth of

$$35[(\mathbf{P}')^4\mathbf{n}(0) + (\mathbf{P}')^3\mathbf{u}(0) + (\mathbf{P}')^2\mathbf{u}(1) + \mathbf{P}'\mathbf{u}(2) + \mathbf{u}(3)]$$

11.3

We want to minimize

$$\begin{aligned} &82.35u_1(0) + 87.56u_2(0) + 70.10u_3(0) + 76.45u_1(1) + 80.90u_2(1) \\ &\quad + 69.55u_3(1) + 59.0u_1(2) + 64.5u_2(2) + 60.5u_3(2) + 37u_1(3) \\ &\quad + 36u_2(3) + 39u_3(3) \end{aligned} \tag{11.1}$$

The constraints are those of equation (6.6), in our present case

$$u_1(0) + u_2(0) + u_3(0) = 0.1809$$

$$-0.2u_1(0) - 0.1u_2(0) - 0.3u_3(0) + u_1(1) + u_2(1) + u_3(1) = 0.15771$$

$$-0.13u_1(0) - 0.16u_2(0) - 0.17u_3(0) - 0.2u_1(1) - 0.1u_2(1) - 0.3u_3(1) + u_1(2) + u_2(2) + u_3(2) = 0.128980$$

$$-0.120u_1(0) - 0.144u_2(0) - 0.110u_3(0) - 0.13u_1(1) - 0.16u_2(1) - 0.17u_3(1) - 0.2u_1(2) - 0.1u_2(2) - 0.3u_3(2) + u_1(3) + u_2(3) + u_3(3) = 0.1038912 \quad (11.2)$$

11.4

The set (11.2) has a very special form. Each successive equation introduces a new set of three variables, and those variables which have appeared in an earlier equation have negative coefficients. We make use of this pattern by formulating the dual of the set. (For the definition of 'dual', see Appendix II.) It is as follows: Maximize

$$0.1809y_1 + 0.15771y_2 + 0.128980y_3 + 0.1038912y_4 \quad (11.3)$$

subject to

$$
\begin{array}{ll}
\text{(i)} & y_1 - 0.2y_2 - 0.13y_3 - 0.120y_4 \leqslant 82.35 \\
\text{(ii)} & y_1 - 0.1y_2 - 0.16y_3 - 0.144y_4 \leqslant 87.56 \\
\text{(iii)} & y_1 - 0.3y_2 - 0.17y_3 - 0.110y_4 \leqslant 70.10 \\
\text{(iv)} & y_2 - 0.2\,y_3 - 0.13\,y_4 \leqslant 76.45 \\
\text{(v)} & y_2 - 0.1\,y_3 - 0.16\,y_4 \leqslant 80.90 \\
\text{(vi)} & y_2 - 0.3\,y_3 - 0.17\,y_4 \leqslant 69.55 \\
\text{(vii)} & y_3 - 0.2\,y_4 \leqslant 59.0 \\
\text{(viii)} & y_3 - 0.1\,y_4 \leqslant 64.5 \\
\text{(ix)} & y_3 - 0.3\,y_4 \leqslant 60.5 \\
\text{(x)} & y_4 \leqslant 37 \\
\text{(xi)} & y_4 \leqslant 36 \\
\text{(xii)} & y_4 \leqslant 39
\end{array}
\quad (11.4)
$$

The set (11.4) exhibits special features which are consequences of those of (11.2), and we shall now take advantage of them.

The last three inequalities show that y_4 cannot exceed 36. Let us then, tentatively, make $y_4 = 36$.

Entering this value for y_4 in the inequalities (vii), (viii), (ix), we have

$$y_3 \leqslant 59.0 + 7.2 = 66.2$$

$$y_3 \leqslant 64.5 + 3.6 = 68.1$$

$$y_3 \leqslant 60.5 + 10.8 = 71.3$$

So y_3 cannot exceed 66.2, and we try $y_3 = 66.2$.

Proceeding in this same way, entering the values of y_3 and y_4 which we have chosen in (iv), (v) and (vi), we have

$$y_2 \leqslant \min (94.37, 93.28, 95.17)$$

so let $y_2 = 93.28$, and then

$$y_1 \leqslant \min (113.922, 112.664, 113.298)$$

hence we make $y_1 = 112.664$.

We do not know, as yet, if these values of the y_j are optimal, but we can test this as follows.

The assumed values of the y_j turn the following inequalities into equations: (xi), (vii), (v), and (ii). They correspond to the original variables $u_2(3)$, $u_1(2)$, $u_2(1)$, $u_2(0)$, and we know from duality theory that these and only these will be positive (and not zero) if our guess of the values of the y_j was correct. Thus the set (11.2) reduces to the triangular set

$$\begin{aligned} u_2(0) \qquad\qquad\qquad\qquad\qquad\qquad &= 0.1809 \\ -0.1u_2(0) + \quad u_2(1) \qquad\qquad\qquad\qquad &= 0.15771 \\ -0.16u_2(0) - \; 0.1u_2(1) + \quad u_1(2) \qquad\qquad &= 0.128980 \\ -0.144u_2(0) - 0.16u_2(1) - 0.2u_1(2) + u_2(3) &= 0.1038912 \end{aligned} \tag{11.5}$$

from which

$$u_2(0) = 0.1809 \qquad u_2(1) = 0.17580$$

$$u_1(2) = 0.175504 \qquad u_2(3) = 0.1931696$$

while all the other u_i are zero.

All these values are non-negative, and hence they are optimal in the set (11.2). In fact, we could be certain that they would turn out to be non-negative, because each equation in (11.5) contains just one new variable with positive coefficient (viz. 1), while the coefficients of the others are all negative.

11.5

Our problem is now solved. As a check, we find that the two objective functions, (11.1) and (11.3), have the same value, 47.3706656. If we add to this

$$(20\mathbf{P}' + 25\mathbf{P}'^2 + 30\mathbf{P}'^3 + 35\mathbf{P}'^4)[0.181, 0.505, 0.314] = 63.8872080$$

which we had originally ignored, then we have the minimal cost of 111.2578736.

The cheapest development of the structures through four steps is as follows:

$$\begin{pmatrix}0.181\\0.505\\0.314\end{pmatrix} \to \begin{matrix}0.1676\\0.3563+0.1809\\0.2952\end{matrix} = \begin{pmatrix}0.1676\\0.5372\\0.2952\end{pmatrix} \to \begin{matrix}0.16304\\0.36516+0.17580\\0.29600\end{matrix}$$

$$= \begin{pmatrix}0.16304\\0.54096\\0.29600\end{pmatrix} \to \begin{matrix}0.162208+0.175504\\0.365296\\0.296992\end{matrix} = \begin{pmatrix}0.337712\\0.365296\\0.296992\end{pmatrix}$$

$$\to \begin{matrix}0.1972416\\0.3472320+0.1931696\\0.2621568\end{matrix} = \begin{pmatrix}0.1972416\\0.5406016\\0.2621568\end{pmatrix}$$

The cost of this is

$$2(0.1809)+3(0.17580)+1(0.175504)+1(0.1931696)$$
$$+20+25+30+35 = 111.2578736$$

as above.

Grinold and Stanford (1974) solve a general system of weak maintainability by an application of dynamic programming, which is equivalent to our method. The latter was first used in Vajda (1976).

11.6

We have just found the cheapest way of maintaining the total membership through four years, starting from [0.181, 0.505, 0.314].

We know that there are other ways of maintaining the total membership. For instance, we could make use of the fact that the initial structure is re-attainable after two steps, with $u_3(0) = 0.181$ and $u_2(1) = 0.212$ (see Section 8.8). We could repeat these recruitment rates, $u_3(2) = 0.181, u_2(3) = 0.212$, and this would, of course, also maintain the total membership throughout. It would be more expensive, though:

$$70.10(0.181)+80.90(0.212)+60.50(0.181)+36(0.212) = 48.4214$$

which is more than 47.3706656.

11.7

We deal now with a somewhat different problem, by stipulating that the initial structure (the same as above) should be re-attained after four steps, while at intermediate steps we merely require recruitment to keep the total membership constant.

We know this to be possible, because we know that the initial structure can be re-attained after two steps, with the total membership retained after one step. We are looking for the cheapest way of obtaining this, but we cannot expect that re-attainment after two steps, though possible, will in fact be part of the optimal path.

11.8

Example 35

Let the costs be the same as in Section 11.2 in the previous example. Our function to be minimized is again that in (11.1).

The first three constraints are those of the set (11.2), but instead of the fourth, we must introduce the requirement that $n(4) = n(0)$. This means, in view of equation (6.4)

$$[\mathbf{I} - (\mathbf{P}')^4]\,\mathbf{n}(0) = (\mathbf{P}')^3\mathbf{u}(0) + (\mathbf{P}')^2\mathbf{u}(1) + \mathbf{P}'\mathbf{u}(2) + \mathbf{u}(3)$$

i.e. when the transition matrix is $\mathbf{P_0}$

$$\begin{aligned}
&0.116u_1(0) + 0.130u_2(0) + 0.104u_3(0) + 0.15u_1(1) + 0.14u_2(1) + 0.15u_3(1)\\
&\qquad + 0.3u_1(2) + 0.1u_2(2) + 0.2u_3(2) + u_1(3) = 0.0845386\\
&0.244u_1(2) + 0.244u_2(0) + 0.166u_3(0) + 0.33u_1(1) + 0.32u_2(1) + 0.17u_3(1)\\
&\qquad + 0.4u_1(2) + 0.5u_2(2) + 0.1u_3(2) + u_2(3) = 0.3281652\\
&0.190u_1(0) + 0.222u_2(0) + 0.150u_3(0) + 0.19u_1(1) + 0.28u_2(1) + 0.21u_3(1)\\
&\qquad + 0.1u_1(2) + 0.3u_2(2) + 0.4u_3(2) + u_3(3) = 0.1587774 \qquad (11.6)
\end{aligned}$$

11.9

This time we cannot use the method of our previous example, because in the last three constraints all coefficients on the left-hand sides are positive, and the argument of Section 11.4 does not apply.

If we did try the same procedure, we would obtain, from the dual set, the upper bounds

$$y_1 = 80.1662 \quad y_2 = 58.886 \quad y_3 = 56.06$$

$$y_4 = 37 \quad y_5 = 36 \quad y_6 = 39$$

However, these are not optimal values, because they would lead to

$$u_2(0) = 0.1809 \quad u_2(1) = 0.17580 \quad u_1(2) = 0.175504$$

as in Section 11.4, when we solved the earlier problem, but then to

$$u_1(3) = -0.0162416 \quad u_2(3) = 0.157568 \quad u_3(3) = 0.0518432$$

and one of these is negative.

We must therefore try another method for minimizing (11.1), subject to the constraints (11.6). The simplex method produces the final answer

$$u_2(0) = 0.1809 \quad u_2(1) = 0.17580 \quad u_1(2) = 0.094296$$

$$u_2(2) = 0.081208 \quad u_2(3) = 0.1494472 \quad u_3(3) = 0.0356016$$

all other $u_i(t) = 0$, and the minimum equal to 47.6317656.

This is larger than the optimal value of the previous problem, quoted in Section 11.5. This must be so, because we have introduced a more restrictive constraint. On the other hand, it is less, and hence better, than 48.4214, which we would obtain by the procedure of Section 11.6, which would also lead back to the initial structure.

11.10

If we add again 63.8872080 to the minimal value obtained, then we obtain 111.5189736 as the cheapest cost for the present problem. The optimal path to re-attainment after four steps, with retaining totals at each intermediate step is

$$\begin{pmatrix}0.181\\0.505\\0.314\end{pmatrix} \to \begin{matrix}0.1676\\0.3563+0.1809=\\0.2952\end{matrix} \begin{pmatrix}0.1676\\0.5372\\0.2952\end{pmatrix} \to \begin{matrix}0.16304\\0.36515+0.17580\\0.29600\end{matrix}$$

$$= \begin{pmatrix}0.16304\\0.54096\\0.29600\end{pmatrix} \to \begin{matrix}0.162208+0.094296\\0.365296+0.081208=\\0.296992\end{matrix} \begin{pmatrix}0.256504\\0.446504\\0.296992\end{pmatrix}$$

$$\to \begin{matrix}0.1810700\\0.3555528+0.1494472=\\0.2783984+0.0356016\end{matrix} \begin{pmatrix}0.181\\0.505\\0.314\end{pmatrix}$$

Its cost is

$$2(0.1809) + 3(0.17580) + 1(0.094296) + 3(0.081208) + 1(0.1494472) + 4(0.0356016) + 20 + 25 + 30 + 35 = 111.5189736$$

as above.

11.11

In Section 11.2 we concentrated the costs on the $u_i(t)$, incorporating those of the $n(t)$. Alternatively, we could base all calculations on the $n_i(t)$, and substitute

$$n_j(t+1) - \sum_{i=1}^{k} p_{ij} n_i(t)$$

for u_j. Translating the costs of the u_j into linear combinations of those of the $n_j(t)$, we obtain the following costs in our examples:

$n_1(0)$	$n_2(0)$	$n_3(0)$	$n_1(1)$	$n_2(1)$	$n_3(1)$
			20	20	20
−0.9	−0.3	−0.6	3	2	2
−0.8	−1.0	−0.2	−1.2	−0.4	−0.8
−0.2	−0.6	−0.8	−1.2	−1.5	−0.3
			−0.5	−1.5	−2.0
−1.9	−1.9	−1.6	20.1	18.6	18.9

$n_1(2)$	$n_2(2)$	$n_3(2)$	$n_1(3)$	$n_2(3)$	$n_3(3)$
25	25	25	30	30	30
4	3	5	1	3	6
−0.3	−0.1	−0.2	−0.6	−0.2	−0.4
−1.2	−1.5	−0.3	−0.4	−0.5	−0.1
−0.6	−1.8	−2.4	−0.4	−1.2	−1.6
26.9	24.6	27.1	29.6	31.1	33.9

$n_1(4)$	$n_2(4)$	$n_3(4)$
35	35	35
2	1	4
37	36	39

We have to minmize

$$-1.9n_1(0) - 1.9n_2(0) - 1.6n_3(0) + 20.1n_1(1) + 18.6n_2(1) + 18.9n_3(1) + 26.9n_1(2) + 24.6n_2(2) + 27.1n_3(2) + 29.6n_1(3) + 31.1n_2(3) + 33.9n_3(3) + 37n_1(4) + 36n_2(4) + 39n_3(4)$$

subject to the constraints

$$\mathbf{n}(t+1) - \mathbf{P}_0'\mathbf{n}(t) \geqslant 0$$

with given $\mathbf{n}(0)$.

If we substitute in the objective function the values $n_i(t)$ found in Section 11.5, viz.

$$\mathbf{n}(0) = [0.181, 0.505, 0.314] \qquad \mathbf{n}(1) = [0.1676, 0.5372, 0.2952]$$

and so on, then we obtain again the value 111.2578736, as we must.

If we substitute those from Section 11.00 (they differ from those in Section 11.5 in that n_3 and n_4 are different), then we obtain once more 111.5189736.

11.12

In our examples above costs were assumed which changed with time. If they are independent of time, then we can make some statements about optimizing with an infinite horizon.

In such a case we must decide which function of the successive structures we wish to minimize. Two possibilities suggest themselves: the objective function may be either

$$\text{(a)} \qquad \lim_{T\to\infty} T^{-1} \sum_{t=0}^{T-1} \mathbf{c}'\mathbf{n}(t)$$

where $\mathbf{c} = [c_1, \ldots, c_k]$ is the cost vector of $\mathbf{n}(t)$. This cost vector is assumed to be independent of time. Or

(b) $\sum_{t=0}^{\infty} v^t \mathbf{c}'\mathbf{n}(t)$

where $v < 1$ is a discounting factor.

We consider first (a).

Denote $T^{-1}\sum_{t=0}^{T-1}\mathbf{n}(t)$ by $\mathbf{y}(T)$. Since $\mathbf{n}(t) \geqslant \mathbf{P}'\mathbf{n}(t-1)$, we have

$$\mathbf{y}(T) \geqslant T^{-1}\sum_{t=1}^{T-1}\mathbf{P}'\mathbf{n}(t-1) = \mathbf{P}'\mathbf{y}(T) - T^{-1}\mathbf{P}'\mathbf{n}(T-1) \tag{11.7}$$

and, with $T \to \infty$ and $\mathbf{y} = \lim_{T\to\infty}\mathbf{y}(T)$,

$$\mathbf{y} \geqslant \mathbf{P}'\mathbf{y} \tag{11.8}$$

It is also easily seen that $\mathbf{y}'\mathbf{e} = 1$ if $\mathbf{n}'(t)\mathbf{e} = 1$ for all t. Hence if we minimize $\mathbf{c}'\mathbf{y}$ subject to

$$\mathbf{y} \geqslant \mathbf{P}'\mathbf{y} \quad \mathbf{y}'\mathbf{e} = 1 \tag{11.9}$$

then the resulting $\mathbf{c}'\mathbf{y}$ will be a lower limit of the

$$\text{minimum of } \lim_{T\to\infty} T^{-1}\sum_{t=0}^{T-1}\mathbf{c}'\mathbf{n}(t) \tag{11.10}$$

where the $\mathbf{n}(t)$ are subject to

$$\mathbf{n}(t) \geqslant \mathbf{P}'\mathbf{n}(t-1) \quad \mathbf{n}'(t)\mathbf{e} = 1 \tag{11.11}$$

11.13

It remains for us to investigate if this lower limit can be obtained by appropriate $n(t)$, $t = 0, 1, \ldots$.

Now the constraints (11.9) are those of obtaining the set of strictly maintainable structures, and the minimum of $\mathbf{c}'\mathbf{y}$ will be obtained at a vertex of the set. We know that such a vertex indicates a structure which requires recruitment into one single state only. Let this be the state i_0.

If we start from any initial structure, and recruit at each subsequent step the necessary numbers into state i_0, then we approach asymptotically the stationary state given by the solution of $\mathbf{y}$ above, and the limiting value of the average sums of $\mathbf{n}(t)$, multiplied by the costs, will be $\mathbf{c}'\mathbf{y}$. Thus the lower limit can be obtained.

11.14

The formulation of this problem with infinite horizon is due to Grinold and Stanford (1974), though they deal with it by a slightly different argument.

They deal also with the case when it is not the total membership, but rather the total efficiency which needs preserving. We know (Section 5.25) that the structures will again converge to a stationary one. Therefore our argument above can again be applied, except for one point to be remembered: it might not always be possible to supply the required efficiency by non-negative recruiting. For instance, it will be impossible if we start from, or if we reach on the way, a structure not in the set of those whose efficiency can be maintained for one step (see Section 7.21). In such a case the minimum of $\mathbf{c}'\mathbf{y}$, subject to the constraints (11.9) will merely be a lower bound.

11.15

Grinold and Stanford (1974) consider also the case of further conditions being imposed, and give necessary and sufficient conditions for such constraints remaining satisfied by all subsequent structures. Moreover, in their paper a transient finite horizon is joined to a stationary infinite problem. We do not consider such situations here.

11.16

We deal briefly with case (b) above, in Section 11.12. Define $\mathbf{z} = \Sigma_{t=0}^{\infty} v^t \mathbf{n}(t)$, so that the objective function to be minimized is $\mathbf{c}'\mathbf{z}$. The constraints can again be written in terms of $\mathbf{z}$, and this leads to a lower bound of the value of $\mathbf{c}'\mathbf{z}$. Grinold and Stanford (1974), and also Grinold (1976) deal with this case in some detail.

11.17

We have seen that it is not always possible to obtain a desired structure from a given one in a given number of steps. In such a case one might have to accept deviations from the required result, and decide on some priorities, taking into account more or less adverse effects of discrepancies, and the cost of recruitment and of the support of states. Even if the required result could be achieved with (necessarily non-negative) recruitment, we might still decide to accept discrepancies, in order to keep within a given budget allowance.

In the literature of this subject, this approach has been described as 'goal programming'.

11.18

Example 36

In the context considered, discrepancies consist of overmanning or undermanning of states. For illustration, consider the following penalties due to these possibilities:

Overmanning in state	1	2	3
penalty per unit	2	3	8
undermanning in state	1	2	3
penalty per unit	5	4	6

Also, let the cost of recruiting into

state	1	2	3
be per unit	6	3	2

let the budget ceiling be B, relevant to the cost of recruiting, and assume that we wish to reach in one step the structure [0.37, 0.37, 0.26] from the structure [0.32, 0.43, 0.25].

We know that this aim cannot be achieved (see equation (7.3)), and that therefore some penalties will have to be incurred.

In linear programming terms, we have the constraints (using again $\mathbf{P}_0$)

$$u_1 + 0.3(0.32) + 0.1(0.43) + 0.2(0.25) + g_1 - f_1 = 0.37$$

$$u_2 + 0.4(0.32) + 0.5(0.43) + 0.1(0.25) + g_2 - f_2 = 0.37$$

$$u_3 + 0.1(0.32) + 0.3(0.43) + 0.4(0.25) + g_3 - f_3 = 0.26$$

$$s + 6u_1 + 3u_2 + 2u_3 = B$$

(where s is the amount by which the cost of recruitment remains below the budget ceiling) and we wish to minimize

$$2f_1 + 5g_1 + 3f_2 + 4g_2 + 8f_3 + 6g_3$$

The cost of supporting the states is here irrelevant for optimization, because we have decided which states we want to have.

Transferring all numerical terms to the right-hand side, we have in tableau form

	(2) f_1	(3) f_2	(6) g_3	u_1	u_2	u_3	
(5) g_1	−1			1			0.181
(4) g_2		−1			1		0.002
(8) f_3			−1			−1	0.001
s				6	3	2	B
	−7	−7	−14	5	4	−8	0.921

(Regarding the numbers in brackets, and the construction of the last row, see Appendix II, Section II.4.)

The continuation depends on the size of B. When $B \leqslant 0.006$, then the final tableau is

	(2) f_1	(3) f_2	(6) g_3	u_1	s	u_3	
(5) g_1	−1			1			0.181
(4) g_2		−1		−2*	−1/3	−2/3	$0.002 - B/3$
(8) f_3			−1			−1	−0.001
u_2				2	1/3	2/3	$B/3$
	−7	−7	−14	−3	−4/3	−32/3	$0.921 - 4B/3$

Interpretation

We can transfer [0.32, 0.43, 0.25] into [0.189, 0.368 + $B/3$, 0.261] and the cost of recruiting is B, i.e. all that is available for this purpose. The objective function cannot be made zero, as long as B is less than or equal to 0.006: discrepancies must be accepted.

When $0.006 \leqslant B \leqslant 1.092$, then the final tableau is

	(2) f_1	(3) f_2	(6) g_3	(4) g_2	s	u_3	
(5) g_1	−1	−1/2		1/2	−1/6*	−1/3	0.182 − $B/6$
u_1		1/2		−1/2	1/6	1/3	−0.001 + $B/6$
(8) f_3			−1			−1	0.001
u_2		−1		1			0.002
	−7	−11/2	−14	−3/2	−5/6	−29/3	0.918 − $5B/6$

Interpretation

We can transfer [0.32, 0.43, 0.25] into [0.188 + $B/6$, 0.370, 0.261] and the cost of recruiting is B, i.e. all that is available for that purpose. The objective function cannot be made zero for the assumed range of B: discrepancies must be accepted.

When $B \geqslant 1.092$, then the final tableau is

	(2) f_1	(3) f_2	(6) g_3	(4) g_2	(5) g_1	u_3	
s	6	3		−3	−6	2	B − 1.092
u_1	−6				1		0.181
(8) f_3			−1			−1	0.001
u_2		−1		1			0.002
	−2	−3	−14	−4	−5	−8	0.008

Interpretation

We can transfer [0.32, 0.43, 0.25] into [0.370, 0.370, 0.261] and the cost of recruiting is 1.092. Even if we used more (which the budget might allow), we would still have to accept at least the discrepancy in n_3, viz. overmanning. This can obviously not be improved by recruitment, however high the budget is.

11.19

We consider yet another example, viz. the possibility of transferring [0.9, 0, 0.1] into [0.37, 0.37, 0.26] in one step. We know already that without a budget ceiling this is possible (Section 7.14).

We have now in tableau form

	(2) f_1	(3) f_2	(8) f_3	u_1	u_2	u_3	
(5) g_1	-1			1			0.08
(4) g_2		-1			1		0
(6) g_3			-1			1	0.13
s				6	3	2	B
	-7	-7	-14	5	4	6	1.18

Continuing, we obtain, when $B \leqslant 0.26$,

	(2) f_1	(3) f_2	(8) f_3	u_1	u_2	s	
(5) g_1	-1			1			0.08
(4) g_2		-1			1		0
(6) g_3			-1	-3	$-3/2$	$-1/2$	$0.13 - B/2$
u_3				3	$3/2$	$1/2$	$B/2$
	-7	-7	-14	-13	-5	-3	$1.18 - 3B$

With B given and less than or equal to 26, the most preferable transformation, in the sense of minimizing total penalties, is

$$[0.9, 0, 0.1] \rightarrow [0.29, 0.37, 0.13 + B/2]$$

When $0.26 \leqslant B \leqslant 0.74$

	(2) f_1	(3) f_2	(8) f_3	u_1	(6) g_3	s	
(5) g_1	-1			1			0.08
(4) g_2		-1	$-2/3$	-2*	$2/3$	$-1/3$	$(0.26 - B)/3$
u_2			$2/3$	2	$-2/3$	$1/3$	$(B - 0.26)/3$
u_3			-1		1		0.13
	-7	-7	$-32/3$	-3	$-10/3$	$-4/3$	$(2.24 - 4B)/3$

(The value of g_2 is negative, hence we continue)

	(2) f_1	(3) f_2	(8) f_3	(4) g_2	(6) g_3	s	
(5) g_1	-1	$-1/2$	$-1/3$	$1/2$	$1/3$	$-1/6$	$(0.74 - B)/6$
u_1		$1/2$	$1/3$	$-1/2$	$-1/3$	$1/6$	$(B - 0.26)/6$
u_2		-1		1			0
u_3			-1		1		0.13
	-7	$-11/2$	$-29/3$	$-3/2$	$-13/3$	$-5/6$	$(3.7 - 5B)/6$

With B in this bracket, the smallest total penalty is paid when we transfer [0.9, 0, 0.1] into $[(3.70 + B)/6, 0.37, 0.26]$. The cost of recruiting is then B.

When $B \geqslant 0.74$,

	(2) f_1	(3) f_2	(8) f_3	(4) g_2	(6) g_3	(5) g_1	
s	6	3	2	−3	−2	−6	$B - 0.74$
u_1	−1					1	0.08
u_2		−1		1			0
u_3			−1		1		0.13
	−2	−3	−8	−4	−6	−5	0

If the budget is high enough, the desired transformation is possible. The cost of recruiting is 0.74.

For an application of goal programming, see, for instance, Charnes and co-workers (1970).

12

Choice of Transition Rates

12.1

In Part I, and also until now in Part II, we have assumed that the transition rates were given, and only the recruitment rates could be controlled. Now we change our attitude in this respect and we assume that it is also possible to control the rates of transition between states.

On the other hand, we shall still assume that the wastage rates are determined by external causes.

Unless we make remarks to the contrary, we also assume that we wish to retain the total membership of the population.

12.2

As in previous chapters, let n_i be the proportion of members in state i, p_{ij} the transition rate from state i to state j, and w_i the wastage rate from state i. We denote $p_{ij}n_i$ by q_{ij}, $1 - w_i$ by r_i, and $r_i n_i$ by s_i. The relationship between the structure n, and a resulting structure $\bar{\mathbf{n}} = \mathbf{P}'\mathbf{n} + \mathbf{u}$, after one step ($\mathbf{P}$ being the transition matrix and u_i the rate of recruitment into state i) can then be described concisely by Table 17, where we have written W for $\Sigma_{i=1}^{k} n_i w_i$.

In Table 17 each row, and each column adds up to its value on the margin. This constitutes $2k + 1$ constraints on the q_{ij} and u_i. The sums of the vertical, and of the horizontal marginal totals are $\Sigma_i \bar{n}_i = \Sigma_i s_i + W$, so that only $2k$ of the constraints are independent.

Table 17

Totals	$\bar{n}_1$	$\bar{n}_2$	$\ldots$	$\bar{n}_k$
s_1	q_{11}	q_{12}	$\ldots$	q_{1k}
s_2	q_{21}	q_{22}	$\ldots$	q_{2k}
$\vdots$	$\vdots$	$\vdots$		$\vdots$
s_k	q_{k1}	q_{k2}	$\ldots$	q_{kk}
W	u_1	u_2	$\ldots$	u_k

12.3

Table 17 in the previous section can be considered to be one of the transportation problem of linear programming (see Appendix II). It is always possible to find non-negative q_{ij} and u_i for any marginal totals. Any set of values satisfying the constraints lies in the convex hull of basic solutions, i.e. those which contain (not more than) $2k$ positive values and have a tree structure. This means that if each row and each column is represented by a node in a graph, and links are drawn corresponding to positive entries in their intersections, then this graph is a tree. (We ignore the complication of possible degeneracy, when fewer than $2k$ values are positive.)

If the p_{ij} are only restricted by $1 - \Sigma_{j=1}^{k} p_{ij} = w_i$ (given), then the problem of fitting q_{ij} and u_i into a table with given n_i (or s_i) and $\bar{n}_i$ is trivial. We shall therefore restrict the form of the transition matrix which we consider.

12.4

If we think of the states as grades in a hierarchy, the rank being given by the subscripts $i = 1, 2, \ldots, k$ in increasing order, then the transfer rates mean promotion when $j > i$, and demotion when $j < i$. We shall now assume that demotions are inadmissible, i.e. that $p_{ij} = 0$ when $j < i$. Hence also $q_{ij} = 0$ in such a case.

However, we shall not assume in general that promotions are possible only into the next higher rank. Thus p_{ij} may be positive even if $j > i + 1$.

With these assumptions, Table 17 above reduces to Table 18.

We shall investigate which $\bar{\mathbf{n}}$ can be attained from a given $\mathbf{n}$ in one step, and also from which $\mathbf{n}$ a given $\bar{\mathbf{n}}$ can be attained.

12.5

An inspection of Table 18 shows that solutions in non-negative q_{ij} and u_i do not exist for all pairs $(\mathbf{n}, \bar{\mathbf{n}})$. For instance, because of $s_k = q_{kk}$, a solution can only exist if

$$\bar{n}_k \geqslant s_k = (1 - w_k) n_k \tag{12.1}$$

Table 18

Totals	$\bar{n}_1$	$\bar{n}_2$	$\ldots$	$\bar{n}_{k-1}$	$\bar{n}_k$
s_1	q_{11}	q_{12}	$\ldots$	$q_{1,k-1}$	q_{1k}
s_2	0	q_{22}	$\ldots$	$q_{2,k-1}$	q_{2k}
$\vdots$	$\vdots$	$\vdots$		$\vdots$	$\vdots$
s_{k-1}	0	0	$\ldots$	$q_{k-1,k-1}$	$q_{k-1,k}$
s_k	0	0	$\ldots$	0	q_{kk}
W	u_1	u_2	$\ldots$	u_{k-1}	u_k

Also, if $p_{11} = q_{11} = 0$, then u_1 must equal $\bar{n}_1$. If

$$\bar{n}_1 + \bar{n}_2 + \ldots + \bar{n}_t = 1 \quad \text{and} \quad \bar{n}_{t+1} = \ldots = \bar{n}_k = 0 \tag{12.2}$$

then necessarily

$$s_{t+1} = \ldots = s_k = 0 \tag{12.3}$$

In particular, if $\bar{n}_k = 0$, then $s_k = 0$, and if $\bar{n}_1 = 1$, then $n_2 = \ldots = n_k = 0$, and hence $n_1 = 1$.

If any partitioning of W is admissible, then all structures are attainable from $[1, 0, \ldots, 0]$. For instance, if $r_1 \leqslant \bar{n}_1$, we take

$$q_{11} = r_1 \quad u_1 = \bar{n}_1 - r_1 \quad u_j = \bar{n}_j \qquad \text{for } j = 2, \ldots, k \tag{12.4}$$

If $\bar{n}_1 + \ldots + \bar{n}_t \leqslant r_1 \leqslant \bar{n}_1 + \ldots + \bar{n}_{t+1}$, then we take

$$\begin{aligned} &q_{11} = \bar{n}_1, \ldots, q_{1t} = \bar{n}_t \quad q_{1,t+1} = r_1 - \bar{n}_1 - \ldots - \bar{n}_t \\ &u_{t+1} = \bar{n}_{t+1} - (r_1 - \bar{n}_1 - \ldots - \bar{n}_t) \quad u_{t+j} = \bar{n}_{t+j} \quad (j = 2, \ldots, k - t) \end{aligned} \tag{12.5}$$

12.6

If any partitioning of W is admissible, then every structure is strictly maintainable: we do not transfer at all, and make up wastage by $u_i = w_i$. But if the partitioning of W is subject to conditions, then we must proceed differently. For instance, if $W = u_1$, i.e. wastage is to be made up by entries into state 1, then we find the basic solutions for strictly maintainable structures shown in Table 19.

12.7

These are the basic solutions in (q_{ij}, u_i)-space. We shall now want to know what they mean in **n**-space. This depends on the values of the w_i. Assume $\mathbf{w} = [0.2, 0.1, 0.3]$. Then, in order to have non-negative entries in Table 19(I) above, we must have

$$0.8n_1 - 0.1n_2 - 0.3n_3 \geqslant 0 \quad 0.1n_2 + 0.3n_3 \geqslant 0$$

$$0.9n_2 - 0.3n_3 \geqslant 0 \quad 0.3n_3 \geqslant 0 \quad 0.2n_1 + 0.1n_2 + 0.3n_3 \geqslant 0$$

The last two inequalities are satisfied for $n_i \geqslant 0$, and we solve the first three inequalities by linear programming, which will give us the vertices in **n**-space. We obtain the following results:

$$\begin{pmatrix} 0.238 \\ 0.191 \\ 0.571 \end{pmatrix} \quad \begin{pmatrix} 0.111 \\ 0.889 \\ 0.000 \end{pmatrix} \quad \begin{pmatrix} 1 \\ 0 \\ 0 \end{pmatrix}$$

Similarly, we obtain for Table 19(II)

$$\begin{pmatrix} 0.273 \\ 0 \\ 0.727 \end{pmatrix} \quad \begin{pmatrix} 0.111 \\ 0.889 \\ 0 \end{pmatrix} \quad \begin{pmatrix} 1 \\ 0 \\ 0 \end{pmatrix}$$

Table 19

I	n_1	n_2	n_3
$r_1 n_1$	$n_1 - W$	$w_2 n_2 + w_3 n_3$	
$r_2 n_2$		$n_2 - w_2 n_2 - w_3 n_3$	$w_3 n_3$
$r_3 n_3$			$n_3 - w_3 n_3$
W	W		
II			
$r_1 n_1$	$n_1 - W$	$w_2 n_2$	
$r_2 n_2$		$n_2 - w_2 n_2$	
$r_3 n_3$			$n_3 - w_3 n_3$
W	W		
III			
$r_1 n_1$	$n_1 - W$	n_2	$w_2 n_2 + w_3 n_3 - n_2$
$r_2 n_2$			$n_2 - w_2 n_2$
$r_3 n_3$			$n_3 - w_3 n_3$
W	W		
IV			
$r_1 n_1$	$n_1 - W$		$w_2 n_2 + w_3 n_3$
$r_2 n_2$		n_2	$-w_2 n_2$
$r_3 n_3$			$n_3 - w_3 n_3$
W	W		

Similar tables can be constructed for $W = u_2$, and for $W = u_3$.

and for Table 19(III)

$$\begin{pmatrix} 0.238 \\ 0.191 \\ 0.571 \end{pmatrix} \quad \begin{pmatrix} 0.273 \\ 0 \\ 0.727 \end{pmatrix} \quad \begin{pmatrix} 1 \\ 0 \\ 0 \end{pmatrix}$$

while Table 19(IV) is not feasible at all.

12.8

These results must now be interpreted in terms of the p_{ij}.

For instance, take

$$\begin{pmatrix} 0.238 \\ 0.191 \\ 0.571 \end{pmatrix}$$

a vertex in case (I). (We would, in fact, get identical results if we took it to be a vertex in case (III).) Then Table 19(I) looks as follows:

	0.238	0.191	0.571
0.191	0	0.191	
0.171		0	0.171
0.400			0.400
0.238	0.238		

and in terms of $p_{ij} = q_{ij}/n_i$, this is to be interpreted as

	p_{ij}	
0	0.80	
	0	0.90
		0.70

Similarly, consider the vertices of case (II)

$$\begin{pmatrix} 0.273 \\ 0 \\ 0.727 \end{pmatrix} \quad \text{and} \quad \begin{pmatrix} 0.111 \\ 0.889 \\ 0 \end{pmatrix}$$

The tables are

	0.273	0	0.727
0.218	0	0	0.218
0		0	
0.509			0.509
0.273	0.273		

and

	0.111	0.889	0
0.089	0	0.089	0
0.800		0.800	
0			0
0.111	0.111		

which we interpret as

	p_{ij}	
0	0	0.8
	0.9	
		0.7

	p_{ij}	
0	0.8	0
	0.9	
		0.7

Any structure in the convex hull of such vertices can be strictly maintained, with entries into state 1 only.

12.9

For instance, take

$$0.2\begin{pmatrix} 0.238 \\ 0.191 \\ 0.571 \end{pmatrix} + 0.3\begin{pmatrix} 0.273 \\ 0 \\ 0.727 \end{pmatrix} + 0.5\begin{pmatrix} 0.111 \\ 0.889 \\ 0 \end{pmatrix} = \begin{pmatrix} 0.185 \\ 0.483 \\ 0.332 \end{pmatrix}$$

We obtain the table

	0.185	0.483	0.332
0.148	0	0.083	0.065
0.435		0.400	0.035
0.232			0.232
0.185	0.185		

and

p_{ij}		
0	0.45	0.35
	0.83	0.07
		0.70

These q_{ij} are, of course, those of the three tables above, multiplied respectively by the weights 0.2, 0.3, 0.5.

12.10

Now let the initial structure **n**, and the structure $\bar{\mathbf{n}}$, the one we wish to reach after one step, be given. The basic solution will contain (not more than) $2k$ positive values, i.e. one less than the sum of the number of rows and of columns.

As an illustration, take $\mathbf{n} = [0.32, 0.43, 0.25]$ and $\bar{\mathbf{n}} = [0.37, 0.37, 0.26]$. We have then the table

	0.37	0.37	0.26
0.8(0.32) = 0.256	q_{11}	q_{12}	q_{13}
0.9(0.43) = 0.387	0	q_{22}	q_{23}
0.7(0.25) = 0.175	0	0	q_{33}
0.182	u_1	u_2	u_3

A basic solution has six positive entries, so that three of the admissible cells will remain empty.

We start with a solution which we have exhibited in Appendix II (though the order of rows was different there)

(A)	0.370	0.370	0.260
0.256	0.188	0.068	
0.387		0.302	0.085
0.175			0.175
0.182	0.182		

Interpreting this in terms of the p_{ij}, we have the transition matrix

$$\begin{pmatrix} 0.588 & 0.212 & \\ & 0.702 & 0.198 \\ & & 0.700 \end{pmatrix}$$

Indeed, with this matrix we have

$$\begin{pmatrix} 0.32 \\ 0.43 \\ 0.25 \end{pmatrix} \rightarrow \begin{matrix} 0.188 + 0.182 \\ 0.370 \\ 0.260 \end{matrix} = \begin{pmatrix} 0.37 \\ 0.37 \\ 0.26 \end{pmatrix}$$

This may be compared with Section 7.8, equation (7.3), we found that $\mathbf{P}_0$ was not a suitable transition matrix for the pair of $\mathbf{n}$ and $\bar{\mathbf{n}}$ we are considering now.

We find other basic solutions by filling in some admissible cell which is as yet empty, and adjusting the entries to keep the marginal totals satisfied (this is the classical method for solving the transportation problem). In this manner we obtain the following other basic solutions:

(B)			(C)			(D)		
0.188		0.068	0.256			0.256		
	0.370	0.017		0.370	0.017		0.302	0.085
		0.175			0.175			0.175
0.182			0.114		0.068	0.114	0.068	

to be interpreted, as transition matrices, as follows:

0.588		0.212	0.800			0.800		
	0.860	0.040		0.860	0.040		0.702	0.198
		0.700			0.700			0.700

12.11

We were able to proceed in the way we did, because we had a first basic solution readily available, and continued from there. However, when a basic solution is not known, and this will certainly be the case when none exists, then we can start from any arbitrary solution, using the inadmissible cells as well, and then proceed to minimize the total cost of transitions (see Appendix II, Section II.8), attaching a zero cost to admissible, and some positive cost to inadmissable cells. If the minimizing solution still contains an entry in an inadmissible cell, then this indicates that no feasible solution exists.

As an example of such a solution, consider the transition from [0.32, 0.43, 0.25] to [0.40, 0.43, 0.17]. We know that this is impossible, because 0.175 is already larger than 0.17.

We start from

	0.400	0.430	0.170	shadow costs	
0.256	0.256			0	
0.387	0.144	0.243		c	(>0)
0.175		0.175^-	$+$	$2c$	
0.182		0.012^+	0.170^-	c	
shadow costs	0	$-c$	c		

Adjustments of 170 are indicated by the + and – signs. This leads to

	0.400	0.430	0.170	shadow costs
0.256	0.256			0
0.387	0.144^-	0.243^+		c
0.175		0.005	0.170	$2c$
0.182	+	0.182^-		c
shadow costs	0	$-c$	$-2c$	

	0.400	0.430	0.170	shadow costs
0.256	0.256			0
0.387		0.387		0
0.175		0.005	0.170	c
0.182	0.144	0.038		
shadow costs	0	0	$-c$	

The last table is 'optimal' but it contains 0.005 in an inadmissible cell: the desired transition is impossible with any transition matrix which does not allow demotions.

12.12

We now turn to the question of determining those $\bar{\mathbf{n}}$ which are attainable from a given structure $\mathbf{n}$. The unknowns are now $\bar{\mathbf{n}}$, $\mathbf{u}$, and $\mathbf{P}$.

To begin with, we define restrictions on the size of the region of attainable structures $\bar{\mathbf{n}}$.

Consider the equations

$$\bar{n}_j = \sum_{i=1}^{k} p_{ij} n_i + u_j \tag{12.6}$$

where, incidentally, the upper limit of summation could be j, because $p_{ij} = 0$ when $i > j$. We add equation (12.6) for $j = 1, \ldots, t$ and have

$$\sum_{j=1}^{t} \bar{n}_j = \sum_{j=1}^{t} \sum_{i=1}^{j} p_{ij} n_i + \sum_{j=1}^{t} u_j$$

$$= \sum_{i=1}^{t} \sum_{j=i}^{t} p_{ij} n_i + \sum_{j=1}^{t} u_j \tag{12.7}$$

Now

$$\sum_{j=i}^{t} p_{ij} n_i \leqslant n_i(1 - w_i) \tag{12.8}$$

with equality when $p_{ij} = 0$ for $j > t$ and

$$\sum_{j=1}^{t} u_j \leqslant \sum_{j=1}^{k} u_j = \sum_{i=1}^{k} w_i n_i \tag{12.9}$$

with equality when $u_j = 0$ for $j > t$.

Hence

$$\sum_{j=1}^{t} \bar{n}_j \leqslant \sum_{i=1}^{t} n_i(1 - w_i) + \sum_{j=1}^{k} u_j = \sum_{i=1}^{t} n_i + \sum_{i=t+1}^{k} w_i n_i \tag{12.10}$$

The upper limit is obtained with the conditions for equality mentioned after inequalities (12.8) and (12.9).

12.13

We illustrate the algorithm derived from the transportation problem, with $\mathbf{n} = [0.32, 0.43, 0.25]$, so that $W = 0.182$.

We constrain W to be equal to one of u_1, u_2, or u_3, and thus four variables will be positive. When $W = u_1$, we obtain

(1)	0.438	0.387	0.175
	0.256		
		0.387	
			0.175
	0.182		

(2)	0.182	0.643	0.175
		0.256	
		0.387	
			0.175
	0.182		

(3)	0.182	0.387	0.431
			0.256
		0.387	
			0.175
	0.182		

(4)	0.438	0	0.562
	0.256		
			0.387
			0.175
	0.182		

(5)	0.182	0.256	0.562
		0.256	
			0.387
			0.175
	0.182		

(6)	0.182	0	0.818
			0.256
			0.387
			0.175
	0.182		

When $W = u_2$, we obtain

(1)	0.256	0.569	0.175
	0.256		
		0.387	
			0.175
		0.182	

(2)	0	0.825	0.175
		0.256	
		0.387	
			0.175
		0.182	

(3)	0	0.569	0.431
			0.256
		0.387	
			0.175
		0.182	

(4)	0.256	0.182	0.562
	0.256		
			0.387
			0.175
		0.182	

(5)	0	0.438	0.562
		0.256	
			0.387
			0.175
		0.182	

(6)	0	0.182	0.818
			0.256
			0.387
			0.175
		0.182	

When $W = u_3$, we obtain

(1)	0.256	0.387	0.457	(2)	0	0.643	0.457	(3)	0	0.387	0.613
	0.256					0.256					0.256
		0.387				0.387				0.387	
			0.175				0.175				0.175
			0.182				0.182				0.182
(4)	0.256	0	0.744	(5)	0	0.256	0.744	(6)	0	0	1.000
	0.256					0.256					0.256
			0.387				0.387				0.387
			0.175				0.175				0.175
			0.182				0.182				0.182

Any combination of two or more of such basic solutions, with non-negative weights adding up to unity, will again produce solutions.

Once more, it is easy to interpret the tables in terms of transition matrices.

The tables show the basic solutions in $(\bar{\mathbf{n}}, \mathbf{u}, \mathbf{P})$-space. If we project them onto $\mathbf{n}$-space, then their convex hull has the vertices

(1) and (4) of $W = u_1$, i.e. $[0.438, 0.387, 0.175]$ and $[0.438, 0, 0.562]$

(2) of $W = u_2$, i.e. $[0, 0.825, 0.175]$

and

(6) of $W = u_3$, i.e. $[0, 0, 1]$

The region is restricted by $\bar{n}_1 \leqslant 0.438$ $(= n_1 + 0.1n_2 + 0.3n_3)$ and $\bar{n}_1 + \bar{n}_2 \leqslant 0.825$ $(= n_1 + n_2 + 0.3n_3)$, in accordance with inequality (12.10).

It follows, for instance, that $[0, 0, 1]$ can be reached, but not $[1, 0, 0]$ or $[0, 1, 0]$.

12.14

It follows from the illustrative example in Section 12.8 that $[0.37, 0.37, 0.26]$ must lie in the feasible region. Now inspection shows that a point with $\bar{n}_1 = 0.37$ cannot lie in the convex hull of the vertices corresponding to $W = u_2$, or $W = u_3$, so it must lie in the convex hull of the vertices (1) to (6) for $W = u_1 = 0.182$.

If we look for three basic solutions in whose triangle $\bar{\mathbf{n}} = [0.37, 0.37, 0.26]$ lies, we find that there are six of them, (a) to (f), and the corresponding weights which produce $\bar{\mathbf{n}}$ are these:

	(1)	(2)	(3)	(4)	(5)	(6)
(a)	0.514	0.266		0.220		
(b)	0.734	0.045			0.221	
(c)	0.734	0.134				0.132
(d)	0.734		0.132	0.220		
(e)	0.650		0.266		0.134	
(f)	0.734		0.222			0.044

If we apply these weights to the transfer rates in the basic solutions (1) to (6), we find that (a) and (b) form the solution (A) in Section 12.10, (e) and (f) are solution (B), while (c) and (d) are the non-basic solution $\frac{1}{2}$ [(A) + (B)], as follows:

	0.37	0.37	0.26
0.256	0.188	0.034	0.034
0.387		0.336	0.051
0.175			0.175
0.182	0.182		

Though we cannot have $u_1 = 0$ to obtain $\bar{n}_1 = 0.37$, it does not follow that we must have $u_1 = 0.182$. However, we must have at least $u_1 = 0.114$ (see solutions (C) and (D)), because $q_{11} \leqslant 0.256$ and hence $u_1 \geqslant 0.370 - 0.256$.

12.15

If we have to make analogous computations for a number of initial structures n, then it is useful to have a list of thise structures attainable from $[1, 0, \ldots, 0]$, $[0, 1, \ldots, 0]$, ... and from $[0, 0, \ldots, 0, 1]$. We then combine the results with weights $n_1, n_2, \ldots, n_k$ respectively.

For instance, using again our case with $W = u_1 = 0.182$, we note that we can attain

from $[1, 0, 0]$ the basic solutions $[1, 0, 0]$, $[0.2, 0.8, 0]$ and $[0.2, 0, 0.8]$

from $[0, 1, 0]$ the basic solutions $[0.1, 0.9, 0]$ and $[0.1, 0, 0.9]$

and

from $[0, 0, 1]$ the basic solution $[0.3, 0, 0.7]$

Multiplying one from the first triple by 0.32, one of the second pair by 0.43, and the last structure by 0.25, and adding, we obtain one of the results (1), . . . , (6).

12.16

If we want to consider an expanding population with given rate $1 + \alpha$, then we use $W + \alpha$ instead of W. If the population contracts at this rate, then we use $W - \alpha$. Clearly this is only possible if $\alpha < W$.

12.17

When we ask from which $\mathbf{n}$ a given structure $\bar{\mathbf{n}}$ can be obtained, then the unknowns are $\mathbf{n}$, $\mathbf{u}$, and $\mathbf{P}$.

Adding the equations (12.6) this time for $j = t + 1, \ldots, k$ we have

$$\begin{aligned}
\sum_{j=t+1}^{k} \bar{n}_j &= \sum_{j=t+1}^{k} \sum_{i=1}^{j} p_{ij}n_i + \sum_{j=t+1}^{k} u_j \\
&= \sum_{j=t+1}^{k} \left(\sum_{i=1}^{t} p_{ij}n_i + \sum_{i=t+1}^{j} p_{ij}n_i \right) + \sum_{j=t+1}^{k} u_j \\
&= \sum_{j=t+1}^{k} \sum_{i=1}^{t} p_{ij}n_i + \sum_{i=t+1}^{k} \sum_{j=i}^{k} p_{ij}n_i + \sum_{j=t+1}^{k} u_j \\
&\geqslant \sum_{i=t+1}^{k} \sum_{j=i}^{k} p_{ij}n_i = \sum_{i=t+1}^{k} s_i n_i
\end{aligned} \tag{12.11}$$

with equality when $u_j = 0$ for $j = t + 1, \ldots, k$ and $p_{ij} = 0$ for $i = 1, \ldots, t$, and $j = t + 1, \ldots, k$.

Thus we have an attainable upper bound for the region of possible $\mathbf{n}$, when $\bar{\mathbf{n}}$ is given.

The structure $[0, 0, \ldots, 1]$ can be attained from any $\mathbf{n}$ by making $p_{ik} = 1 - w_i$ $(i = 1, \ldots, k)$, and $W = u_k$.

The structure $[1, 0, \ldots, 0]$ can obviously only be attained from itself, if we do not allow demotions. In Section 12.5 we have seen that from this, any other structure can also be attained.

12.18

If we are merely interested in the structures which answer our question, then we can solve $\mathbf{P}'\mathbf{n} = \bar{\mathbf{n}} - \mathbf{u}$ for $\mathbf{n}$. We show this for $k = 3$, $\bar{\mathbf{n}} = [0.37, 0.37, 0.26]$ and for $\mathbf{u}$ to be restricted to one single state, and assuming $p_{13} = 0$. Expressing u_i as $\Sigma_{i=1}^{k} w_i n_i$, replacing p_{12} by $0.8 - p_{11}$ and p_{23} by $0.9 - p_{22}$, we obtain the following expressions:

when $W = u_1$

$$n_1 = (0.074 + 0.07p_{22})/D_1 \qquad n_2 = (0.093 + 0.44p_{11})/D_1 \qquad n_3 = 1 - n_1 - n_2 \tag{12.12}$$

where $D_1 = 0.16 - 0.2p_{11} - 0.1p_{22} + p_{11}p_{22}$,

when $W = u_2$

$$n_1 = (0.37p_{22} - 0.74)/D_2 \qquad n_2 = (-0.259 + 0.44p_{11})/D_2 \qquad n_3 = 1 - n_1 - n_2 \tag{12.13}$$

where $D_2 = -0.2p_{11} + p_{11}p_{22}$,

when $W = u_3$

Table 20

	$0.37 - W$		$0.63 - s_2 - s_3$		$0.37 - W$	$0.63 - s_2 - s_3$	
(1)		0.37	$s_2 - 0.37$	(2)		$s_2 + s_3 - 0.26$	$0.26 - s_3$
			s_3				s_3
	W				W		
	(0.3, 0.7, 0) (0.59, 0.41, 0) (0.22, 0.41, 0.37)				(0.3, 0.7, 0) (0.71, 0.29, 0) (0.63, 0, 0.37) (0.22, 0.41, 0.37)		
	$0.37 - W$	0.37	$0.26 - s_2 - s_3$		$0.37 - W$	$0.37 - s_2$	$0.26 - s_3$
(3)			s_2	(4)		s_2	
			s_3				s_3
	W				W		
	(0.71, 0.29, 0) (1, 0, 0) (0.63, 0, 0.37)				(0.59, 0.41, 0) (1, 0, 0) (0.63, 0, 0.37) (0.22, 0.41, 0.37)		
	0.37		$s_1 - 0.37$		0.37	$s_1 - 0.37$	
(5)		$0.37 - W$	$0.63 - s_1 - s_3$	(6)		$s_2 + s_3 - 0.26$	$0.26 - s_3$
			s_3				s_3
		W				W	
	(0.46, 0.54, 0) (0.71, 0.29, 0) (0.46, 0.17, 0.37)				(0.46, 0.54, 0) (0.71, 0.29, 0) (0.63, 0, 0.37) (0.46, 0.17, 0.37)		

(7)	0.37	$0.37 - W$	$0.26 - s_2 - s_3$	(8)	0.37	$s_1 + s_3 - 0.63$	$0.26 - s_3$
			s_2			s_2	
			s_3				s_3
		W				W	
	(0.63, 0, 0.37) (1, 0, 0) (0.71, 0.29, 0)				(0.63, 0, 0.37) (0.46, 0.54, 0) (1, 0, 0) (0.46, 0.17, 0.37)		
(9)	0.37		$s_1 - 0.37$	(10)	0.37	$s_1 - 0.37$	
		0.37	$s_2 - 0.37$			$0.74 - s_1$	$s_1 + s_2 - 0.74$
			s_3				s_3
			W				W
	(0.46, 0.54, 0) (0.59, 0.41, 0) (0.46, 0.41, 0.13)				(0.46, 0.54, 0) (0.92, 0.08, 0) (0.92, 0, 0.08) (0.46, 0.41, 0.13)		
(11)	0.37	0.37	$s_1 - 0.74$	(12)	0.37	$0.37 - s_2$	$s_1 + s_2 - 0.74$
			s_2			s_2	
			s_3				s_3
			W				W
	(1, 0, 0) (0.92, 0.08, 0) (0.92, 0, 0.08)				(0.59, 0.41, 0) (1, 0, 0) (0.92, 0, 0.08) (0.46, 0.41, 0.13)		

$$n_1 = 0.37p_{11}/D_3 \qquad n_2 = (0.74p_{11} - 0.296)/D_3 \qquad n_3 = 1 - n_1 - n_2 \quad (12.14)$$

where $D_3 = p_{11}p_{22}$.

This gives us the values as they depend on **P**, but it does not give us, conveniently, the ranges of **n**, or the form of **P**. We look therefore for a more informative alogorithm.

12.19

The following algorithm is again derived from that of the transportation problem, but its interpretation is more involved than it was in earlier cases, because now the q_{ij}s depend on **n**.

In Table 20 we show tables for $W = u_i$ ($i = 1, 2, 3$). They exhibit the vertices in (**u**, **P**)-space for given **n**. By observing the ranges of **n** which make the elements of **P** non-negative, we obtain the regions of those **n** from which $\bar{\mathbf{n}}$ can be attained.

12.20

We have also shown above the projection of the vertices onto **n**-space for each of the basic solutions, to two decimals.

To show how these vertices were obtained, we use solution (1) as an example. We require $n_i \geqslant 0$ for all i, and

$$\begin{aligned}
&0.37 - 0.2n_1 - 0.1n_2 - 0.3n_3 \geqslant 0\\
&0.63 - 0.9n_2 - 0.7n_3 \geqslant 0\\
&0.9n_2 - 0.37 \geqslant 0\\
&0.7n_3 \geqslant 0\\
&n_1 + n_2 + n_3 = 1
\end{aligned} \qquad (12.15)$$

We solve the set (12.15) by linear programming and remark that the last inequality is equivalent to $n_3 \geqslant 0$. We do not need it as a separate constraint, because all variables are supposed to be non-negative in any case.

In tableau form, with a_i as slack variables, we have

	n_1	n_2	n_3	
a_1	0.2	0.1	0.3	0.37
a_2		0.9	0.7	0.63
a_3		−0.9		−0.37
s	1.0	1.0	1.0	1.00

dropping s

	n_2	n_3	
a_1	−0.1	0.1	0.17
a_2	0.9	0.7	0.63
a_3	−0.9		−0.37
n_1	1.0	1.0	1.00

and then

a_2	n_3	
0.111	0.177	0.240
1.111	0.777	0.700
1.000	0.700	0.260
1.111	0.223	0.300

	a_3	n_3	
a_1	−0.111	0.1	0.211
n_2	−1.111		0.411
a_2	1.000	0.7	0.260
n_1	1.111	1.0	0.589

	a_3	a_2	
a_1	−0.253	0.143	0.174
n_2	−1.111		0.411
n_3	1.429	1.429	0.371
n_1	−0.318	−1.429	0.218

These give the (projections of the) vertices, to two decimal places,

$$[0.59, 0.41, 0] \quad [0.3, 0.7, 0] \quad [0.22, 0.41, 0.37].$$

The region of feasible n is restricted by

$$n_3 \leqslant 0.37 \quad \text{and} \quad 0.9n_2 + 0.7n_3 \leqslant 0.63$$

which is in accordance with equations (12.11).

The values of W corresponding to the vertices exhibited above are 0.1300, 0.1589, 0.1960 and case (1) above looks as follows (to two decimal places)

	0.37	0.37	0.26
0.24	0.24		0
0.63		0.37	0.26
0			0
0.13	0.13		

	0.37	0.37	0.26
0.47	0.21		0.26
0.37		0.37	0
0			0
0.16	0.16		

	0.37	0.37	0.26
0.17	0.17		0
0.37		0.37	0
0.26			0.26
0.20	0.20		

12.21

The tables in Section 12.19 (Table 20) exhibit those vertices which refer to cases where entries take place into a single state. Other structures in $(\mathbf{u}, \mathbf{P})$-space are obtained by combining any two or three of them, with non-negative weights adding up to unity. We shall determine the vertices of such regions in $\mathbf{n}$- space.

To obtain these cases, when two of the u_i are positive, we proceed as follows. We choose pairs of tables in the same row in Table 20 of Section 12.19 (i.e. cases where the same p_{ij} is zero) where the columns of that u_i which is zero are identical. Such a pair is, for instance, that of cases (8) and (12), where $u_1 = 0$, and $p_{23} = 0$. The first column is the same in both cases. We have to find a convex combination which makes one more u_ip_{ij} equal to zero, because one of these u_i, which are now zero, will be positive. Thus, starting from that pair, either $(s_1 + s_3 - 0.63)t + (0.37$

$-s_2)(1-t)=0$, or $(0.26-s_3)t+(s_1+s_2-0.74)(1-t)=0$ is required, with $0 \leqslant t \leqslant 1$. In the first case we shall have $p_{12}=0$, and in the second case $p_{13}=0$, by making $t=(0.37-s_2)/W$ or $t=(0.74-s_1-s_2)/W$ respectively.

The two new vertices are then

0.37		$s_1-0.37$
	s_2	
		s_3
	$0.37-s_1$	$0.63-s_1-s_2$

and

0.37	$s_1-0.37$	
	s_2	
		s_3
	$0.74-s_1-s_2$	$0.26-s_3$

For some pairs only one combination is effective, and (3) and (7) cannot be combined at all, because it would require a negative t.

Some new vertices come about from two different combinations. Altogether, we obtain (with an indication of which pairs have led to them)

s_1		
	$s_2+s_3-0.26$	$0.26-s_3$
		s_3
$0.37-s_1$	$0.63-s_2-s_3$	

(2, 6)

$s_1+s_3-0.26$		$0.26-s_3$
	s_2	
		s_3
$0.63-s_1-s_3$	$0.37-s_2$	

(4, 8)

s_1		
	0.37	$s_2-0.37$
		s_3
$0.37-s_1$		$0.63-s_2-s_3$

(1, 9)

$s_1-0.37$	0.37	
		s_2
		s_3
$0.74-s_1$		$0.26-s_2-s_3$

(3, 11)

$s_1+s_2-0.37$	$0.37-s_2$	
	s_2	
		s_3
$0.74-s_1-s_2$		$0.26-s_3$

(4, 12)

0.37	$s_1-0.37$	
		s_2
		s_3
	$0.74-s_1$	$0.26-s_2-s_3$

(6, 10) and (7, 11)

0.37	$s_1-0.37$	
	s_2	
		s_3
	$0.74-s_1-s_2$	$0.26-s_3$

(6, 10) and (8, 12)

0.37		$s_1-0.37$
	s_2	
		s_3
	$0.37-s_2$	$0.63-s_1-s_3$

(8.12)

The ranges of those **n** which do not make any of the entries negative are easily determined. We notice also the following results.

The combination (5, 9) is only possible if $n_2=0.37/0.9=0.41$, and the result is the case (9), which is identical with (12) in this situation.

If

$n_1 = 0.37/0.8 = 0.46$, then (5) = (6) and (9) = (10)
$n_2 = 0.37/0.9 = 0.41$, then (1) = (4) and (9) = (12)
$n_3 = 0.26/0.7 = 0.37$, then (2) = (4) and (6) = (8).

Moreover, if

$s_2 + s_3 = 0.63$, then (1) = (2)
$s_2 + s_3 = 0.26$, then (2) = (3), and (6) = (7)
$s_1 + s_3 = 0.63$, then (5) = (8)
$s_1 + s_3 = 0.74$, then (10) = (12).

Finally, if none of the u_i is restricted to zero, then we have

s_1		
	s_2	
		s_3
$0.37 - s_1$	$0.37 - s_2$	$0.26 - s_3$

and the limits of the n_i are then, of course,

0.37/0.8   0.37/0.9   0.26/0.7

12.22

The structure **n** = [0.32, 0.43, 0.25] is one of those from which [0.37, 0.37, 0.26] can be reached, as we know (Section 12.10). Now **n** can be located in a number of triangles whose vertices are some of those mentioned in Section 12.19.

For instance (see solution (1) in Table 20)

$$0.260\ [0.59, 0.41, 0] + 0.066\ [0.3, 0.7, 0] + 0.674\ [0.22, 0.41, 0.37]$$

If we apply the weights 0.260, 0.066, 0.674 respectively to the transition matrices corresponding to the vertices, as shown in Section 12.19, then we obtain solution (B) of Section 12.10.

12.23

We shall now ask which structures can be reached from any other structure, even if not necessarily after one single step.

We know that (0, 0, . . . , 0, 1) is attainable from any other structure in one step (Section 12.17). Our question can thus be reduced to the question of which structures can be reached from (0, 0, . . . , 0, 1), after an arbitrary number of steps.

In one step, we can obtain any structure in the convex hull of

$$\begin{pmatrix} w_k \\ 0 \\ 0 \\ \vdots \\ 0 \\ 0 \\ r_k \end{pmatrix} \begin{pmatrix} 0 \\ w_k \\ 0 \\ \vdots \\ 0 \\ 0 \\ r_k \end{pmatrix} \cdots \begin{pmatrix} 0 \\ 0 \\ 0 \\ \vdots \\ 0 \\ w_k \\ r_k \end{pmatrix} \begin{pmatrix} 0 \\ 0 \\ 0 \\ \vdots \\ 0 \\ 0 \\ 1 \end{pmatrix}$$

One of these structures is

$$[a_1 w_k, a_2 w_k, \ldots, a_{k-1} w_k, r_k] \tag{12.16}$$

$a_1 + a_2 + \ldots + a_{k-1} = 1 \quad a_i \geqslant 0$ for all i.

From the structure (12.16) we obtain in one step

$$\begin{pmatrix} r_1 & & & & \\ & r_2 & & & \\ & & \ddots & & \\ & & & r_{k-1} & \\ & & & & r_k \end{pmatrix} \begin{pmatrix} a_1 w_k \\ a_2 w_k \\ \vdots \\ a_{k-1} w_k \\ r_k \end{pmatrix} + \begin{pmatrix} u_1 \\ 0 \\ \vdots \\ 0 \\ 0 \end{pmatrix}$$

$$= [b_1, a_2 r_2 w_k, \ldots, a_{k-1} r_{k-1} w_k, r_k^2] \tag{12.17}$$

Where b_1 is such that the components add up to unity. It is easily seen that this is achieved by making

$$u_1 = (a_1 w_1 + a_2 w_2 + \ldots a_{k-1} w_{k-1} + r_k) w_k \tag{12.18}$$

(Remember that, by definition, $r_k + w_k = 1$.)

After the next step we obtain, in the same manner,

$$[b_2, a_2 r_2^2 w_k, \ldots, a_{k-1} r_{k-1}^2 w_k, r_k^3] \tag{12.19}$$

and, after n steps

$$[b_n, a_2 r_2^n w_k, \ldots, a_{k-1} r_{k-1}^n w_k, r_k^{n+1}] \tag{12.20}$$

All those points with $n = 0, 1, \ldots$ can be reached from any other point. This is certainly possible via $[0, 0, \ldots, 0, 1]$, but perhaps also otherwise.

This means that all points can be reached from any other point, though those where $\bar{n}_k = 0$ only arbitrarily closely.

Appendix I

Matrix Theory and Related Matters

We mention here a few facts from matrix theory, assuming that the reader is familiar with the concepts of matrix and determinant, and with the rules of matrix multiplication and the evaluation of determinants.

I.1

Consider a set of k linear homogeneous algebraic equations in k variables,

$$\mathbf{A}\mathbf{x} = 0 \tag{I.1}$$

Such a system has always the 'trivial' solution $\mathbf{x} = 0$. Other solutions exist if and only if the matrix of coefficients $\mathbf{A}$ is 'singular', i.e. if its determinant $D = |\mathbf{A}|$ is zero.

$|\mathbf{A}|$ is zero, if the k equations are not linearly independent. If r of them are linearly independent, we say that the matrix has 'rank' r. In that case the highest order of these subdeterminants of $|\mathbf{A}|$, which are not zero, is r.

If the rank of the matrix $\mathbf{A}$ is r, then $\mathbf{A}\mathbf{x} = 0$ has $k - r$ linearly independent solutions. If, in particular, $r = k - 1$, then a solution is proportional to

$$[D_{i1}, \ldots, D_{ik}] \quad \text{(any } i\text{)} \tag{I.2}$$

where the 'co-factors' or 'signed minors' D_{ij} are the subdeterminants of $|\mathbf{A}|$ obtained by omitting the ith row and the jth column, multiplied by $(-1)^{i+j}$.

If $\mathbf{A}$ is not singular, then the 'inverse matrix' $\mathbf{A}^{-1}$ exists, defined by $\mathbf{A}\mathbf{A}^{-1} = \mathbf{I}$, where $\mathbf{I}$ is the 'identity matrix', with ones in the diagonal, and zero everywhere else.

The inverse matrix can be computed as

$$\mathbf{A}^{-1} = \begin{pmatrix} D_{11}/D & \ldots & D_{k1}/D \\ \vdots & & \vdots \\ D_{1k}/D & \ldots & D_{kk}/D \end{pmatrix} \tag{I.3}$$

The elements of any column are a solution of $\mathbf{A}\mathbf{x} = 0$, if the rank of $\mathbf{A}$ is $k - 1$ (in which case $\mathbf{A}^{-1}$ does not exist).

I.2

Consider now a matrix $\mathbf{A}$. We want to find values λ for which $\mathbf{A} - \lambda\mathbf{I}$ is singular, i.e. such that the determinant

$$|\mathbf{A} - \lambda\mathbf{I}| = \begin{vmatrix} a_{11} - \lambda & a_{12} & \ldots & a_{1k} \\ a_{21} & a_{22} - \lambda & \ldots & a_{2k} \\ \vdots & \vdots & & \vdots \\ a_{k1} & a_{k2} & \ldots & a_{kk} - \lambda \end{vmatrix} = 0 \qquad \text{(I.4)}$$

$\lambda = 0$ will be such a value if and only if **A** is singular.

Equation (I.4) is an algebraic equation of degree k, the 'characteristic equation' of **A**. Its roots are called 'latent roots', or 'characteristic values', or 'eigenvalues' of **A**.

The k latent roots, the solutions of equation (I.4), are not necessarily all different, but in this book we shall always assume that they are. For causes of equal roots the theory becomes much more complicated, and we refer, for these cases, to such textbooks as Frazer, Duncan, and Collar (1946), or Gantmacher (1959).

I.3

It can be shown – though we do not prove it here – that any matrix satisfies its own characteristic equation (the 'Cayley–Hamilton theorem'). Hence any power of **A** higher than $k - 1$ can be expressed as a linear combination of $\mathbf{I}, \mathbf{A}, \mathbf{A}^2, \ldots, \mathbf{A}^{k-1}$.

Example

Let

$$\mathbf{A} = \begin{pmatrix} 0.7 & 0.5 \\ 0.3 & 0.5 \end{pmatrix}$$

The characteristic equation is

$$\begin{vmatrix} 0.7 - \lambda & 0.5 \\ 0.3 & 0.5 - \lambda \end{vmatrix} = \lambda^2 - 1.2\lambda + 0.2 = 0. \qquad \text{(I.5)}$$

The characteristic roots are therefore $\lambda_1 = 1.0$, $\lambda_2 = 0.2$. Substituting **A** for λ, the characteristic equation is

$$\begin{pmatrix} 0.64 & 0.60 \\ 0.36 & 0.40 \end{pmatrix} - \begin{pmatrix} 0.84 & 0.60 \\ 0.36 & 0.60 \end{pmatrix} + \begin{pmatrix} 0.2 & 0 \\ 0 & 0.2 \end{pmatrix} = \begin{pmatrix} 0 & 0 \\ 0 & 0 \end{pmatrix} \qquad \text{(I.6)}$$

Consequently

$$\mathbf{A}^2 = 1.2\mathbf{A} - 0.2\mathbf{I} \quad \mathbf{A}^3 = 1.2\mathbf{A}^2 - 0.2\mathbf{A} = 1.24\mathbf{A} - 0.24\mathbf{I}, \qquad \text{(I.7)}$$

and so on.

I.4

When λ is a latent root, then $(\mathbf{A} - \lambda\mathbf{I})\mathbf{x} = 0$, i.e. $\mathbf{Ax} = \lambda\mathbf{x}$, has a non-trivial solution **x**. This is a 'latent vector', or 'characteristic vector', or 'eigenvector' of **A**, corresponding to λ. If **x** is a latent vector, then so is $s\mathbf{x}$, for any number s.

Let λ be a latent root of the matrix **A**, and let $[x_1, \ldots, x_k]$ be a corresponding latent vector. Then

$$a_{i1}x_1 + \ldots + a_{ik}x_k = \lambda x_i \quad (i = 1, \ldots, k) \tag{I.8}$$

and hence

$$|a_{i1}||x_1| + \ldots + |a_{ik}||x_k| \geqslant |\lambda||x_i| \tag{I.9}$$

Denote the component of **x** with the largest absolute value by x_m. Then

$$\begin{aligned} |a_{i1}| + \ldots + |a_{ik}| &\geqslant |a_{i1}||x_1/x_m| + \ldots + |a_{ik}||x_k/x_m| \\ &\geqslant \lambda |x_i/x_m| \quad \text{for } i = 1, \ldots, k \end{aligned} \tag{I.10}$$

It follows that

$$\lambda \leqslant |a_{m1}| + \ldots + |a_{mk}| \tag{I.11}$$

This applies to any latent root.

In particular, if all a_{ij} are real and non-negative, and if

$$a_{i1} + \ldots + a_{ik} < 1 \tag{I.12}$$

for all i and hence also for $i = m$, whichever m may be, then 1 cannot be a latent root of **A**, and $(\mathbf{I} - \mathbf{P})^{-1}$ will exist.

Because the latent roots of **A** are the same as those of **A**′, the sum of the absolute values of the elements in any column of **A** is also an upper bound for the absolute value of any latent root, if $a_{ij} + \ldots + a_{kj} < 1$ for all j.

I.5

Another restriction on the values of latent roots is given by the following theorem (Brauer, 1946).

Let the real matrix $\mathbf{A} = (a_{ij})$ have no zero row, let all its roots add up to zero, and let $a_{ij} \geqslant 0$ when $i \neq j$, hence $a_{ii} < 0$ for all i. Then all latent roots are either zero, or have negative real parts.

Proof

Let λ be a latent root and $[x_1, \ldots, x_k]$ the corresponding latent vector. If x_m is the component with the largest absolute value, then

$$|\lambda - a_{mm}||x_m| \leqslant \sum_{\substack{j=1 \\ j \neq m}}^{k} a_{mj}|x_m| = -a_{mm}|x_m| \tag{I.13}$$

and hence

$$|\lambda - a_{mm}| \leqslant -a_{mm} \tag{I.14}$$

This means that λ will lie in the complex plane within, or on, a circle with centre a_{mm} (negative) and radius $-a_{mm}$. This circle can reach 0, but otherwise it will have only points with negative real part.

I.6

If $|a_{i1}| + \ldots + |a_{ik}| < 1$ for all i, then a_{ij}^t converges, with increasing t, to zero. In this case we can find an algebraic expression for $(\mathbf{I} - \mathbf{A})^{-1}$. We have

$$\begin{aligned} \mathbf{I} - \mathbf{A} &= \mathbf{I} - \mathbf{A} \\ \mathbf{A}(\mathbf{I} - \mathbf{A}) &= \mathbf{A} - \mathbf{A}^2 \\ &\vdots \\ \mathbf{A}^t(\mathbf{I} - \mathbf{A}) &= \mathbf{A}^t - \mathbf{A}^{t+1} \\ &\vdots \end{aligned}$$

Adding, we obtain

$$(\mathbf{I} - \mathbf{A})(\mathbf{I} + \mathbf{A} + \ldots + \mathbf{A}^t + \ldots) = \mathbf{I}$$

hence

$$(\mathbf{I} - \mathbf{A})^{-1} = \mathbf{I} + \mathbf{A} + \ldots + \mathbf{A}^t + \ldots \tag{I.15}$$

I.7

If $\mathbf{v}_i$ is the latent vector corresponding to the latent root λ_i, then $\mathbf{A}\mathbf{v}_i = \lambda_i \mathbf{v}_i$, hence $\mathbf{A}^2 \mathbf{v}_i = \lambda_i \mathbf{A}\mathbf{v}_i = \lambda_i^2 \mathbf{v}_i$ and, by induction,

$$\mathbf{A}^t \mathbf{v}_i = \lambda_i^t \mathbf{v}_i \tag{I.16}$$

for all non-negative integers t.

If all latent roots are different, then their latent vectors are linearly independent, i.e. there do not exist values $c_1, \ldots, c_k$ not all zero, such that $c_1\mathbf{v}_1 + \ldots + c_k\mathbf{v}_k = 0$.

Proof

If such c_i did exist, then multiplying by $\mathbf{A}$, we would also have

$$\begin{aligned} c_1\lambda_1\mathbf{v}_1 + \ldots + c_k\lambda_k\mathbf{v}_k &= 0 \\ &\vdots \\ c_1\lambda_1^{k-1}\mathbf{v}_1 + \ldots + c_k\lambda_k^{k-1}\mathbf{v}_k &= 0 \end{aligned} \tag{I.17}$$

and this set would apply, severally, to the first, . . . , kth component of the vectors. But the determinant

$$\begin{vmatrix} 1 & 1 & \ldots & 1 \\ \lambda_1 & \lambda_2 & & \lambda_k \\ \vdots & \vdots & & \vdots \\ \lambda_1^{k-1} & \lambda_2^{k-1} & \ldots & \lambda_k^{k-1} \end{vmatrix}$$

equals the product of all differences $\lambda_i - \lambda_j$, and this is not zero when all latent roots are different. Therefore the set (I.17) could only have the solution with all components of all vectors being zero, which is impossible by the definition of the latent vectors.

I.8

Because of the linear independence of the latent vectors $\mathbf{v}_1, \ldots, \mathbf{v}_k$ any vector $\mathbf{v}$ of k components can be expressed in the form

$$\mathbf{v} = a_1\mathbf{v}_1 + \ldots + a_k\mathbf{v}_k \tag{I.18}$$

Then

$$\mathbf{A}\mathbf{v} = \sum_{i=1}^{k} a_i\mathbf{A}\mathbf{v}_i = \sum_{i=1}^{k} a_i\lambda_i\mathbf{v}_i$$

also, by induction,

$$\mathbf{A}^t\mathbf{v} = \sum_{i=1}^{k} a_i\lambda_i^t\mathbf{v}_i \tag{I.19}$$

I.9

A determinant does not change its value if it is transposed, i.e. if rows and columns are exchanged. Therefore the latent roots of $\mathbf{A}'$, the transpose of the matrix $\mathbf{A}$, are the same as those of $\mathbf{A}$.

The latent vectors $\mathbf{w}_i$ of $\mathbf{A}'$ are the solutions of $(\mathbf{A}' - \lambda_i\mathbf{I})\mathbf{w}_i = 0$ ($i = 1, \ldots, k$), i.e. those of

$$\mathbf{w}_i'(\mathbf{A} - \lambda_i\mathbf{I}) = 0 \tag{I.20}$$

We call these vectors $\mathbf{w}_i$ the 'left-hand latent vectors' of $\mathbf{A}$, to distinguish them from the 'right-hand latent vectors' $\mathbf{v}_i$ previously defined.

Again, if $\mathbf{w}_i$ is a left-hand latent vector, then so is $c\mathbf{w}_i$ for any c.

It can be shown that

$$\mathbf{w}_i'\mathbf{v}_i \neq 0 \tag{I.21}$$

and

$$\mathbf{w}_i'\mathbf{v}_j = 0 \quad \text{when } i \neq j \tag{I.22}$$

Proof

$$\lambda_j\mathbf{w}_i'\mathbf{v}_j = \mathbf{w}_i'\mathbf{A}\mathbf{v}_j = \lambda_i\mathbf{w}_i'\mathbf{v}_j \tag{I.23}$$

If $\lambda_i \neq \lambda_j$, then equation (I.22) follows, and hence the non-diagonal elements of the matrix

$$(\mathbf{w}_1', \ldots, \mathbf{w}_k')[\mathbf{v}_1, \ldots, \mathbf{v}_k] \tag{I.24}$$

are zero. But due to the linear independence of the $\mathbf{v}_i$ and of the $\mathbf{w}_j$, this product is not singular, hence (I.21).

The vectors $\mathbf{v}_i$ and $\mathbf{w}_j$ can be chosen so that $\mathbf{w}_i'\mathbf{v}_i = 1$. In this case the matrix (I.24) equals $\mathbf{I}$.

I.10

Let $\mathbf{w}_i'\mathbf{v}_i = 1$ for $i = 1, \ldots, k$, so that

$$(\mathbf{v}_1, \ldots, \mathbf{v}_k)^{-1} = [\mathbf{w}_1', \ldots, \mathbf{w}_k'] \tag{I.25}$$

By equation (I.16) we have

$$\mathbf{A}^t(\mathbf{v}_1, \ldots, \mathbf{v}_k) = (\lambda_1^t\mathbf{v}_1, \ldots, \lambda_k^t\mathbf{v}_k) \tag{I.26}$$

and hence, by equation (I.25)

$$\mathbf{A}^t = (\lambda_1^t\mathbf{v}_1, \ldots, \lambda_k^t\mathbf{v}_k)[\mathbf{w}_1', \ldots, \mathbf{w}_k'] = \sum_{i=1}^{k} \lambda_i^t\mathbf{v}_i\mathbf{w}_i' = \sum_{i=1}^{k} \lambda_i^t\mathbf{B}_i \tag{I.27}$$

where

$$\mathbf{B}_i = \mathbf{v}_i\mathbf{w}_i' \tag{I.28}$$

is a matrix, to be distinguished from $\mathbf{w}_i'\mathbf{v}_i$, a scalar.

Equation (I.27) is the 'spectral representation' of $\mathbf{A}^t$, and the matrices $\mathbf{B}_1, \ldots, \mathbf{B}_k$ form the 'spectrum' of $\mathbf{A}$. They have the following properties:

$$\begin{aligned} &\sum_i \mathbf{B}_i = \mathbf{I} \qquad \mathbf{B}_i\mathbf{v}_i = \mathbf{v}_i \quad (\text{all } i) \\ &\mathbf{B}_i\mathbf{v}_j = 0 \quad (\text{when } i \neq j) \end{aligned} \tag{I.29}$$

It follows that if

$$\mathbf{v} = \sum_{j=1}^{k} a_j\,\mathbf{v}_j \quad (\text{equation (I.18)})$$

then

$$\mathbf{A}^t\mathbf{v} = \sum_{i=1}^{k} \lambda_i^t\mathbf{B}_i\mathbf{v} = \sum_{i=1}^{k} \lambda_i^t\mathbf{B}_i \sum_{j=1}^{k} a_j\mathbf{v}_j = \sum_{i=1}^{k} \lambda_i^t a_i\mathbf{v}_i$$

which is equation (I.19).

$\mathbf{A}^t$ can also be written (see equation (I.27))

$$(\mathbf{v}_1, \ldots, \mathbf{v}_k)\begin{pmatrix} \lambda_1^t & 0 & \ldots & 0 \\ 0 & \lambda_2^t & \ldots & 0 \\ \vdots & \vdots & & \vdots \\ 0 & 0 & \ldots & \lambda_k^t \end{pmatrix}\begin{pmatrix} \mathbf{w}_1' \\ \vdots \\ \mathbf{w}_k' \end{pmatrix} \tag{I.30}$$

and hence (by equation (I.25))

$$\begin{pmatrix} \mathbf{w}_1' \\ \vdots \\ \mathbf{w}_k' \end{pmatrix}\mathbf{A}^t(\mathbf{v}_1, \ldots, \mathbf{v}_k) = \begin{pmatrix} \lambda_1^t & 0 & \ldots & 0 \\ 0 & \lambda_2^t & \ldots & 0 \\ \vdots & \vdots & & \vdots \\ 0 & 0 & \ldots & \lambda_k^t \end{pmatrix} \tag{I.31}$$

I.11

Let **A** be a matrix whose elements are real and non-negative. We are, in particular, interested in 'irreducible' non-negative matrices. A matrix is irreducible if it cannot be transformed into the form

$$\begin{pmatrix} \mathbf{R} & \mathbf{0} \\ \mathbf{S} & \mathbf{T} \end{pmatrix}$$

(where **R** and **T** are square matrices and **0** is here the matrix whose elements are all 0) by the same permutation of rows and columns, i.e. after some renumbering of the states.

Equivalently, an irreducible matrix can be defined as being a transition matrix such that each state can be reached from any other state after a finite number of steps, not necessarily the same number of steps for all pairs.

I.12

We quote results from Frobenius (1912, pp. 456–77).

(i) A non-negative irreducible matrix **A** has a positive latent root λ_0, say with corresponding strictly positive right-hand and left-hand latent vectors. The latent root λ_0 is simple, and not smaller than the absolute value of any other latent root of **A**.

(ii) If there are $h - 1$ other latent roots of equal absolute value $|\lambda_0| = r$, say, then they are the distinct roots of $\lambda^h - r^h = 0$.

It can be shown (e.g. Gantmacher, 1959, vol. II, pp. 64–6) that λ_0 is the smallest value μ for which $\mathbf{Ax} \leqslant \mu\mathbf{x}$ can be solved with non-negative $\mathbf{x} \neq 0$. The theorem of Frobenius shows that all components of the vector **x** corresponding to $\mu = \lambda_0$ are, in fact, positive.

Incidentally, it is also true that

$$\lambda_0 = \max_{\mathbf{x} \geqslant 0} \min_i (\mathbf{Ax})_i/\mathbf{x}_i = \min_{\mathbf{x} > 0} \max_i (\mathbf{Ax})_i/\mathbf{x}_i \qquad \text{(I.32)}$$

It is also shown in Gantmacher (1959, vol II, pp. 63ff.) that

$$\min_i \sum_j a_{ij} \leqslant r \leqslant \max_i \sum_j a_{ij} \qquad \text{(I.33)}$$

and that an irreducible non-negative matrix cannot have two linearly independent non-negative characteristic vectors.

I.13

Section I.12 referred to irreducible matrices. For reducible non-negative matrices we can merely assert that there exists always a non-negative latent root such that no absolute value of any other latent root exceeds it. The corresponding latent vector can be made non-negative (Gantmacher, 1959, vol II, p. 66).

Moreover, we show now that the smallest value $\mu \geqslant 0$ for which $\mathbf{Ax} \leqslant \mu\mathbf{x}$ has a solution $\mathbf{x} \geqslant 0$, $\mathbf{x} \neq 0$ is a latent root of $\mathbf{A}$ even when $\mathbf{A}$ is reducible (though it is then not necessarily the latent root with largest absolute value).

If $\mathbf{A}$ has a column consisting of zeros only, then the smallest non-negative latent root is 0, and the result is then trivially true.

We now assume that $\mathbf{A}$ has no null column. Let λ_0 be the smallest non-negative value of μ for which $\mathbf{Ax} \leqslant \mu\mathbf{x}$, $\mathbf{x} \geqslant 0$, $\mathbf{x} \neq 0$ exists. If λ_0 is not a latent root, let $\mathbf{x}_0 \geqslant 0$, $\mathbf{x} \neq 0$ be such that $\mathbf{Ax}_0 \leqslant \lambda_0 \mathbf{x}_0$. In that case $\mathbf{Ax}_0 - \lambda_0 \mathbf{x}_0 = \mathbf{d}$, say has at least one negative component, while the other components are zero.

Since $\mathbf{A}$ has no null column, it follows that

$$\mathbf{Ad} < 0 \quad \text{i.e.} \quad \mathbf{A}(\mathbf{Ax}_0 - \lambda_0 \mathbf{x}_0) < 0$$

Write $\mathbf{Ax}_0 = \mathbf{y}_0$ ($\geqslant 0$), hence

$$\mathbf{Ay}_0 - \lambda_0 \mathbf{y}_0 < 0$$

But then λ_0 is not the smallest value of μ for which $\mathbf{Ax} - \mu\mathbf{x} \leqslant 0$ has a solution $\mathbf{x} \geqslant 0$, $\mathbf{x} \neq 0$.

This proves our statement.

I.14

A non-negative matrix with the additional property that the elements in each row add up to unity is called 'stochastic'. Equivalently, a matrix is stochastic if and only if it has a right-hand latent vector whose components are all unity. The corresponding latent root is also 1.

It follows from (I.11) that no latent root can have an absolute value larger than 1. Also, if the matrix is irreducible, then there will be one single latent root of value 1. There may be, though, others of absolute value 1.

Because the right-hand vector of a stochastic matrix, corresponding to the latent root 1 is $[1, 1, \ldots, 1]$, we conclude from equation (I.22) that all left-hand latent vectors corresponding to the other latent roots must have components which add up to 0.

I.15

An irreducible stochastic matrix with no latent roots of absolute value 1, apart from the single real root, is called 'ergodic', otherwise it is 'periodic'. If it is ergodic, then with increasing t,

$$\mathbf{A}^t = \sum_{i=1}^{k} \lambda_i^t \mathbf{B}_i \tag{I.27}$$

will converge to

$$\mathbf{B}_1 = [\mathbf{w}'_1, \ldots, \mathbf{w}'_1] \tag{I.34}$$

If the stochastic matrix is periodic, then the latent roots of absolute value 1 are distinct roots of unity. In this case $\mathbf{A}^t$ will not converge, but will pass periodically through the same series of values, when t increases.

Example

The matrix

$$\mathbf{A} = \begin{pmatrix} 0 & 1 & 0 \\ 0 & 0 & 1 \\ 1 & 0 & 0 \end{pmatrix}$$

has the characteristic equation $(\lambda - 1)(\lambda^2 + \lambda + 1) = 0$, and hence the latent roots 1, $(-1 + i\sqrt{3})/2$, $(-1 - i\sqrt{3})/2$. We have

$$\mathbf{A}^2 = \begin{pmatrix} 0 & 0 & 1 \\ 1 & 0 & 0 \\ 0 & 1 & 0 \end{pmatrix} \quad \text{and} \quad \mathbf{A}^3 = \begin{pmatrix} 1 & 0 & 0 \\ 0 & 1 & 0 \\ 0 & 0 & 1 \end{pmatrix} = \mathbf{I}$$

$\mathbf{A}^4 = \mathbf{A}$, $\mathbf{A}^5 = \mathbf{A}^2$, $\mathbf{A}^6 = \mathbf{I}$, and so on.

I.16

We turn now to some applications of matrix theory, in particular to the use of latent roots and of latent vectors. In the present section we shall deal, in particular, with difference equations.

Consider a set of difference equations

$$n_i(t+1) = a_{1i}n_1(t) + a_{2i}n_2(t) + \ldots + a_{ki}n_k(t) \quad (i = 1, \ldots, k) \tag{I.35}$$

One solution is $n_i(t) = 0$ for all i and all t, but we are looking for other solutions.

Let us assume that the solution is of the form

$$n_i(t+1) = \lambda n_i(t) \tag{I.36}$$

then the set (I.35) will read

$$\begin{aligned} (a_{11} - \lambda)n_1(t) + a_{21}n_2(t) + \ldots + a_{k1}n_k(t) &= 0 \\ a_{12}n_1(t) + (a_{22} - \lambda)n_2(t) + \ldots + a_{k2}n_k(t) &= 0 \\ &\vdots \\ a_{1k}n_1(t) + a_{2k}n_2(t) + \ldots + (a_{kk} - \lambda)n_k(t) &= 0 \end{aligned} \tag{I.37}$$

This system has a non-trivial solution $n(t) = \lambda^t n(0)$, if the matrix of coefficients is singular, i.e. if λ is a latent root of the matrix (a_{ij}).

We assume that the matrix has k different latent roots. Then the corresponding latent vectors $\mathbf{v}_j = [v_{j1}, \ldots, v_{jk}]$ $(j = 1, \ldots, k)$ are linearly independent, and therefore

$$n_i(t) = c_1\lambda_1^t\mathbf{v}_{1i} + \ldots + c_k\lambda_k^t\mathbf{v}_{ki} \tag{I.38}$$

with arbitrary c_j is also a solution.

Given the initial vector $\mathbf{n}(0)$ we can compute the c_j, and so equation (I.38) is the general solution of the set (I.35).

If the matrix (a_{ij}) is stochastic, then precisely one latent root equals 1, and if it is ergodic, then the corresponding latent vector $\mathbf{v}$ will give a stationary structure, thus

$$\mathbf{v} = \mathbf{A}'\mathbf{v} = (\mathbf{A}')^2\mathbf{v} = \ldots = (\mathbf{A}')^t\mathbf{v} = \ldots \tag{I.39}$$

Given any structure $\mathbf{n}(0)$, its progression in time due to a stochastic transition matrix $\mathbf{A}$ can be described by $\mathbf{n}(t) = (\mathbf{A}')^t\mathbf{n}(0)$, with elements independent of time. Such a sequence is called a 'Markov chain'. For more detail see, for instance, Cox and Miller (1965).

I.17

Let a single difference equation be given, in the form

$$n(t+1) = a_0 n(t) + a_1 n(t-1) + \ldots + a_t n(0) \tag{I.40}$$

where n is a scalar function. We can solve it by finding the roots of its characteristic equation

$$\lambda^{t+1} - a_0\lambda^t - \ldots - a_{t-1}\lambda - a_t = 0 \tag{I.41}$$

If this polynomial equation has $t+1$ different roots $\lambda_0, \lambda_1, \ldots, \lambda_t$ then the general solution of equation (I.40) is

$$n(s) = c_0\lambda_0^s + \ldots + c_t\lambda_t^s \tag{I.42}$$

where $c_0, \ldots, c_t$ are arbitrary constants, which can be determined if $\mathbf{n}(s)$ is known for $t+1$ values of s. In most cases this will be for $s = 0, 1, \ldots, t$.

I.18

A set of differential equations can be dealt with in a manner analogous to the treatment of difference equations, described in Section I.16.

Consider the set

$$\mathrm{d}n_i(t)/\mathrm{d}t = b_{1i}n_1(t) + \ldots + b_{ki}n_k(t) \quad (i = 1, \ldots, k) \tag{I.43}$$

Assuming that the solution has the form

$$n_i(t) = n_i(0)\exp(\lambda t) \tag{I.44}$$

the set (I.43) reads, after dividing each equation by $\exp(\lambda t)$,

$$\begin{array}{l} (b_{11} - \lambda)n_1(0) + b_{21}n_2(0) + \ldots + b_{k1}n_k(0) \\ b_{12}n_1(0) + (b_{22} - \lambda)n_2(0) + \ldots + b_{k2}n_k(0) \\ \quad\vdots \qquad\qquad \vdots \qquad\qquad\qquad \vdots \\ b_{1k}n_1(0) + b_{2k}n_2(0) + \ldots + (b_{kk} - \lambda)n_k(0) \end{array} \tag{I.45}$$

This system has a non-trivial solution $\mathbf{n}(0)$ if λ is a latent root of the matrix of coefficients. If the matrix has k different latent roots, then we obtain

$$n_i(t) = c_1 \exp(\lambda_1 t)v_{1i} + \ldots + c_k \exp(\lambda_k t)v_{kt} \tag{I.46}$$

where the constants c_j depend on the initial vector $\mathbf{n}(0)$.

Appendix II

Linear Programming. The Simplex Method, and the Transportation Problem

II.1

Consider a system of m simultaneous linear equations in n ($> m$) variables, where all variables are to have non-negative values and add up to unity.

If we choose $n - m$ variables to be zero, and if the system in the remaining variables is not contradictory, then we can solve it as a system of linear equations, and provided the resulting values are non-negative, then we have obtained a solution to the original system. We call a solution basic, and all solutions of the system lie in the convex hull of the basic solutions, i.e. they are linear combinations of the basic solutions, with the weights adding up to unity. The basic solutions are equivalent to the vertices of the set of solution vectors.

II.2

It would be rather time-consuming to determine all basic solutions by choosing all the $\binom{n}{m}$ combinations of $n - m$ out of n variables, setting them equal to zero, determining whether the remaining system has a solution at all, and if it has, whether it is non-negative. Therefore we make use of a method which enables us to find all basic solutions from one of them.

For this purpose it is necessary to find an initial basic solution.

If each equation contains a variable whose coefficient has the same sign as the right-hand side, or if the latter is zero, any sign, and which does not appear in any other equation as well, then we can make all other variables zero, and have found, by solving the remaining system, altogether n non-negative variables which solve the original system.

If there is no such variable in every equation, then we introduce an 'artificial' variable in each equation which lacks a suitable variable. For instance, let the system, in variables x_i and u_j, be

$$\begin{aligned} u_1 + 0.3x_1 + 0.1x_2 + 0.2x_3 &= 0.37 \\ u_2 + 0.4x_1 + 0.5x_2 + 0.1x_3 &= 0.37 \\ u_3 + 0.1x_1 + 0.3x_2 + 0.4x_3 &= 0.26 \\ x_1 + \quad x_2 + \quad x_3 &= 1.00 \end{aligned} \tag{II.1}$$

Each of the first three equations contains just one of the u_i. The last equation contains no such suitable variable to start off with. Therefore we add to it the artificial variable, s, changing it into

$$s + x_1 + x_2 + x_3 = 1.00 \qquad \text{(II.2)}$$

We now set $x_1 = x_2 = x_3 = 0$, and obtain the solution

$$u_1 = 0.37 \quad u_2 = 0.37 \quad u_3 = 0.26 \quad s = 1.00$$

We call these basic variables and the others – those which have value zero – non-basic variables.

However, this is not a solution of the set (II.1), which did not contain s at all as a variable. We construct therefore a system equivalent to the set (II.1) which contains another variable, not s, in just one equation. Let us choose x_1 to be this variable.

From equation (II.2) we have $x_1 = 1.00 - x_2 - x_3 - s$. Substituting into the first three equations of (II.2) we obtain

$$u_1 - 0.3s - 0.2x_2 - 0.1x_3 = 0.07$$

$$u_2 - 0.4s + 0.1x_2 - 0.3x_3 = 0.03$$

$$u_3 - 0.1s + 0.2x_2 + 0.3x_3 = 0.16$$

$$x_1 + s + x_2 + x_3 = 1.00$$

or, in 'tableau' form

	s	x_2	x_3	
u_1	–0.3	–0.2	–0.1	0.07
u_2	–0.4	0.1	–0.3	–0.03
u_3	–0.1	0.2	0.3	0.16
x_1	1.0	1.0	1.0	1.00

Now we have come up against another difficulty: if we put $s = x_2 = x_3 = 0$, then u_2 will have the negative value –0.03.

Therefore we carry out another exchange, choosing x_3 rather than u_2 to appear in one equation only.

We have $x_3 = 0.1 + 0.333x_2 - 1.333s + 3.333u_2$, and after substitution into the first, third and fourth equations, in tableau form

	x_2	s	u_2	
u_1	–0.233	–0.167	–0.333	0.08
x_3	–0.333	1.333	–3.333	0.10
u_3	0.300	–0.500	1.000	0.13
x_1	1.333	–0.333	3.333	0.90

to be read

$$u_1 - 0.233x_2 - 0.167s - 0.333u_2 = 0.08$$

etc.

In fact, the column of s can now be ignored, because s already has the value zero, and is of no further interest. Without s, we are back at our original set.

We have found a basic solution, with non-negative variables, viz.

$$u_1 = 0.08 \quad u_2 = 0 \quad u_3 = 0.13 \quad x_1 = 0.9 \quad x_2 = 0 \quad x_3 = 0.1$$

This is not the only basic solution, though. For instance, we could exchange u_2 and u_3, by substituting

$$u_2 = 0.13 - 0.3x_2 - u_3$$

into the first, second, and fourth equations. We obtain then

	x_2	u_3	
u_1	−0.133	0.333	0.123
x_3	0.667	3.333	0.533
u_2	0.300	1.000	0.130
x_1	0.333	−3.333	0.467

another basic solution:

$$u_1 = 0.123 \quad u_2 = 0.130 \quad u_3 = 0 \quad x_1 = 0.467 \quad x_2 = 0 \quad x_3 = 0.533$$

On the other hand, we could not have exchanged u_1 and u_2, because that would have produced a negative u_2.

We compute one more basic solution, by exchanging u_2 and x_2, i.e. from the third equation in the last tableau

$$x_2 = 0.433 - 3.333u_2 - 3.333u_3$$

and the next tableau is

	u_2	u_3	
u_1	0.444	0.778	0.181
x_3	−2.222	1.111	0.245
x_2	3.333	3.333	0.433
x_1	−1.111	−4.444	0.322

that is

$$u_1 = 0.181 \quad u_2 = 0 \quad u_3 = 0 \quad x_1 = 0.322 \quad x_2 = 0.433 \quad x_3 = 0.245$$

There are no other basic feasible solutions in this case. All solutions, basic or not, can be described as linear combinations of these three, as follows:

$$
\begin{aligned}
x_1 &= 0.9\ \rho_1 + 0.467\rho_2 + 0.322\rho_3\\
x_2 &= \qquad\qquad\qquad\quad 0.433\rho_3\\
x_3 &= 0.1\ \rho_1 + 0.533\rho_2 + 0.245\rho_3\\
u_1 &= 0.08\rho_1 + 0.123\rho_2 + 0.181\rho_3\\
u_2 &= \qquad\quad 0.130\rho_2\\
u_3 &= 0.13\rho_1
\end{aligned}
$$

with

$$\rho_1 + \rho_2 + \rho_3 = 1 \qquad \rho_1, \rho_2, \rho_3 \geqslant 0$$

The three basic solutions are obtained by making one of the ρ_i equal to one.

II.3

We have just shown, by an example, how to obtain basic solutions of a 'linear programming' problem, i.e. of a set of linear equations in non-negative variables. We describe now the general rules for the procedure.

If we wish to exchange the basic variable y_i, say, for the non-basic variable y_j, then we call the coefficient of y_j in the y_i row the 'pivot' of exchange, and the procedure of changing one tableau into the next is defined by the following rules of the simplex method of linear programming:

1. Interchange the labels of y_i and y_j.
2. Replace the pivot by its reciprocal.
3. Divide all other entries in the row of the pivot by the pivot.
4. Divide all other entries in the column of the pivot by the pivot, and change the sign.
5. Replace all remaining entries a_{uv} by $a_{uv} - a_{uc}a_{rv}/a_{rc}$, where r is the row, and c is the column of the pivot.

As long as some variable is negative, we choose in its row a negative entry for a pivot, in order to make the variable which we exchange for it positive. If there is no negative entry in such a row, then there is no feasible (i.e. non-negative) solution.

When all variables are non-negative, i.e. when we have found a basic feasible solution, then we can carry out a further exchange by choosing, in any column, that entry as a pivot which makes the ratio of the basic variable in its row divided by the pivot as small as possible (otherwise the exchange would make some other variable negative).

Any artificial variable can be dropped after it has become non-basic. If it cannot be made non-basic by applying the rules given above, then the original system has no feasible solution.

If we are merely interested in a subset of the variables, say the x_i in the example above, then the vectors consisting of these components of a solution form again a convex set, but the vectors which we obtain in this way from the vertices in the space of the original system are not necessarily also vertices of the convex region in the subspace onto which the original space was projected.

II.4

In general, a system such as we consider will have more than one basic feasible solution. We might then wish to single out that basic feasible solution whose variables minimize a given linear expression in the variables, the 'objective function' z say. It can be shown that by finding that basic feasible solution which minimizes z we find, in fact, the minimum of z over all feasible solutions – not merely the basic ones.

We may be able to express z in terms of the non-basic variables $z_1, \ldots, z_r$, by using the given equations, thus

$$z - c_1 z_1 - \ldots - c_r z_r = c_0 \tag{II.3}$$

and add this row to the tableau. If some c_i is negative (i.e. some $-c_i$ is positive), then z can be further reduced by making z_i basic, and we shall then perform an iteration by exchanging z_i for another variable, which is at present basic.

If we cannot express z conveniently in terms of the non-basic variables, then we can find the z-row to be added to the tableau as follows:

Let the tableau have the form

	(c_{m+1}) x_{m+1}	$\ldots$	(c_n) x_n	
$(c_1)x_1$	$z_{1,m+1}$	$\ldots$	z_{1n}	x_{10}
	$\vdots$		$\vdots$	
$(c_m)x_m$	$z_{m,m+1}$	$\ldots$	z_{mn}	x_{m0}

If the original form of the objective function was

$$z = c_1 x_1 + \ldots + c_n x_n \tag{II.4}$$

then the row to be added reads

$$z \qquad z_{0,m+1} \quad \ldots \quad z_{0n} \quad z_{00}$$

where

$$z_{0,m+j} = c_1 z_{1,m+j} + \ldots + c_m z_{m,m+j} - c_{m+j} \qquad (j = 1, 2, \ldots, n-m) \tag{II.5}$$

and

$$z_{00} = c_1 x_{10} + \ldots + c_m x_{m0} \tag{II.6}$$

(which follows, of course, from equation (II.4), which defines z).

In the last tableau we have added the c_i in brackets, next to the variables to which they belong, for convenience.

II.5 Parametric linear programming

If the right-hand sides of the equations depend on a parameter α, then we proceed in a similar manner, to obtain basic feasible solutions, for all possible values of that parameter.

For instance, starting from the tableau

	x_1	x_2	x_3	
u_1	0.3	0.1	0.2	$0.37\,(1+\alpha)$
u_2	0.4	0.5	0.1	$0.37\,(1+\alpha)$
u_3	0.1	0.3	0.4	$0.26\,(1+\alpha)$
s	1.0	1.0	1.0	1.00

we proceed to (dropping s)

	x_2	x_3	
u_1	−0.2	−0.1	$0.07+0.37\alpha$
u_2	0.1	−0.3	$-0.03+0.37\alpha$
u_3	0.2	0.3	$0.16+0.26\alpha$
x_1	1.0	1.0	1.00

This is already a basic solution, as long as $\alpha \geqslant 3/37$.
Other vertices can be obtained by exchanging now

u_2 and x_2 as long as $\alpha \leqslant 13/37$ (but still $\geqslant 3/37$)

or x_1 and x_2 as long as $\alpha \geqslant 13/37$

also u_3 and x_3 as long as $\alpha \leqslant 7/13$ (but still $\geqslant 3/37$)

or x_1 and x_3 as long as $\alpha \geqslant 7/13$

If $\alpha \leqslant 3/37$, then we can exchange u_2 and x_3 to begin with, and carry on from there.

No solution exists at all if $\alpha < -13/63$.

II.6

We give now a brief description of the transportation problem and of a method for solving it.

Suppose a_i items ($i = 1, \ldots, m$) are available at locations P_i, and that we wish to transport them to locations Q_j ($j = 1, \ldots, n$), each Q_j receiving b_j items. We have

$$\sum_i a_i = \sum_j b_j \tag{II.7}$$

If the number of items moved from P_i to Q_j is x_{ij} ($\geqslant 0$), then

$$\sum_{\substack{j=1 \\ (\text{all } i)}}^{n} x_{ij} = a_i \qquad \sum_{\substack{i=1 \\ (\text{all } j)}}^{m} x_{ij} = b_j \tag{II.8}$$

These $m + n$ equations are not independent. Because of

$$\sum_{i=1}^{m} \sum_{j=1}^{n} x_{ij} = \sum_{i=1}^{m} a_i = \sum_{j=1}^{n} b_j = \sum_{j=1}^{n} \sum_{i=1}^{m} x_{ij} \tag{II.9}$$

one equation is redundant, and only $m + n - 1$ are independent.

We have here a special case of a linear programming problem. Basic solutions will have (not more than) $m + n - 1$ positive components; the remaining $mn - (m + n - 1) = (m - 1)(n - 1)$ variables are zero.

The data can be described, concisely, by the table

	b_1	$\ldots$	b_n
a_1	x_{11}	$\ldots$	x_{1n}
$\vdots$	$\vdots$		$\vdots$
a_m	x_{m1}	$\ldots$	x_{mn}

where the rows and columns of the x_{ij} add up to the marginal totals.

II.7

A solution can easily be started by making x_{11} equal to the smaller of a_1 and b_1. If this is a_1 (or b_1), then subtract a_1 (or b_1) from b_1 (or a_1), omit the first row (or first column) and continue in the same way with the remaining table. This produces a basic feasible solution.

For instance, take the following problem with its first solution:

	370	370	260
182	182		
256	188	68	
387		302	85
175			175

Other basic solutions are found by moving around as many items as possible, filling in one empty cell and emptying another cell, taking care that the row and column balances are preserved.

For instance, in our example we can move 68 from cell (2, 2) into cell (2, 3), subtracting it from (3, 3), and adding it to (3, 2), to obtain

	370	370	260
182	182		
256	188		68
387		370	17
175			175

In this manner we can continue, until all basic feasible solutions are found. (We ignore the slight complication which occurs when less than $m + n - 1$ cells are filled in with positive values.)

II.8

If we attach costs to the various transports, then we might be interested in finding that particular distribution which minimizes the total cost. Because this is a linear programming problem, we know that the minimum cost will be produced by a basic feasible solution.

A simple way of ascertaining if a given basic solution is the minimizing one is as follows.

Attach 'shadow costs' to the rows and columns, in such a way that for each cell with a positive entry the sum of the shadow costs of its row and its column equals the cost of that cell. (One of the shadow costs can be chosen arbitrarily, say equal to zero.)

If, then, in all other cells (the empty ones) that sum of shadow costs is smaller than the cost of the cell, then the minimum cost solution has been reached. Otherwise one of the cells in which this is not so should be entered, and another basic solution computed. Eventually the optimal solution will be obtained.

For instance, let the costs in our example above be as follows:

	2	5	3
	3	6	1
	3	4	2
	4	6	3

Then the shadow costs of the first solution will be (for instance)

				0
				3
				−1
				0
	2	5	3	

Since 3 + 3 is larger than 1, it is worthwhile entering cell (2, 3). This gives the second solution above, with shadow costs

				1
				2
				1
				2
	1	3	1	

This is, for the given costs, the minimizing solution.

II.9

The 'dual problem' of a linear programming problem

$$\begin{aligned} a_{11}x_1 + \ldots + a_{1k}x_k &= b_1 \\ &\vdots \\ a_{m1}x_1 + \ldots + a_{mk}x_k &= b_m \\ x_1, \ldots, x_k &\geqslant 0 \\ \text{minimize } c_1x_1 + \ldots + c_kx_k & \end{aligned}$$

is another linear programming problem, defined as follows:

$$\begin{aligned} a_{11}y_1 + \ldots + a_{m1}y_m + z_1 &= c_1 \\ &\vdots \\ a_{1k}y_1 + \ldots + a_{mk}y_m + z_k &= c_k \\ \text{maximize } b_1y_1 + \ldots + b_my_m & \end{aligned}$$

(Note that $y_j \geqslant 0$ is not required.)

We mention here those parts of duality theory which are required in the main text, in particular in Chapter 11.

If one of a dual pair of problems has a finite solution, then so has the other.

The minimal value and the maximal value of the two respective objective functions are equal.

If in the final answer to the maximizing problem z_r is not zero, then in the minimizing problem $x_r = 0$.

For instance, the dual to

(a)
$$\begin{aligned} x_1 + 2x_2 + 3x_3 &= 1 \\ 4x_1 + 2x_2 + 2x_3 &= 1 \\ x_1, x_2, x_3 &\geqslant 0 \\ \text{minimize } x_1 + x_2 + x_3 & \end{aligned}$$

is the problem

(b)
$$\begin{aligned} y_1 + 4y_2 + z_1 &= 1 \\ 2y_1 + 2y_2 + z_2 &= 1 \\ 3y_1 + 2y_2 + z_3 &= 1 \\ \text{maximize } y_1 + y_2 & \end{aligned}$$

The solution to (b) is

$$y_1 = y_2 = 1/5 \quad z_1 = 0 \quad z_2 = 1/5 \quad z_3 = 0.$$

Therefore we set $x_2 = 0$, and solve, in (a)

$$\begin{aligned} x_1 + 3x_3 &= 1 \\ 4x_1 + 2x_3 &= 1 \end{aligned}$$

i.e.

$$x_1 = 0.1 \qquad x_2 = 0 \qquad x_3 = 0.3$$

Both $x_1 + x_2 + x_3$ and $y_1 + y_2$ equal 0.4.

Appendix III

The Transition Matrix $\mathbf{P}_0$

$$\mathbf{P}_0 = \begin{pmatrix} 0.3 & 0.4 & 0.1 \\ 0.1 & 0.5 & 0.3 \\ 0.2 & 0.1 & 0.4 \end{pmatrix} \qquad \mathbf{w} = \begin{pmatrix} 0.2 \\ 0.1 \\ 0.3 \end{pmatrix}$$

$$\mathbf{P}_0^2 = \begin{pmatrix} 0.15 & 0.33 & 0.19 \\ 0.14 & 0.32 & 0.28 \\ 0.15 & 0.17 & 0.21 \end{pmatrix} \qquad \mathbf{P}_0\mathbf{w} = \begin{pmatrix} 0.13 \\ 0.16 \\ 0.17 \end{pmatrix}$$

$$\mathbf{P}_0^3 = \begin{pmatrix} 0.116 & 0.244 & 0.190 \\ 0.130 & 0.244 & 0.222 \\ 0.104 & 0.166 & 0.150 \end{pmatrix} \qquad \mathbf{P}_0^2\mathbf{w} = \begin{pmatrix} 0.120 \\ 0.144 \\ 0.110 \end{pmatrix}$$

$$\mathbf{P}_0^4 = \begin{pmatrix} 0.0972 & 0.1874 & 0.1608 \\ 0.1078 & 0.1962 & 0.1750 \\ 0.0778 & 0.1396 & 0.1202 \end{pmatrix} \qquad \mathbf{P}_0^3\mathbf{w} = \begin{pmatrix} 0.1046 \\ 0.1170 \\ 0.0824 \end{pmatrix}$$

$$(\mathbf{I} - \mathbf{P}_0)^{-1} = \begin{pmatrix} 27/13 & 25/13 & 17/13 \\ 12/13 & 40/13 & 22/13 \\ 11/13 & 15/13 & 31/13 \end{pmatrix}$$

$$= \begin{pmatrix} 2.077 & 1.923 & 1.308 \\ 0.923 & 3.077 & 1.692 \\ 0.846 & 1.154 & 2.385 \end{pmatrix}$$

Bibliography

(The pages on which an item is cited are given in square brackets.)

D. J. Bartholomew (1973). *Stochastic Models for Social Processes*, 2nd ed, Wiley, Chichester. [2, 9, 89]

D. J. Bartholomew (1974). Stochastic models and their application: a review. In: D. J. Clough, C. C. Lewis and A. L. Oliver (Eds), *Manpower Planning Models*, English Universities Press, London. pp. 81–90. [2]

D. J. Bartholomew and A. R. Smith (Eds) (1971). *Manpower and Management Science*, English Universities Press, London. [2]

H. Bernardelli (1941). Population waves. *J. Burma Res. Soc.*, **31**, 1–18. [27]

L. Brand (1966). *Differential and Difference Equations*, Wiley, New York. [56]

A. Brauer (1946). Limits for the characteristic roots of a matrix. *Duke Math. J.*, **13**, 387–95. [51, 183]

A. Charnes, W. W. Cooper, R. J. Niehaus and D. Sholtz (1970). A model for civilian manpower management and planning in the U.S. Navy. In: A. R. Smith (Ed.) *Models for Manpower Systems*, English Universities Press, London. pp. 247–63. [161]

D. J. Clough, C. C. Lewis and A. L. Oliver (Eds) (1974). *Manpower Planning Models*, English Universities Press, London. [2]

D. R. Cox and H. D. Miller (1965). *The Theory of Stochastic Processes*, Methuen, London. [190]

G. S. Davies (1973). Structural control in a graded manpower system. *Management Sci.*, **20**, 76–84. [102, 111, 122]

G. S. Davies (1975). Maintainability of structures in Markov chain models under recruitment control. *J. Appl. Probability*, **12**, 376–82. [122, 132]

W. Feller (1941). On the integral equation of renewal theory. *Ann. Math. Statistics*, **12**, 243–67. [57]

A. F. Forbes (1970). Promotion and recruitment policies for the control of quasi-stationary hierarchical systems. In: A. R. Smith (Ed.), *Models for Manpower Systems*, English Universities Press, London. pp. 401–16. [77]

A. F. Forbes (1971). Markov chain models for manpower systems. In: D. J. Bartholomew and A. R. Smith (Eds), *Manpower and Management Science*, English Universities Press, London. pp. 93–113. [9]

R. A. Frazer, W. J. Duncan and A. R. Collar (1946). *Elementary Matrices*, Cambridge University Press, Cambridge. [182]

G. Frobenius (1912). Über matrizen aus nicht-negativen elementen. *Sitz.-ber. kgl. Preuss. Akad. Wiss. Berlin*, 456–477. [187]

J. Gani (1963). Formulae for projecting enrolment and degrees awarded in universities. *J. R. Statist. Soc. A*, **126**, 400–9. [2, 38]

F. R. Gantmacher (1959). *The Theory of Matrices* (2 vols.), Chelsea Publishing Co., New York. [182, 187]

J. Graunt (1662). *Natural and political observations . . . upon Bills of Mortality . . .* John Martyn, London. [1]

R. C. Grinold (1976). Input policies for a longitudinal manpower flow model. *Management Sci.*, **22**, 570–5. [157]

R. C. Grinold and K. T. Marshall (1977). *Manpower Planning Models*. North Holland, Amsterdam. [15]

R. C. Grinold and R. E. Stanford (1974). Optimal control of a graded manpower system. *Management Sci. B*, **20**, 1201–16. [82, 152, 156, 157]

R. C. Grinold and R. E. Stanford (1976). Limiting distributions in a linear fractional flow model. *SIAM J. Appl. Math.*, **30**, 402–6. [104]

J. Haig (1976). Private communication. [133]

S. Kakeya (1912/3). On the limits of the roots of an algebraic equation with positive coefficients. *Tohoku Math. J.*, **2**, 140–2. [27]

G. A. Keenay, R. W. Morgan and K. H. Ray (1974). The use of steady-state models for career planning in an expanding organisation. In: D. J. Clough, C. C. Lewis and A. L. Oliver (Eds), *Manpower Planning Models*, English Universities Press, London. pp. 151–9. [92]

J. G. Kemeny and J. L. Snell (1960). *Finite Markov Chains*, Van Nostrand, New York. [15]

K. F. Lane and J. E. Andrews (1955). A method of labour turnover analysis. *J. R. Statist. Soc. A*, **118**, 296–323. [9]

P. H. Leslie (1945). On the use of matrices in certain population genetics. *Biometrika*, **33**, 183–212. [27]

E. G. Lewis (1942). On the generation and growth of a population. *Sankhyā*, **6**, 93–6. [27]

J. H. Pollard (1973). *Mathematical Models for the Growth of Human Populations*, Cambridge University Press, Cambridge. [2]

H. L. Seal (1945). The mathematics of a population composed of k stationary strata . . . *Biometrika*, **33**, 226–30. [2, 65]

A. R. Smith (Ed.) (1970). *Models for Manpower Systems*, English Universities Press, London. [2]

A. R. Smith (Ed.) (1976). *Manpower Planning in the Civil Service*, HMSO, London. [46]

S. Vajda (1947). The stratified semi-stationary population. *Biometrika*, **34**, 243–54. [2, 66, 74]

S. Vajda (1948). Introduction to a mathematical theory of the graded stationary population. *Bull. Ass. Actuaires Suisses*, **48**, 251–73. [2, 64]

S. Vajda (1975). Mathematical aspects of manpower planning. *Operational Res. Q.*, **26**, 527–42. [132]

S. Vajda (1976). On recruitment for a graded population. *Symposia Mathematica XIX*, Istituto Nazionale di alta matematica. Acad. Press [152]

S. Vajda (1977). Maintainability and preservation of a graded population structure. *Management Sci.*, in the press. [66]

P. C. G. Vassiliou (1976). A Markov chain model for wastage in manpower systems. *Operational Res. Q.*, **27**, 57–70. [90]

N. A. B. Wilson (Ed.) (1969). *Manpower Research*, English Universities Press, London. [2]

A. Young (1971). Demographic and ecological models for manpower planning. In: D. J. Bartholomew and B. R. Morris (Eds), *Aspects of Manpower Planning*, English Universities Press, London. [9, 82, 90]

A. Young and G. Almond (1961). Predicting distributions of staff. *Computer J.*, **3**, 246–50. [2, 89]

Index